Little Cold Warriors

Little Cold Warriors

American Childhood in the 1950s

VICTORIA M. GRIEVE

OXFORD
UNIVERSITY PRESS

Oxford University Press is a department of the University of Oxford. It furthers
the University's objective of excellence in research, scholarship, and education
by publishing worldwide. Oxford is a registered trade mark of Oxford University
Press in the UK and certain other countries.

Published in the United States of America by Oxford University Press
198 Madison Avenue, New York, NY 10016, United States of America.

© Oxford University Press 2018

First issued as an Oxford University Press paperback, 2020

Library of Congress Cataloging-in-Publication Data
Names: Grieve, Victoria, 1972– author.
Title: Little cold warriors : American childhood in the 1950s / Victoria M. Grieve.
Description: New York, NY : Oxford University Press, [2018]
Identifiers: LCCN 2017054098 | ISBN 9780190675684 (hardcover : alk. paper) |
ISBN 9780197532904 (paperback : alk. paper) | ISBN 9780190675707 (epub)
Subjects: LCSH: Children and war—United States—History—20th century. |
Children in popular culture—United States—History—20th century. |
Children and politics—United States—History—20th century. | Propaganda,
American—History—20th century. | Cold War—Social aspects—United States. |
United States—Foreign relations—1989—Social aspects. |
Cold War—Influence. | Nineteen fifties.
Classification: LCC HQ784.W3 G75 2018 | DDC 303.6/6083—dc23
LC record available at https://lccn.loc.gov/2017054098

CONTENTS

ACKNOWLEDGMENTS

This book has been a long time in the making, and many people have contributed to it along the way. It is my pleasure to finally acknowledge everyone who helped make it possible.

I presented portions of Chapter 1 at a meeting of the American Studies Association; versions of Chapters 2 and 5 were presented at the Society for the History of Childhood and Youth. Friends and colleagues provided helpful feedback and suggestions to improve the manuscript at every stage.

Utah State University's History Department and the College of Humanities and Social Sciences provided financial support for research and travel. Endless encouragement and many lunchtime conversations with friends and colleagues, especially Daniel McInerney and Tammy Proctor, helped me refine my thinking on several issues in this book. The Friends of the Princeton University Library; Duke University's Hartman Center for Sales, Advertising, and Marketing History; and the Eisenhower Presidential Library and Museum provided travel grants that allowed me to complete archival research. The archivists at these institutions, as well as Marva Felchlin at the Autry Museum of the American West and Wendy Chmielewski and Mary Beth Sigado at the Swarthmore College Peace Collection, were gracious hosts and valuable sources of knowledge and expertise. Thanks also to Marilyn Holt and Dawn Moore for responding to email inquiries and requests for assistance.

Finally, this book would not be in your hands without the constant support of my husband Paul, and my children, Nathan and Naomi, who have inspired me in countless ways over the past 11 years. I hope that they, like many of the young people in this book, recognize the complexity of the world and continue to fight for justice, peace, and true "world friendship."

Little Cold Warriors

Introduction

Duck-and-cover. *Leave It to Beaver*. Dr. Spock. The Baby Boom. The polio scare. Juvenile delinquency. Is this American childhood and youth in the 1950s? Yes—and no.

American childhood in the 1950s is best understood as an era of political mobilization. Although Americans are comfortable with the patriotic history of children "helping" with the war effort during World War II—saving their nickels for war bonds, planting Victory Gardens, and collecting rubber and tin—we tend to think of the 1950s as the decade when children "returned" to being children after decades of depression and war. Both conservative and liberal Baby Boomers have romanticized the 1950s as an age of innocence—of pickup ball games and Howdy Doody, when mom stayed home and the economy boomed. And the drama of the divided Sixties made the Fifties seem even tamer by comparison. These nostalgic narratives obscure many other histories of postwar childhood, one of which has more in common with the war years and the Sixties, when children were mobilized and politicized by the US government, private corporations, and individual adults to fight the Cold War both at home and abroad.

From the late 1940s through the 1960s, all Americans mobilized to wage a global struggle against communist expansion. As they were reminded repeatedly, the fate of America's children, national survival, and the very future of freedom were at stake. Ideological mobilization occurred in a vast array of public and private spaces, from the White House to the private suburban home, in Congress and in public schools, in the pages of science textbooks and Betty Crocker cookbooks. Over the past decade, historians of American childhood and foreign relations have begun to explore how different groups of Americans, including children, experienced and participated in Cold War politics. But, in popular memory, American children's experiences continue to be summed up inadequately with easy references to Bert the Turtle and "duck and cover," which do little to explain children's real lives and merely create images of victimized youngsters. In fact, American children actively fought the Cold War on the home front and abroad in many ways. Children watched their heroes battle communism in its various guises on television, in the movies, and in comic books; children themselves practiced safety drills, joined civil preparedness groups, and helped to build and stock bomb shelters in the backyard. Children collected coins for UNICEF, exchanged art with other children around the world, prepared for nuclear war through the Boy and Girl Scouts, raised funds for Radio Free Europe, sent clothing to refugee children, and donated books to restock the diminished library shelves of war-torn Europe. Rather than rationing and saving, Americans were told to spend and consume in order to maintain the engine of American prosperity. In these capacities, American children functioned as ambassadors, cultural diplomats, and representatives of the United States.

The politicization of childhood during the Cold War era was not a new phenomenon. Visual and rhetorical images of children had been used for political purposes by Progressive reformers like Lewis Hine at the turn of the twentieth century to condemn child labor, to justify federal relief programs during the Great Depression, and to mobilize the home front during both World War I and World War II. The world wars mobilized not only images of children, but their bodies and minds as well. Dominique Marshall has demonstrated how Herbert Hoover's Progressive-era focus on children's bodies as natural resources resulted in an emphasis on food and health in post–World War I international aid programs. Food campaigns emphasized the dependency and innocence of European children rather than their interdependence and embeddedness in politically suspect families. In order to arouse sympathy, aid organizations depicted children as passive victims of wartime circumstances beyond their control despite children's own active assertions to the contrary. For example, rather than expressing the expected gratitude for relief, some Belgian children wrote to their sponsors about equality and universal entitlement. One letter-writer boldly reminded his readers that their donations were not charity but an obligation due to the people who had lived with the enemy from people whose homes remained untouched by the devastation of war. The post–World War I representation of children as universal and innocent beings—unstained by nationalism—was an important means of establishing the neutrality of humanitarian aid and remained so after World War I and World War II.[1] By definition, an inherently "neutral child" was apolitical; his or her actions could not be construed as political. A politicized child, therefore, was the product of external sociopolitical forces or, as the United States argued in the case of Soviet children, brainwashing and ideological indoctrination. Throughout the Cold War, Americans frequently accused the Soviet Union of brainwashing their youngest citizens to accept and embrace communism while maintaining that American children were free from state-sponsored propaganda.

The concepts of neutral and politicized children were central to postwar cultural diplomacy as well. If childhood was a universal stage of life and children were naturally innocent, then not only were foreign children deserving of humanitarian assistance, but American children's voluntary labor for international aid programs could be defined as apolitical and impartial rather than politically motivated. The contradiction of inherently "neutral" American children engaging in political work intensified throughout the Cold War years. American children engaged in political work by representing the United States in a multitude of international projects, from the Future Farmers of America to the Girl Scouts, by raising money for hundreds of causes, by writing essays and engaging in People-to-People diplomacy. The State Department, for example, viewed the volunteer labor and global engagement of financially secure, "apolitical" American children as a demonstration of the superiority of American capitalism over Soviet communism. As physical manifestations of the American "way of life," the healthy and cared-for bodies of American children and the material goods they donated to less fortunate children around the world functioned as propaganda. But because American children were constructed as apolitical, their work could be framed instead as innocent efforts to establish "world friendship." The rhetoric surrounding children's voluntary labor therefore supported the foreign policy goal of American "benevolent supremacy," a term I borrow from Melanie McAlister. McAlister argued that Americans understood US Cold War policy as a form of "benevolent supremacy" in which the United States embraced independence movements in the postcolonial world but feminized developing nations by circumscribing their role within a US-dominated order akin to the consensual but unequal union in a traditional marriage. This discourse of US power defined it as "inevitably global in scope, benevolent in intent, and benign in effect."[2] As I will demonstrate, children learned about appropriate roles in this relationship through popular culture, particularly popular Westerns such as *The Lone Ranger*, as well as through a variety of public and private voluntary efforts. American children understood that they were "lucky" to have been born in the United States, which was assuming its inevitable role as a world leader, and that continued national supremacy and political freedom depended on their active and well-intentioned participation in world affairs to maintain that position.

This is not to say that American children would not benefit from these relationships as well. In return for their global engagement and humanitarian assistance, American children would learn valuable lessons about responsible citizenship, train for life in a democracy, and undertake international obligations. Camp Fire Girls, Boy Scouts, and the Junior Red Cross are examples of youth organizations that equated the civic participation required by their programs with life in a democracy while simultaneously spreading the gospel of American benevolent supremacy. Adults encouraged American youth to learn about other nations, engage in world problems, and accept the nation's new role as a global superpower and all the obligations that accompanied it. Because the home front became the battleground during the Cold War, children engaged in defense work to an unprecedented degree and in new ways.[3]

Since the early 1990s, scholars of American diplomatic history have insisted on the importance of culture in understanding how nations exercise power and attempt to influence world opinion and global affairs.[4] This study contributes to that conversation by showing how American children served as semi-official diplomats and cultural ambassadors during the Cold War and how they understood their own actions. The term "cultural diplomacy" has been used to describe a particular type of public diplomacy. I use the term to describe explicit efforts by the federal government to use the visual arts, music, and literature to influence foreign opinion in favor of the United States. Public diplomacy refers to efforts by a variety of stakeholders, including the federal government, businesses, and private individuals, to influence foreign opinion in favor of the United States. Public diplomacy can flow from governments to foreign citizens or from private citizen to citizen and is related to the use of "soft power" in making particular American traits attractive or preferred among foreign populations. Public diplomacy can be ideologically driven in the sense of insisting upon the superiority of US capitalism, most often by state actors, or ideals-driven, in the sense of promoting a better life, most often from non-state actors or humanitarian groups.[5] In all of these cases, the actions of children became important during the Cold War, based largely on the assumption of children's political innocence. I analyze the ideological underpinnings of children's cultural activities, as well as the actions and beliefs of private individuals, nongovernmental organizations, and federal programs.[6] In short, the Cold War can no longer be adequately explained through the actions of politicians, diplomats, and generals. Not only do we need to consider artists and intellectuals as crucial actors in creating and maintaining the nation, but also ordinary Americans, including children.[7]

Cold warriors relied to a surprising degree on the power of American culture to win the hearts and minds of young people around the world. American literature, modern art, theater, dance, and music, not to mention traveling industrial exhibitions and World's Fairs, were considered prime areas in which to showcase American high culture and material progress. In part, American policy-makers were determined to discredit Soviet accusations of the materialism and crass consumerism of American life. More importantly, the State Department hoped to influence opinion-makers, groups that included educators, intellectuals, artists, and youth. The US government specifically targeted young people, particularly the future leaders of unaligned nations and those trapped behind the Iron Curtain. If the world's young people could be converted to "the American Way" through Hollywood films, US Information Agency (USIA) lending libraries, jazz music broadcast over the Voice of America (VOA), and art exchange programs, the United States could secure the nation's future. Scholars have made the case for understanding the Cold War beyond traditional state politics and through cultural politics, but they have largely ignored the Cold War battle for the world's youth. Historical investigations into the democratization of diplomacy expose the tensions that underlie children's diplomacy and highlight the ambiguous nature of their "voluntary" nationalistic activities.

By examining neglected aspects of Cold War childhood, including the politicization and mobilization of children, and by searching out and listening to their voices in the historical record, we can understand more about how children used the tools at their disposal to actively shape their own lives as well as the meanings of nationhood and citizenship. In order to understand the broad range of activities that might be considered "political," for the purposes of this study, I focus on school-aged children and young people in their teens. Most typically pictured ducking under school desks during a nuclear attack drill, children in the 1950s were not simply victims. They exercised agency in their chosen volunteer activities, engaged with popular culture on a variety of levels, and intentionally participated (or perhaps refused to participate) in particular school and extracurricular programs. Because I am interested in "typical" children's experiences of the decade, this study does not include the explicitly political activities of communist or leftist children, such as the Young Pioneers or communist summer camps. Children who attended interracial summer camps, such as Wo-Chi-Ca, Lakeland, or Kinderland, participated in radically different activities than their peers, and they were certainly a distinct minority of American youth.[8] But children of all races, classes, ethnicities, and geographical locations engaged in Cold War culture, civil defense, and internationalist cultural activities, and it is these experiences that I examine. Because it can be difficult to hear children's voices in the historical record, I also analyze how the idea of childhood functioned in popular culture, art exchange programs, public and private book programs, advertising, and the public schools.

Scholars of childhood have raised important questions about the use of the term "agency" and the implicit assumptions upon which it rests, including Enlightenment ideas emphasizing the coherence of the individual, reason, and self-determination. All human beings, adults as well as children, act within a universe of limited options and possibilities. Although it is important to understand the special constraints that can limit some children's choices, these constraints vary over time and place, and according to gender, race, nationality, class, and many other factors. The question of agency, therefore, might best be understood as one more paradox at the heart of Cold War American childhood. If, on the one hand, children were vulnerable, imagined as potential victims of communist indoctrination or nuclear war, the most precious of democratic society's resources, its future and its reason for fighting Soviet communism around the globe, then they were also political weapons, as Margaret Peacock has pointed out. Children's innocence constituted the basis for their political activities on behalf of the state. This paradox lies at the heart of my analysis.

THE RISE OF PUBLIC DIPLOMACY

Understanding how and why American children became important actors in Cold War diplomacy requires an understanding of postwar American propaganda and public diplomacy efforts more broadly. America's Cold War propaganda apparatus took root during World War II. In June 1942, President Franklin D. Roosevelt created the Office of War Information (OWI), charged with administering information programs both at home and abroad. From its inception, Republicans saw the OWI as a mechanism for encouraging support for New Deal policies, and their opposition to "information programs" continued well into the postwar decades. Nevertheless, the OWI recruited employees from the media, academia, and, in particular, the advertising industry. These men, who brought their marketing expertise to US diplomacy, "knew how to package and market soft drinks, automobiles, and breakfast cereal. . . . Now their client was the United States government, and their job was to sell" America's wartime policies.[9]

The United States had been slow to develop propaganda systems compared to other nations. Moscow, Berlin, London, and Paris had launched radio networks to reach foreign audiences and colonial possessions in the 1920s and 1930s. Nelson Rockefeller, the director of the US Office of International Affairs, used shortwave radio to counter Nazi propaganda in Latin America beginning in 1940, but when the Japanese attacked Pearl Harbor, the US government had fewer than a dozen transmitters capable of overseas broadcasting. By 1945, however, the OWI ran 39 transmitters worldwide and assisted a wide variety of print media organizations, from foreign-language magazines and books to film, pamphlets, matchbooks, photo exhibits, and leaflets. The postwar denazification and democracy education programs established in occupied Germany and Japan set important precedents for later USIA activities. Beginning in 1945, US Army officers established an extensive network of Amerika Hauser (America Houses), small cultural institutes that included libraries, lecture rooms, and English-language learning classrooms. Housed within the State Department, the Office of Information Coordination maintained a global network of 76 branch offices and 67 USIS information centers and libraries that stocked books, displayed exhibits, and showed films about the United States.[10] Postwar authorities also created an exchange program that brought German journalists, teachers, and businessmen to the United

States to experience democratic society firsthand. Wartime programming of the VOA set another crucial precedent. By the end of the war, the VOA carried daily news and feature stories from Washington to nations across the globe and broadcast the VOA in 24 languages. However, when the war ended, so did the justification for the OWI, and Congressional Republicans moved quickly to shutter the organization.

President Truman, however, recognized the crucial importance of information activities to American foreign policy. He abolished the Office of War Information on August 31, 1945, and transferred its functions to the Interim International Information Service (IIIS), a new office housed in the State Department under William B. Benton, the Assistant Secretary of State for Public Affairs. Like many men who became government propaganda experts, Benton had enjoyed a prewar career in advertising and journalism, and he believed in the power of words and ideas, both to spread democracy and to discredit the Soviet Union and communism.[11] At IIIS, however, Benton presided over a much-reduced organization whose main responsibilities were supervising American re-education programs in Germany and Japan, developing America's relationship with UNESCO, and working doggedly to persuade reluctant congressmen of the importance of the information program. Although bolstered by George Kennan's 1946 "Long Telegram," which warned of aggressive Soviet propaganda efforts, many congressmen who viewed the information program as leftist and elitist, not to mention expensive, further trimmed the budget of the newly named Office of International Information and Cultural Affairs. The agency's 1946 budget appropriation of $45 million was trimmed by almost half, to $25.4 million, in 1947. Despite budgetary woes, the IIIS identified "political organizations, trade unions, youth groups, farmers, and cultural and scientific societies" as key target audiences. From the beginning, US propagandists focused on winning the hearts and minds of young people.[12]

The information program remained a neglected stepchild of foreign policy until 1947, when the Soviet threat in Eastern Europe and the Balkans aroused Congress. Truman's unprecedented request for direct military and economic aid for Greece and Turkey further established the need for America to explain its motives in the emerging Cold War against the Soviet Union. Senators Karl Mundt (R-SD) and Alexander Smith (R-NJ) sponsored legislation that would give the information programs a permanent home in the State Department. In September 1947, a bipartisan group of a dozen congressmen toured 22 nations in Europe and the Near East and came home convinced of the need to counter the USSR's far more advanced and aggressive psychological warfare efforts. Upon their return to Washington, they argued that the United States had to "counteract the insidious undermining of the free forces resisting communism" and explain "US ideals, motives, and objectives to a demoralized and groping Europe." Despite lingering congressional opposition to overseas information programs, on January 16, 1948, Congress passed the US Information and Educational Exchange Act, more popularly known as the Smith-Mundt Act, to "promote a better understanding of the United States in other countries, and to increase mutual understanding between the people of the United States and the people of other countries."[13] President Truman signed the law on January 30, 1948, officially establishing public diplomacy as a basic component of American foreign policy. Long before Joseph Nye coined the term "soft power," the United States sought to create "world understanding" through information programs and both public and private global outreach efforts. Through such efforts, US power was represented as benevolent—spreading democracy, freedom, and wealth—and benign in effect—increasing rather than limiting education, opportunity, and material comforts.

As the Cold War heated up between 1947 and 1950, US information campaigns and propaganda efforts expanded rapidly. The National Security Act of 1947 created the Central Intelligence Agency (CIA), with the authority to engage in covert psychological warfare and "other functions," which eventually included the use "black propaganda" to subvert existing governments, endorse coups, and encourage assassinations of foreign leaders. CIA money subsidized unattributed publications, most famously the Congress for Cultural Freedom's flagship journal, *Encounter* (1953–1991) and helped to prevent communist victories in the 1948 French and Italian elections.[14] When the Cold War expanded to Asia with the outbreak of the Korean War in 1950, the Soviet Union launched a vicious propaganda campaign accusing the US military of using biological weapons, killing 300,000 North Korean women and children and targeting schools, libraries, and rest homes. Radio Moscow produced 502 hours per week of programming, compared to only 203 hours broadcast over the VOA.[15] In the spring and summer of 1950, the United States committed to full-scale propaganda activities to roll back communism across the globe. NSC-68, the blueprint for US Cold War policy, recommended the creation of the Psychological Strategy Board (PSB) in an attempt to consolidate and organize the various propaganda and information programs scattered throughout the federal bureaucracy, including more aggressive psychological and covert activities to foment unrest and revolt in communist-dominated areas. As the Cold War intensified, Soviet authorities retaliated with a campaign to reduce Western influence by expelling private organizations such as the YMCA, CARE, and the American Friends Service Committee, nongovernmental organizations whose presence had served to counter anti-American propaganda.[16] Edward Barrett, a *Newsweek* editor and propaganda expert during World War II, became Assistant Secretary of State for Public Affairs and reinvigorated the Truman administration's propaganda offensive. In April 1950, Truman announced a broad "Campaign of Truth." Declaring that the Cold War was "a struggle, above all else, for the minds of men," Truman called for a sustained ideological warfare program. In hearings led by the Senate Foreign Relations Committee, Secretary of State Dean Acheson, Generals George Marshall and Dwight Eisenhower, and foreign affairs expert John Foster Dulles urged Congress to create a new agency to direct ideological warfare and to combat Soviet propaganda in Korea. In response, the Republican-led Congress more than doubled federal funding for information activities to $79.1 million.[17] In practice, this "Campaign of Truth" targeted vulnerable children who were represented as victims of Soviet propaganda.

By the time Eisenhower took office in January 1953, the United States had established an extensive global propaganda structure. VOA broadcasts reached 100 countries in 46 languages, the US press service supplied

materials to 10,000 foreign newspapers every single day, the motion picture service reached more than 300 million viewers. And US information
centers sponsored libraries and a variety of cultural programs in 60 countries and 190 cities across the globe. Despite these gains, Secretary of State
John Foster Dulles warned in the midst of the Korean War that "[t]he
communists to date in Asia have won hands down, the propaganda war,
with the result that in most of the world today we stand morally convicted
of vile atrocities."[18]

Eisenhower wholeheartedly embraced psychological warfare and
cultural diplomacy, testifying before Congress in 1947, "We should dis-
seminate the truth about the United States to the peoples of the world
by every means at our disposal." Throughout the Cold War, and particularly during Eisenhower's presidency, the US government developed a
"camouflaged" approach to propaganda that relied on a unique public–
private approach involving "independent news media, nongovernmental
organizations, and private individuals" to communicate the government's
propaganda messages. By working through existing youth groups, educational exchanges, and pen pals, as well as professional artists, writers, and
musicians, psychological warfare experts blurred the distinctions between
domestic and international propaganda by targeting Americans *and* by
using them "as active participants in a war of persuasion." In a campaign
speech on October 8, 1952, Eisenhower made clear his intention to move
beyond established channels of official diplomacy in the global war of
ideas. The American people themselves, including children, would spread
ideas through "every medium of communication, mutual economic assistance, trade and barter, and friendly contacts through travel, correspondence, and sports."[19]

When Eisenhower took office, he created the Committee on
International Information Activities, informally known as the Jackson
Committee, to review the nation's existing propaganda structure. The
ultimate psychological warrior of the Eisenhower administration, C. D.
Jackson had headed the wartime Psychological Warfare Division and, in
1952, was a vice-president at media company Time-Life, Inc. In June 1953,
the Jackson Committee recommended elevating psychological warfare to

the same level of importance as political, economic, and military strategies; integrating information activities into the general conduct of foreign
policy; replacing Truman's Psychological Strategy Board (PSB) with the
Operations Coordinating Board (OCB); and giving the director of the IIA
a higher rank within the State Department. Despite these suggestions, both
the Jackson Committee and President Eisenhower eventually conceded to
the wishes of Secretary of State John Foster Dulles, who insisted that the
information program be removed from the State Department. On July 1,
1953, President Eisenhower announced the creation of the USIA, a federal
agency incorporating all government information programs, including
the VOA radio network, overseas libraries and information centers, the
film service, and press and publication agencies. The mission of the new
agency was to "persuade foreign peoples that it is in their own interest to
take actions which are also consistent with the national objectives of the
United States."[20] Only the Fulbright Exchange program remained in the
State Department, at Senator William Fulbright's insistence.[21]

Under President Eisenhower, the USIA rapidly expanded. Unlike
Truman's PSB, the OCB enjoyed a place in the executive branch and an
official relationship with the National Security Council. By March 1954,
the USIA employed 48 staff and operated a $450 million budget, which
Director Theodore Streibert used to launch a "cultural offensive" against
Soviet propaganda. Overseas lectures, art exhibits, concerts, films, radio
and television programs, trade fairs, and literature traveled abroad to
highlight the achievements and freedom of American culture. By 1954,
the International Exchange Service (IES) had established programs in
more than 70 countries to support a broad campaign to combat communism and other "anti-American forces" that the State Department accused
of "sowing mistrust" of US policies. Streibert worked with US businesses
to create the Business Council for International Understanding, modeled
on the Ad Council, to carry out public relations projects abroad using
USIA themes. It was under Streibert that the United States launched its
most ambitious program to mobilize the private sector, the People-to-
People program. Despite its increased stature in the federal bureaucracy,
however, the USIA did not become an official member of the National

Security Administration (NSA) or the OCB until 1955, and Eisenhower did not include Striebert in cabinet meetings until 1956. The information programs never achieved parity with military or economic strategies during the Cold War, but, under Eisenhower, American propaganda efforts reached their peak and recruited all Americans, including children, to represent their nation as cultural diplomats and ambassadors.[22]

Eisenhower's military background and global travels throughout World War II strengthened his personal belief in the efficacy of a broad-based, democratic approach to diplomacy. He instituted these ideas in organizations like the Crusade for Freedom (1950–60), the People-to-People Program (1955), and the President's Physical Fitness program (1956).[23] In his 1958 State of the Union Address, Eisenhower focused on security and peace, emphasizing defense spending and economic aid to allied nations. But he also repeatedly called on the American people to sacrifice as necessary for the larger cause of international peace. "Federal action can do only a part of the job," the President insisted.

> In both education and research, redoubled exertions will be necessary on the part of all Americans if we are to rise to the demands of our times. This means hard work on the part of state and local governments, private industry, schools and colleges, private organizations and foundations, teachers, parents, and—*perhaps most important of all—the student himself, with his bag of books and his homework.*[24]

Administration officials presented cultural exchange to the public in terms that appealed to an idealized construction of American national identity, one that took for granted the superiority of American civilization. The federal government asked ordinary Americans to enlighten and uplift the peoples of the world by extending the virtues of their society to the less fortunate. Although they didn't practice traditional colonialism or imperialism, Cold War policies encouraged Americans to interpret US foreign policy in terms of a "benevolent supremacy," the practice of welcoming other nations into the protective circle of American security if they accepted American ideas and policies. Educational and cultural exchange efforts in the 1950s and 1960s, for example, were assumed to increase "mutual understanding" but in practice more often meant "prov-ing" the good intentions of the United States.[25] Since the inception of the Cold War, the federal government considered American youth crucial to this project. From 1945 to 1963, under Presidents Truman, Eisenhower, and Kennedy, the federal government specifically mobilized children and young people to engage in public diplomacy and to win the Cold War.

DOMESTIC INFORMATION CAMPAIGNS

The 1948 Smith-Mundt Act authorized the State Department and the USIA to distribute propaganda abroad but prohibited "the domestic dis-semination of information intended for foreign audiences." How, then, did the federal government convince the American people, young and old, to support Cold War policies such as the nuclear arms race and civil preparedness? The answer is twofold. It is now well-known that the federal government secretly funneled money and ideas into a variety of cultural organizations, including Radio Free Europe and the Congress for Cultural Freedom, in an effort to manipulate their public messages. The Federal Civil Defense Administration and the Atomic Energy Commission directly targeted children through civil defense films and grade-level books about atomic energy distributed through the schools. But the far more influential means of reaching ordinary Americans was advertising.

For the most part, Madison Avenue and private corporations con-structed the "information campaigns" that Americans experienced every day—over the radio and television, in print and outdoor ads, in public school programs, and in their communities. The primary organization for creating and distributing public information campaigns was the Ad Council, which originated as the War Advertising Council in 1942 to sell war bonds and explain the nation's war aims to the American people. In the postwar years, the Ad Council worked with the federal govern-ment to identify important public issues, many of which mirrored the State Department's foreign propaganda campaigns, such as the superior-ity of capitalism and the evils of communism. Funded by corporations that donated public advertisements and the ad agencies that constructed the ads for free, the Ad Council leaned toward conservative positions and tended to support ideas that benefitted big business. This close relationship between the federal government and corporate America created some ethical problems. Historian Megan Barnhart has argued that the Ad Council's roots in corporate America conflicted with public education efforts, such as the atomic energy campaign, since "promoting public awareness of the need for international control of atomic energy provided no tangible benefit to corporate America."[26] The typical Ad Council strategy first educated the public about a particular issue and then motivated the public to action through appeals to fear, patriotism, or the like. The first year of the atomic energy campaign for example, from August 1946 through March 1947, focused on disseminating facts—the devastating power of atomic weapons—and the need for Americans to educate themselves about nuclear power. A 1946 Ad Council radio spot warned:

> The discovery of atomic weapons of warfare . . . with their terrific destructive power . . . has raised one of the most vital problems ever to face you and the rest of the world. But you must know about atomic energy itself before you can have any idea what to do about it. Learn all you can about what leading scientists have to say about the atom. Be informed. Remember . . . ignorance may be bliss, . . . but in this case it's a keg of dynamite, . . . and you're sitting on it.[27]

These ads reached more than 6 million Americans in 1946–1947 and aired during children's television programs such as *Quiz Kids*. This first phase, however, failed to offer Americans an avenue for action and resulted, according to 1947 opinion polls, in Americans feeling helpless before the nuclear threat. With no clear path for action, most Americans disengaged from the political issues surrounding atomic energy control.[28] Later Ad Council campaigns, such as the Crusade for Freedom, would offer clear and direct means of action for Americans eager to fight the Cold War at home and abroad.

More pervasive than Ad Council public information campaigns, corporate advertising, which during the 1950s and 1960s echoed many of the themes sent abroad as foreign propaganda, offered another way for

Americans to negotiate appropriate responses to the Cold War. Again and again, diverse consumer products from life insurance and air travel to televisions and packaged foods promised *security*. As Elaine Tyler May and other historians have argued, atomic-age Americans were anxious, and millions turned inward—to marriage, to home, to family, to domesticity—to foster a sense of safety and security. White, middle-class Americans, in their new suburban homes filled with babies and young children, required an unprecedented amount of consumer goods. The Baby Boom ensured that children and childhood innocence provided a ready vocabulary to sell those consumer goods, but the Cold War supplied the emotional imperative. Advertising executives used Cold War fears and anxiety to sell products and used consumer products to sell the Cold War. Americans were exposed to the same ideas as foreigners through popular culture, corporate advertising, patriotic pageantry, and government public information campaigns.

American children and youth, politicized by the federal government as well as by private organizations, corporate America, and the public schools, became little Cold Warriors, ambassadors, and representatives of the nation. From this perspective, the 1950s look more like the war years and the 1960s than Americans typically acknowledge.

NOTES

1. Dominique Marshall, "Children's Rights and Children's Action in International Relief and Domestic Welfare: The Work of Herbert Hoover Between 1914–1950," *Journal of the History of Children and Youth* 1.3 (Fall 2008): 351–388.
2. Melanie McAlister, *Epic Encounters: Culture, Media, and US Interests in the Middle East Since 1945* (Oakland: University of California Press, 2005): 46.
3. Jennifer Helgren, *American Girls and Global Responsibility* (New Brunswick, NJ: Rutgers University Press, 2017).
4. Akira Iriye, "Culture and International History," in Michael Hogan and Thomas Paterson, eds. *Explaining the History of American Foreign Relations* (Cambridge: Cambridge University Press, 1991): 214–215. Iriye argued that a cultural approach to diplomatic history examines "international affairs in terms of dreams, aspirations, and other manifestations of human consciousness" such as "memory, ideology, emotions, life styles, scholarly and artistic work, and other symbols."

5. The past decades have seen a rapid increase in scholarly work in the field of public diplomacy. See Gregory Tomlin, *Murrow's Cold War: Public Diplomacy for the Kennedy Administration* (Lincoln, NE: Potomac Books, 2016); Ien Ang, Yudhishthir Raj Isar, and Phillip Mar, "Cultural Diplomacy: Beyond the National Interest?," *International Journal of Cultural Policy* 21.4 (2015): 365–381; Nicholas Cull, *The Cold War and the United States Information Agency: American Propaganda and Public Diplomacy, 1945–1989* (London: Cambridge University Press, 2008); Kenneth Osgood, *Total Cold War: Eisenhower's Secret Propaganda Battle at Home and Abroad* (Lawrence: University of Kansas Press, 2006). On "soft power," see Joseph Nye, *Bound to Lead: The Changing Nature of American Power* (New York: Basic Books, 1990).

6. Iriye, "Culture and International History," 214–225. Originally published as "Culture," *Journal of American History* 77.1 (June 1990): 99–107.

7. Studies of traditional political and economic power have dominated the field of diplomatic and Cold War history, but recent studies approach the topic with a more holistic view. See Osgood, *Total Cold War* (2006); Cull, *The Cold War and the United States Information Agency* (2008); Wilson P. Dizard, Jr. *Inventing Public Diplomacy: The Story of the US Information Agency* (Boulder: Lynne Rienner Publishers, 2004); Frances Stonor Saunders, *The Cultural Cold War: The CIA and the World of Arts and Letters* (New York: New Press, 2001); Serge Guibaut, *How New York Stole the Idea of Modern Art* (Chicago: University of Chicago Press, 1985); David Caute, *The Dancer Defects: The Struggle for Cultural Supremacy During the Cold War* (Oxford University Press, 2005); Michael L. Krenn, *Fall-out Shelters for the Human Spirit: American Art and the Cold War* (Chapel Hill: University of North Carolina Press, 2005); Penny M. Von Eschen, *Satchmo Blows Up the World: Jazz Ambassadors Play the Cold War* (Cambridge: Harvard University Press, 2004); Walter L. Hixson, *Parting the Curtain: Propaganda, Culture, and the Cold War* (New York: Palgrave Macmillan, 1999); Laura A. Belmonte, *Selling the American Way: US Propaganda and the Cold War* (Philadelphia: University of Pennsylvania Press, 2008); Sarah Ellen Graham, ed., *Culture and Propaganda: The Progressive Origins of American Public Diplomacy, 1936–1953* (New York: Ashgate Publishing, 2015).

8. Studies of communist youth cultural and political organizations include Judy Kaplan and Linn Shapiro, *Red Diapers: Growing Up in the Communist Left* (Champaign: University of Illinois Press, 1998); Paul Mischler, *Raising Reds: The Young Pioneers, Radical Summer Camps, and Communist Political Culture in the United States* (New York: Columbia University Press, 1999); June Levine and Gene Gordon, *Tales of Wo-Chi-Ca: Blacks, Whites, and Reds at Camp* (San Rafael, CA: Avon Springs Press, 2002).

9. Dizard, *Inventing Public Diplomacy*, 19.

10. Belmonte, *Selling the American Way*, 18; Hixson, *Parting the Curtain*, 5; Department of State, http://eca.state.gov/ivlp/about-ivlp/program-history

11. David F. Krugler, *The Voice of America and the Domestic Propaganda Battles, 1945–1953* (Columbia: University of Missouri Press, 2000): 7.

12. Cull, *The Cold War and the United States Information Agency*, 36–37.

13. Title I, Section 2, United States Information and Educational Exchange Act of 1948. Available at http://www.state.gov/documents/organization/177574.pdf.

14. The Congress for Cultural Freedom (CCF) was an organization of noncommunist Left intellectuals founded in 1950. Its mission was to use the influence of its members, academic journals and conferences, and exhibitions to sway European intellectuals away from communist sympathies to form a united anti-totalitarian global intelligentsia. In 1966, the *New York Times* reported that the CCF had been funded by the CIA.

15. "What Russians Are Told About the War in Korea," *New York Times* (September 24, 1950): E5; "Stepped Up Red Propaganda Saps Hope for Korea Truce, *New York Times* (May 5, 1952): 1; Belmonte, *Selling the American Way,* 47.

16. CARE was founded in 1945 by 22 American aid organizations to provide emergency assistance to European survivors of World War II. On May 11, 1946, the first 15,000 packages were delivered to Le Havre, France. Early packages were leftover US Army surplus food parcels intended to provide one meal for ten soldiers during the planned invasion of Japan. For $10, CARE allowed Americans send the packages to Europe, where millions faced starvation. Later CARE packages included tools, blankets, clothes, books, school supplies, and medicine.

17. "High Leaders Ask Congress for Vast 'Truth Propaganda,'" *New York Times* (July 6, 1950): 1; Hixson, *Parting the Curtain,* 9–16.

18. Hixson, *Parting the Curtain,* 21; "Propaganda War in Korea Proposed," *New York Times* (September 18, 1952): 3.

19. Osgood, *Total Cold War,* 5, 51–53.

20. Hixson, *Parting the Curtain,* 24–26; Dizard, *Inventing Public Diplomacy,* 53–55.

21. Cull, *The Cold War and the United States Information Agency*, 32, 90–91. In September 1945, Senator William Fulbright (D-AR) proposed using funds from the sale of surplus war materials to fund a program of reciprocal educational exchanges. The first Fulbright scholars left for Burma in the fall of 1948.

22. Hixson, *Parting the Curtain,* 136–140.

23. Cull, *The Cold War and the United States Information Agency.*

24. Dwight D. Eisenhower, "State of the Union," (January 9, 1958); emphasis added.

25. Matt Loayza, "'A Curative and Creative Force': The Exchange of Persons Program and Eisenhower's Inter-American Policies, 1953–1961," *Diplomatic History* 37.5 (November 2013): 952–953.

26. Megan Barnhart, "Selling the International Control of Atomic Energy: The Scientists' Movement, the Advertising Council, and the Problem of the Public," in Rosemary B. Mariner and G. Kurt Piehler, eds. *The Atomic Bomb and American Society: New Perspectives* (Knoxville: University of Tennessee Press, 2009): 105.

27. Advertisement text, "Atomic Energy" (November 22, 1946), Federation of American Scientists Records, cited in Barnhart, "Selling the International Control of Atomic Energy," 107–108.

28. Wendy Melillo, "A Keg of Dynamite and You're Sitting on It: An Analysis of the Ad Council's Atomic Energy Campaign," *Journalism History* 38.4 (Winter 2013): 233–239.

1

Cold War Comics

Educating American Children for a New Global Role

In both the United States and the Soviet Union, maintaining public support for the Cold War necessitated a constant stream of foreign and domestic persuasion in a variety of forms: from parades to posters, ad campaigns to atomic films, comic books to cartoons, American and Soviet children learned that they were engaged in a global struggle.[1] But for both historical and ideological reasons, the means of socializing children into the new global balance of power differed in some ways between the two superpowers. In the United States, the "creation story" of the nation, of pioneers settling the western frontier through hard work and individual striving, was pressed into national service to provide a Cold War narrative that explained the role of the United States on new frontiers in Third World nations. One of the primary ways children learned this lesson was through Western-themed popular culture. This chapter concentrates on a variety of Lone Ranger texts in order to understand how America's frontier narrative applied to a larger global struggle and was made understandable to American children.

Lone Ranger comic books served as just one among many popular culture Westerns during the Cold War that suggested to American children an appropriate role for the nation and for them, as its future leaders in a world of global competition. From film and radio came Roy Rogers, Gene Autry, and the Cisco Kid. Wild Bill Hickok, Annie Oakley, Buffalo Bill, Jr., the Range Rider, Zorro, Kit Carson, and even a canine patriot, Rin-Tin-Tin, fought for the cause of law and order on the Western frontier. The Lone Ranger was, and continues to be, one of the most powerful and pervasive representative of the American frontier hero, serviceable to the changing needs of American policies from his introduction in 1933 to his most recent (and poorly received) film in 2013.[2] Film historian Stanley Corkin suggested that many if not most post–World War II Westerns suggested the taming of unruly territories in preparation for the expansion of commerce; in other words, making the West—and the world—safe for capitalism. As the dominant film genre in postwar America, Westerns centered on imperialism and the construction of national identity in an era of nationalism and global hegemony.[3] I argue that in the decades after World War II, the masked hero represented American "benevolent supremacy," which Melanie McAlister contrasted to both traditional European colonialism and Soviet militarism in that the colonial subject freely chose subordination in a relationship akin to marriage.[4] Like Tonto, Third World peoples would yield willingly to a superior political, military, and moral force that would in return ensure prosperity and stability. The Lone Ranger modeled for young viewers in both the United States and colonized nations the appropriate role for the postwar United States as civilizer and savior, not conqueror or colonizer.

THE COMICS AFTER WORLD WAR II

Popular culture for juvenile audiences—comic books, radio, cartoons, and movies—played a crucial role in mobilizing children and explaining why the United States was at war.[5] During World War II, children's contributions to the war effort expanded well beyond school and volunteer activities. With encouragement from the Office of War Information, they collected tin and rubber, bought savings stamps, helped to plant and tend Victory Gardens, scanned the skies for enemy aircraft, and participated in defense drills. Disney, a leader in America's propaganda effort, created a moveable book, *The Victory March: The Mystery of the Treasure Chest* (1942), to encourage children to purchase and collect war savings stamps. Disney's cartoons showcased the worst caricatures and stereotypes of America's German and Japanese enemies. The 1943 animated short "Der Fuehrer's Face" (originally titled "Donald Duck in Nutzi Land") featured Donald Duck trapped in a surrealist nightmare: living in a Nazi-run country, Donald is forced to work 48-hour shifts in an ammunitions factory while he's bombarded incessantly by Nazi propaganda. Designed to sell war bonds, the propaganda cartoon won the Academy Award for Best Animated Short Film in 1943. Spike Jones and his City Slickers' parody song, "Der Fuehrer's Face," topped the charts between October 1942 and January 1943. Disney drafted the lovable Donald in 1942, and fans followed his military exploits in "The Spirit of '43," which featured Donald Duck challenging Americans to "spend for the Axis or save for your taxes." The following year, Donald "Commando" Duck went to war and "wiped out" a Japanese airfield. The US government relied on Disney to create training films for the military as well as propaganda films for general audiences. In 1943, Disney released an animated adaptation of Gregor Ziemer's 1941 bestselling book about the Nazi education system, *Education for Death: The Making of a Nazi*. The same year, RKO Pictures released a feature-length adaptation called *Hitler's Children* for adult audiences.[6] Between 1941 and 1945, Disney Studios produced 32 short films and numerous educational and instructional films for the US government and military.[7]

Comic books, too, responded to the war with a flood of pro-American superheroes. Captain America was born in 1941; the cover of the first issue depicted the ultra-American hero slugging Adolph Hitler in the face, almost a year before the United States declared war on Germany.[8] Americans bought 25 million comic books per month in 1943, totaling $30 million in sales. *Newsweek* attributed the boom to "the well-filled pockets of the nation's school children," but the *New York Times* reported that comic books made up 25% of all magazines shipped abroad to American servicemen. At least 35,000 copies of *Superman* alone shipped out to American GIs.[9] By the end of the war, in November 1945, the US Army newspaper *Yank* reported that comic book sales at military posts across the nation exceeded the combined sales of the *Saturday Evening Post* and *Readers' Digest* by ten to one. The Market Research Company of America estimated that about 70 million Americans—roughly half of the nation's population—read comic books. Approximately 95% of all boys and 91% of all girls between the ages of 6 and 11 and 87% of boys and 81% of girls between 12 and 17 read comics regularly.[10] On the eve of the Cold War, US publishers enjoyed thriving audiences for comic books, at home and abroad.

There were critics, however. Parents, educators, and librarians had long bemoaned children's enthusiasm for the graphic violence, implausible adventures, and questionable morals celebrated in some comic books. Communists described Captain America as an imperialist and accused comic heroes of buttressing an oppressive class system. Such accusations were bad enough when the audience was limited to American children, but as the United States emerged as a global superpower after the war, suddenly comic books took on international significance as representations of the nation's character. According to critics, comics not only poisoned the minds of American children, but, with the dramatic rise of foreign assistance programs, threatened to do the same to youngsters around the world. In 1945, the Women's Council for Post-War Europe announced that comic books would not be included in the 500 Treasure Chests containing juvenile books donated by Americans to the children of war-torn Europe and Asia. Comics, spokeswoman Ninon Talon explained, "give the wrong impression of this country to European and Chinese youngsters" and imply that "the United States is a country of gangsters and shooting." Instead, their committee created a list of several hundred "carefully selected . . . acceptable books" that the public could donate.[11] Talon was not alone in her insistence on the political importance of comic books. One reader of the *New York Times* argued that sending comic books to Germany with Economic Cooperation Administration (ECA) funds "present[ed] the worst and most distorted aspect of American society" and advocated against the democratic process by settling issues through immediate and direct "justice," usually in the form of violence.[12] The Soviet Union likewise charged that *Superman* comic books "fascized" American children, teaching the "army of tomorrow" that "gangsterism is the norm of human relations."[13] One young author of the 1949 Camp Wo-Chi-Ca (Workers Children's Camp, a leftist summer camp) yearbook penned a critical article about comic books, finding them for the most part "ridiculous" and "a bad escape from reality" that often featured only handsome heroes and "bad guys" with "foreign minority-group names." The author asserted, "Most comics, instead of helping us to respect people of different backgrounds, prejudice us against them."[14]

The attacks on comic books culminated with the publication of Dr. Frederic Wertham's *The Seduction of the Innocent* in 1954, Senate investigations of the link between comic books and juvenile delinquency in 1955, and the industry's self-imposed Comics Code Authority (CCA), which impacted the content of comics well through the 1970s. Because of their intentionally clean and patriotic content, however, The Lone Ranger comics largely escaped these public controversies.

THE LONE RANGER AND THE COLD WAR

As America's enemy shifted from fascism to communism after the war, children's popular culture quickly followed. Bradford Wright argued that comics of the 1950s "basically affirm[ed] the triumphalist culture of the United States," expressing "moral certitude about American virtues, confidence in the nation's institutions, and optimism for a new age of affluence." William Savage agreed, noting that comics "boost[ed] morale in the face of a few unthinkable things, including atomic war and/or Communist takeover of the United States."[15] Perhaps patriotic superheroes in so-called clean comics convinced some educators by the late 1940s to accept the inevitable and to use comic books to teach children positive values. Even US government bureaucrats recognized that if violent comics reflected negatively on the United States, then pro-American comics might communicate positive ideals to foreign audiences. In late 1949, the State Department initiated an experimental "picture story series on great Americans" for distribution in Korea, Thailand, Vietnam, and Indonesia.[16] Although the graphic approach was new, the "picture story" itself was a traditional history of the United States that began with Columbus and ended with the creation of the United Nations. The triumphant story concluded with a panoramic image of New York City, foregrounded by major transportation networks including railways, highways, waterways, and an airplane overhead. Fertile agricultural lands stretch from the middle distance to high peaks in the back of the picture frame. Much like the human parade on the front cover, American history is described as a linear progression from the past to the modern present, from Europe to the United States, from wilderness to civilization. The text reiterates the theme of human progress, linking material well-being with political ideals epitomized by the United States: "This story has been one of quest . . . quest for opportunity, for material happiness . . . quest for better ways of doing things . . . and above all, quest for freedom . . . freedom of mind and spirit, for all men created equal in the sight of God."[17]

The Boy Scouts of America's monthly magazine, *Boys' Life*, featured a regular series of similar comic-format lessons in American history titled "How America Grew." The October 1957 story, "How America Grew . . . The Communist Experiment," retells the story of the Pilgrims as a failed communist experiment. Upon settling in the inhospitable New World, the Pilgrims agreed that "all work would be done on a communist basis" for seven years. Dissatisfaction arose, however, when the more industrious workers "grew tired of doing the work of the lazy" and "married men resented" that "their wives had to do the cooking and washing for the unmarried men." In 1523, the Governor assigned parcels of land to each family, and the Puritans ended their communist experiment. Land ownership "gave every man a reason for hard work—his own family's welfare."[18] The fact that Karl Marx wrote *The Communist Manifesto* more than 300 years after this creative historical account seems immaterial. Reinterpretations of US history to privilege Cold War values—individualism, capitalism, and democratic government—were common themes in children's pop culture, both foreign and domestic, throughout the Cold War.

Assuming that children and the cultural products intended for them simply mirrored the Cold War politics of adults, however, or that children, foreign or domestic, readily assimilated the messages embedded in popular culture or government propaganda is too simplistic. Children who consumed comics cannot be understood in direct relation to children as political actors or global citizens during the Cold War. Each individual brought his or her own experiences and personal identity to reading books and playing games, including gender, class, race, and nationality. It is therefore difficult if not impossible to generalize about how individual children interpreted the political content of comic books or played with toys in ways that manufacturers and parents (or bureaucrats) did not intend or anticipate. What we can perhaps understand from the era's juvenile pop culture is how adults conceptualized the American past and the nation's role in contemporary global politics during the Cold War years and the ways social reproduction works through popular texts for children. Beyond official representations, however, toys and comics offered a means by which children could practice and "try out" various roles they saw enacted on screens big and small, in politics and pop culture. If play is understood as a form of repetitive rehearsal for adult roles, we can read comics and other forms of children's pop culture as one way to understand the historical processes by which young people acquire agency as historical actors.

Scholars of children's play Howard Chudacoff and Brian Sutton-Smith define the concept of play as a "component of children's culture" that varies in relationship to each child's social circumstances and that is often limited, constrained, and defined by adults. Chudacoff focuses on four contexts that shaped American children's play experiences between 1600 and the present: the settings where play takes place, the instruments or absence of instruments that facilitate play, the actor(s) taking part in the play activities, and the degree of control and autonomy children have over their play. Particularly in the mid to late twentieth century, commercially manufactured toys became more widely available and perceived (by adults at least) as educational tools to inspire children's creativity or learning. Sutton-Smith argued, however, that "it is not so much what the toy does by itself, but in what way it gives the child an instrument with which to express and manipulate the cultural forces that bear upon him or her."[19] The imaginative world of the Lone Ranger and the Western frontier can be understood as instruments through which American children could make sense of the Cold War.

Dell Publishing, a leader in juvenile comics since 1929, targeted the youngest comic book readers. In 1938, Dell expanded its holdings by securing the rights to the Walt Disney and Warner Brothers cartoon properties through a partnership with Western Publishing. Licensed cartoon characters like Mickey Mouse, Donald Duck, Bugs Bunny, and Porky Pig, as well as Western heroes, secured Dell's market among young readers for the next several decades. Throughout the 1950s, Dell was the largest comic book publisher in the world, selling up to 26 million comic books every month in 1953. In addition to comic book adaptations of popular cartoon characters, Dell bought the rights to the movie and television characters Tarzan, Davy Crockett, Roy Rogers, Gene Autry, and the Lone Ranger.[20] Dell's "clean" comic books included *Roy Rogers, Dale Evans: Queen of the West, Western Roundup, Gene Autry*, and *The Lone Ranger*. Dell's cowboys were so popular that quarterly spin-offs starring Autry's horse, Champion, and Roy Rogers's Trigger, soon appeared. But the Lone Ranger was Dell's most popular Western hero, starring in 145 comic book issues between 1948 and 1962, and prompting two companion publications: the bimonthly comic book *Tonto* appeared in 1951 (31 issues) and a quarterly titled *Hi-Yo Silver, The Lone Ranger's Famous Horse*, began in 1952 (36 issues).[21]

A hero born during the Great Depression, the Lone Ranger debuted on a Detroit radio show in 1933. Over the course of a dozen episodes, the character acquired his now-familiar persona: an expert rider and marksman who never shot to kill; a paragon of virtue; a hero who lived outside the law, but always fought for justice. Tonto was introduced in episode 11 to give the Lone Ranger someone to talk to, a reason for dialogue. By 1939, more than 20 million Americans tuned in three times each week to hear *The Lone Ranger*. An early example of merchandising, the show's producers licensed the manufacture of a vast array of related products, including Lone Ranger guns, costumes, books, and a popular comic strip. Between 1933 and 1971, the Masked Man and his faithful sidekick Tonto starred in radio and television shows, paperback novels, Little Golden Books, films, and comic books. Until 1948, *The Lone Ranger* comic books consisted of reprints of newspaper strips written by Fran Stryker and illustrated by Charles Flanders. From August 1951 through May 1962, artist Tom Gill teamed up with script-writer Paul S. Newman to produce The Lone Ranger comic books. Artist Ernest Nordli painted the cover art from 1948 through mid-1953, when Don Spaulding and Hank Hartman began to share the job. Cover art shifted to photographs of television actor Clayton Moore in October 1957.

During the peak of the Cold War—from 1948 through 1962—the Lone Ranger and Tonto were ubiquitous. The duo appeared in 145 Dell comic books and on television between 1948 and 1962 to wide popular acclaim. By 1953, the show's twentieth anniversary, 249 US stations broadcast the radio show, which enjoyed the highest rating of any radio Western, reaching an estimated 12 million listeners weekly. During the same year, 90 television stations broadcast *The Lone Ranger* program, reaching an estimated audience of 5 million viewers each week. Readers in Norway, Argentina, Finland, France, Brazil, New Zealand, Uruguay, Ecuador, Hong King, South Africa, Cuba, and Canada followed the exploits of the Lone Ranger. The Whitman Publishing Company published 15 Lone Ranger novels, and the comic strip appeared daily in 177 newspapers, 28 of them abroad, and in 119 Sunday papers, 33 of them in foreign countries, for a combined audience of 71 million readers. *The Lone Ranger, Tonto*, and *Hi-Yo Silver* comic books boasted a circulation of 2 million monthly readers.[22]

The thousands of Lone Ranger texts produced from the 1930s through the 1970s told a particular national history, one that could be adapted to contemporary concerns. In the noble adventures of the Lone Ranger and Tonto, Americans saw a flattering self-portrait that glorified the golden age of nineteenth-century Western imperialism as a patriotic and necessary endeavor, explained pioneers' interactions with indigenous peoples as an ideal of good intentions, and portrayed American involvement in colonial wars as an exercise in negotiating local acceptance of US expansionist goals through the strategic employment of indigenous allies.[23] The Lone Ranger was committed to westward expansion and to making the West safe for settlers. After World War II, he became a fitting symbol not only of the Old West, but also of the contemporary nation; he embodied positive "American" values—honesty, hard work, and individualism. He was not so much an icon of the past as an enduring symbol of a widely accepted national mythology. Furthermore, as the embodiment of "American values" during the Cold War, the Lone Ranger–Tonto relationship provided a model of successful relationships that the US government could forge with indigenous peoples in the promotion of American values and goals on both domestic and international frontiers.

The Lone Ranger was not an isolated example of American nationalism; rather, he was part of a broad cultural cooptation of the idea of the US West as a "frontier" during the Cold War. The Westerns that dominated American film and television from 1946 to 1962 repeatedly played out the basic psychology of the Cold War: good versus evil, the rule of law, and courage in the defense of a threatened civilization. The heroes of Westerns provided role models of responsible American adulthood, dedicated to positive social values, love of country, respect for government, and communion with the creators of the nation. From 1947 to 1950, Westerns accounted for about 30% of Hollywood's output, a higher percentage than during any other era.[24] Hollywood's Motion Picture Alliance for the Preservation of American Ideals, founded in 1944 by John Wayne, Walt Disney, and 1,500 members of the film community, in combination with House Un-American Activities Committee (HUAC)'s investigations of Hollywood in 1947 and 1951, had a chilling effect on American film, ensuring that Westerns became a reliable vehicle for pro-American ideals and glorification of the American past.[25] It was not only popular culture that reflected these ideas. President Truman drew on America's frontier past, depicting the United States as a purveyor of civilization to a disorderly world. Just as "courts have marshals" and "counties need sheriffs," the United States had to use its military might to police the globe. Secretary of

States James Byrnes, while conducting negotiations with the Soviet Union, threatened that he had an atomic weapon "in his hip pocket."[26] Western comic books, television shows, and radio programs carried these ideas to wide audiences, particularly young ones.

George Trendle, The Lone Ranger's creator, made no secret of his desire to "entertain as well as quietly instruct and inspire" children. He made sure that the masked hero preached "Americanism through the American Heritage" and practiced "American" values: patriotism, fairness, tolerance, sympathy, religiosity, and pure speech. Trendle created a set of guidelines to ensure that his freelance writers emphasized the Ranger's characteristics in each story, and he offered suggestions for various plot devices that would highlight these traits.[27] One of Dell's most prolific writers, Gaylord Dubois, instilled "old-time moral and emotional values" in his stories, "praying for guidance" as he penned thousands of adventure tales.[28] Trendle accounted for the Lone Ranger's popularity in the dramatization of pioneers' hardships, those who "fought to give us our great American Heritage of opportunity, security and freedom. . . . the Lone Ranger has taught the real meaning of the word, Democracy."[29] In 1953, Senator Homer Ferguson applauded the Lone Ranger for teaching youngsters "the principles of good citizenship, patriotism, fair play, tolerance, and a sympathetic understanding of people and their rights and privileges."[30] How did a radio and television cowboy teach such values? Both congressmen and the Ranger's creators argued that children learned through imitation; children would mimic what they saw and heard their heroes do and say.

The Lone Ranger was broadcast on numerous foreign radio and television stations, through which he became, at least to his creators, "a modern worldwide symbol of freedom and justice" that would "teach Americanism around the world." Frank Meurer noted, "We have Lone Ranger novels in Norwegian and Japanese. . . . We have comic books in all the South American countries, and lately we've had them in England. What this does is teach Americanism around the world."[31] By November 1957, 53 television stations in 11 foreign countries broadcast the show, and more than 200 Sunday and daily newspapers carried the comic strip. Presumably, foreigners would learn Americanism the same way American children did—by imitating their cowboy hero and embracing his values.

Native Americans, Tonto, and Benevolent Supremacy

Congressman Ferguson's praise is insufficient evidence that the Lone Ranger actually accomplished its creators' nationalistic goals. Indeed, while Senator Ferguson thought children were learning fairness and sympathy, they instead may have relished make-believe but ferocious gun battles and the slaughter of imaginary Indians. The variety of ways American children could experience the Lone Ranger certainly mattered—with the entire family gathered around the radio or television, alone with a comic book, or playing scripted or unstructured games of "cowboys and Indians" with neighborhood children in the backyard. Comic books, with their low price of 10 cents, enabled children to exercise consumer choice when they purchased their own. In addition, gender, race, class, ethnicity, and nationality could influence the many ways children might interpret and participate in the masked man's adventures. Given the many variables, it is nearly impossible to imagine how German or Chinese children might have interpreted the Lone Ranger in light of their own experiences.

Furthermore, the variety of Lone Ranger texts should be understood in relation to one another; that is, how representations of the Lone Ranger differed from television to comic books to board games, and how these varied narratives interacted with other contemporary popular culture texts. For example, on television and in film, the Lone Ranger typically made his dramatic entrance pictured against a backdrop of pristine wilderness and blue sky, accompanied by the dynamic *William Tell* Overture. In this visual context, the heroic Lone Ranger entered and occupied the land as a savior and proprietor. The lack of buildings, telephone poles, wires, or modern structures signified the complete absence of civilization. This "emptiness" encouraged viewers to see the Old West as an uninhabited land, waiting for white settlers to make proper use of it and its resources.[32] Classic Westerns shared this characteristic way of picturing the landscape. Like most Westerns in the John Ford tradition, *The Lone Ranger* TV series featured panoramic, wide shots that emphasized the grandeur and the availability of the landscape. In contrast, the small size of the comic panel negated the power of wide shots. How, then, did comic books emphasize the visual availability of the landscape? Typical Lone Ranger comics began as the television show did—by setting the stage. The Ranger is almost always outside in an uninhabited landscape, pictured in a wilderness, if not necessarily an awe-inspiring one. From there, the action moved to headshots that emphasized dialogue or action. The landscape portrayed in comic books could not achieve the same visual power as television and later, film, but a child's familiarity with the television Lone Ranger would supply some of the action, drama, and contextual information that a comic book could not. The different forms of media reinforced one another.

If comic book panels could not summon the same impressive spectacle or proprietary gaze that television achieved, what was the purpose of these views of the open Western landscape, however small? The beauty and availability of the landscape has always been integral to the myth of the winning of the West: in the canonical Western, whites and Indians fought for control over territory, as did the United States and the Soviet Union during the Cold War, at least ideologically and economically. Visually inserting the Lone Ranger—and only the Lone Ranger—into this landscape implies American control. However, the Lone Ranger rarely encountered "bad" Indians. In typical comic book plots, *white* villains threatened to misuse the land or control it by illegal or unfair means. But the absence of bad Indians as well as "good" elided the fact that Indians once owned the land and that they were destroyed or removed. As Ariel Dorfman noted, the fact of their historical destruction was suppressed.[33] To a young comic book reader, the land appeared simply vacant. Like nineteenth-century landscape paintings, depictions of the West as wilderness performed ideological functions; they equated the wilderness with the nation's innocence and its seemingly limitless democratic potential. We can situate Lone Ranger comics in a long tradition of American visual culture and civic religion that portrays Americans as a "chosen people," specially appointed to create a model of freedom for the world. And this exceptionalist rhetoric, rather than the idea of occupying territory, is more to the point of the Lone Ranger. Benevolent supremacy does not require, and in fact repudiates, the direct occupation of land and the colonial relationship it creates. Like the Truman and Eisenhower Doctrines in Korea and Vietnam, the United States fought not for ownership of territory but for the political and economic stability of a global capitalist democracy. The didactic plot lines and narratives of *The Lone Ranger* readily complemented American civil religion, the sacred symbol of the idealized American narrative implied in the Western landscape.

As with the television series, the comic book Lone Ranger rarely confronted Native Americans in his quest for justice. Rather, it was white villains—outlaws, greedy land-grabbers, robbers, and thieves—who threatened the honest people of the West. Michael Ray Fitzgerald argued that "Cold War politics and relentless criticism from the Soviet Union over minority rights in the US made overt conflict between white settlers and American Indians a potential source of diplomatic difficulties between the US and emerging postcolonial nations."[34] Marauding Indian villains of the pre-war Western, as featured in John Ford's 1939 film *Stagecoach*, were replaced by underhanded white villains. When the comic book reader or television viewer did encounter Indians, they were usually attacking one another, thus performing the fantasy that white settlers brought "law and order" to the Wild West. This notion lent itself easily to the idea of benevolent supremacy, that American democratic capitalism was best equipped to bring peace and stability to emerging nations of the Third World. Native Americans and other "natives" needed protection from one another as they were incapable of peaceful co-existence or political stability; the Lone Ranger, a representative of the United States, would provide that protection and strength. By resolving the specific struggles of particular men and women on the western frontier, the Lone Ranger and Tonto symbolically resolved the nation's larger problems of political and cultural unity and explained the nation's foreign responsibilities during the Cold War.[35] As Stanley Corkin argues, Cold War imperialism necessitated the reordering of other lands "according to a distinctly US vision of civil society," in this case, represented by the Lone Ranger and Tonto.[36]

Since native peoples were not the typical villains in *The Lone Ranger*, Tonto's role is crucial to understanding the unequal relationships inherent in the idea of benevolent supremacy. The ideal Indian, Tonto was brave, loyal, and intelligent. As the Lone Ranger's closest friend and companion, readers and viewers understood that "real Americans" did not indulge racial or religious prejudices. In television shows and comic books, there was never a disparaging word about a minority group. But as Chadwick Allen has argued, Tonto operated as an "island of tribalism" in a frontier imagined as overwhelmingly white, supervised, and supported by the authority of the idealized White Ranger. Constructed as "authentic" through his traditional dress and broken English, yet under constant surveillance, Tonto's relationship with the Lone Ranger functioned as an idealized treaty; the repeatedly performed version of this fantasy included Indian complicity in the opening and white settlement of Indian lands.[37] In one episode, caught in a classic case of mistaken identity, Tonto exclaims, "Those fellers think we kill Sherman! What we do?" The Ranger answers confidently, "We tell them the truth!"[38] Tonto was neither overtly subjugated as in nations under communist domination nor "colonized" in the sense of Western European colonialism. As a willing partner in the modernization of his native lands, Tonto modeled the appropriate role for the peoples of emerging nations: freely choosing dependence and indebtedness in return for protection and stability.

The 1950s saw a flood of Western narratives in which the role of the Indian, even if sympathetically portrayed, served as a metaphor for the nation's fears and anxieties. Chris York argues that both the cavalry Western and the Indian Western films that prominently featured Indians rationalized Cold War conflict and politics like "breeches in the chain of command and subversion of the democratic process," thereby "rationaliz(ing) the development of the republican nation-state into an imperial Great Power." Even sympathetic treatment of Native Americans left little room to move beyond stereotypes. In the Western borderlands, the Indian was either part of the wilderness, an obstacle to civilization and progress, or he crossed the ideological border to become a companion or sidekick who "recognizes and chooses to exist within Euro-American civilization." Native Americans were capable of civilization, but only if they adopted Euro-Americans values and beliefs. Tonto and the Lone Ranger were the most recognizable iteration of the hero and sidekick convention in Westerns. Although he was loyal, strong, and intuitive, Tonto was always "subjugated to the authority of the Lone Ranger."[39] Similarly, the "backwardness" of Third World nations and their inability to protect themselves rationalized the military growth of the United States and interference in other nations' affairs. Those who recognized and desired the benefits of American protection had to choose to exist within the framework of American civilization, surrendering a measure of independence to benefit from the relationship. One young American, 17-year-old Ronnie Baker of Washington, Iowa, agreed, noting that the United Nations action was necessary in Korea "to stop the Russians from eventually fighting on United States soil. It's just as if New York started conquering the Eastern part of the country and Iowa stayed out of it till they were at our back door. It works on the same principle."[40]

According to the Lone Ranger's writers, Tonto provided a heroic role model for African-American children. John Todd, the actor who played Tonto on the early television show, saw the relationship between the Lone Ranger and Tonto as one of hero-worship. "He doesn't aspire to be a hero in his own right. And the Lone Ranger doesn't try to teach Tonto anything. He accepts him the way he is. [Tonto] is content just to follow the Ranger. With Tonto, it's a case of hero-worship."[41] However, organized minority groups were quick to point out examples of racism on the show. Writer Fran Stryker recalled that hundreds of African-Americans wrote to protest the depiction of a black character who spoke in dialect. When the Ranger visited the prewar South in another episode, viewers objected to enslaved people in the background singing a song with the word "darkie" in the lyrics.[42] Clearly, American minority groups did not always experience Tonto in the ways expected by his creators.

COLD WAR AMERICANISM

The white villains on America's western frontier shared something in common with communists: they were not distinguished by outward signs of duplicity. Except for a black cowboy hat, the villain might look no different from any other settler, rancher, or farmer. Indeed, the Lone Ranger's enemies often held positions of authority and blended seamlessly into frontier society. For example, the March/April 1948 issue, "The Lone Ranger and the Legion of the Black Arrow," pits the Lone Ranger against "a huge secret organization whose purpose is to overthrow the government! Especially here in the West. . . . " The Ranger described the Black Arrow as a nationwide organization whose unknown leaders had "enlisted the help of outlaws and savages all over the country . . . to overthrow the authorities and set up a government of their own. There are pitifully few of us to stop them!" Jane, the daughter of a man who was killed for trying to leave the organization once he discovered its evil intent, poses as a member of the Legion to learn more about their "big head man in Washington." Eventually, the Lone Ranger, Tonto, and Jane end up trapped in a cave, outnumbered and without ammunition. In a moment of desperation, Jane cries, "We haven't a chance! Surrender to them, and save your lives!" Surrender, however, is not an option for the Lone Ranger. In the end, Silver and Scout come to the rescue, and, against great odds, the three make a "break for freedom."[43] The threat of the unseen enemy, internal subversion, and the ever-present fear of infiltration and espionage were common tropes throughout 1950s popular culture.[44] Like the Nazi villains of World War II comics, one could not distinguish Soviet (or Black Arrow) agents by physical characteristics or outward markers of ethnicity. Ideology was the menace, and it could be hidden through treachery.

Suspicion of domestic spying peaked during the early 1950s, at the height of McCarthyism. With the rapid Soviet advances in nuclear technology and the arrest of Julius and Ethel Rosenberg, Americans feared undercover spies in the State Department, Reds in the schools and universities, and communist ideology camouflaged in film and television scripts. In the May 1948 issue of *The Lone Ranger* comic book, the plots in both stories turned on the theme of impersonation. In the first episode, "The Lone Ranger and the Clever Imposters," two crooks impersonating the Lone Ranger and Tonto were entrusted to deliver a cash payment; when they failed to do so, the Ranger and Tonto were nearly arrested and had to prove their innocence and capture the criminals to clear their names. "The Lone Ranger and the Gold Mine Episode" is predicated on a series of impersonations, disguises, and mistaken identities: a mining syndicate boss offers a cash award for a man "impersonating the Lone Ranger"; the Lone Ranger himself goes into disguise to fool the mine boss and his agent; believing he is an imposter, locals repeatedly attempt to capture the Lone Ranger and are convinced of his identity only after he produces his silver bullets and demonstrates his expert marksmanship.[45] The inability to know someone's true identity and the ability to hide one's political beliefs figure prominently in these stories.

Perhaps the Lone Ranger's most explicit political statement appeared in a June 1948 television episode. When his nephew Dan Reid asked what the Ranger meant by American Heritage, the Ranger responded with a heavy-handed lesson in patriotic duty. This lengthy quotation neatly sums up the nationalist symbolism, individualism, and anticommunism embedded in the Ranger's character, traits of the quintessential Cold Warrior that he aimed to teach to American children. His speech provided a history and civics lesson to millions of American and foreign viewers and, in response to thousands of requests, was printed and distributed to the American public.

> Our forefathers were men among whom uncommon valor was a common virtue. Those men have handed down a great heritage which you, and others like you, must protect and preserve. It is the heritage of every American. The right to live as free people in a land where there is true equality of opportunity. It is your duty to be eternally vigilant—prepared at all times to fight those who dare to challenge our way of life. And you must build. It is your duty to make of this a greater nation—to build homes and farms and villages—mills, factories, and great cities. Property is the fruit of labor. That some should

be rich shows that others may become rich and hence is encouragement to industry and enterprise. Abraham Lincoln said: "Let not him who is houseless pull down the house of another. But let him labor diligently and build one for himself—thus by example—assuring that his own shall be safe from violence when built."

You have for your own a great nation—together with the will—the heart—the courage—to make it even greater. This is your heritage. This is the heritage of every American.[46]

American children learned from this statement that they were responsible for defending their nation's unique history of freedom, which they had to guard constantly from external threats. It was their duty to spread the nation's ideals around the globe, just as their pioneer forebears had done in the West. Financial wealth was not something to be ashamed of, but rather provided a goal for others to aspire to. In this statement, the Lone Ranger summed up America's ideological position in the global war against communism.

Despite the Lone Ranger's association with the wide open spaces of the American West, it is striking how much of the television show takes place indoors, particularly in domestic settings. The first 78 television episodes (1949–1951) were shot in Utah and California, many just north of Hollywood at Iverson Ranch, a center of Western filming from the 1930s through the 1950s. But between 1951 and 1957, filming was generally restricted to studio sound stages; for the final season, filming returned to outdoor locations. For most of the series, therefore, a considerable portion of the action takes place in sheriffs' offices, home interiors, newspaper offices, and stores—a fact that seems to contradict the common trope for Western cowboys—a naturally civilized man untainted by the sins and softness of civilized society. And yet, a natural gentleman, the Lone Ranger felt equally comfortable in the Wild West and in the parlors of frontier homes. These domestic spaces, identified with women and private family life, frequently became the target of external threats. A common theme in Lone Ranger episodes was the homestead or ranch under threat due to the underhanded or illegal actions of outlaws. A January 1951 episode, "Silent

Voice," features the Lone Ranger saving Cleve Ritchie from the hench-men of Dr. Payton, who planted Stella Watson in Cleve's home to care for his ailing grandmother so that Stella could steal a map to an old Spanish treasure that Cleve found to fund the town. In an October 1952 episode, "Jeb's Gold Mine," schemers try to drive out a homesteader, knowing there is gold on his land. As a privileged site of American culture in the 1950s, the family under siege was a visible trope in anticommunist rhetoric as well as a signifier of American national identity.[47] The demands of film-ing structured *The Lone Ranger* television series in ways that privileged the domestic sphere and simultaneously aligned with Cold War ideologies that elevated the nuclear family. The Lone Ranger symbolized American strength, stability, and justice, ensuring the safety of emerging nations just as he did in the American West, promising protection for the "private" yet politicized domestic sphere.

The Lone Ranger's patriotism and incorruptible morals shielded Dell Comics from attack when the comic book industry came under fire in the early 1950s. Dell claimed, with some justification, that anti-comics activists weren't targeting their wholesome comic books and that joining the Association of Comics Magazine Publishers (ACMP) would associate Dell with less scrupulous publishers. The Dell pledge was written in every comic book:

> The Dell trademark *is*, and always has been, a positive guarantee that the comic magazine bearing it contains only clean and wholesome juvenile entertainment. The Dell code eliminates entirely, rather than regulates, objectionable material. That's why when your child buys a Dell Comic you can be sure it contains only good fun and happy adventures. "DELL COMICS ARE GOOD COMICS" is our only credo and our constant goal.[48]

Dell's conservative image spared it from any significant backlash when the company refused to join the ACMP. Given their "target audience of young children," Dell's "steadfastly traditional" comics met parents high expectations, although the Lone Ranger did come in for occasional criticism for "the shooting and violence" that sent "tots to their beds in an emotional lather."[49] Despite significant differences among comic book publishers, from the conservative Dell to the more liberal DC Comics, "all affirmed the basic assumptions of an American Cold War consensus." DC Comics' superheroes—firmly on the side of law and order—and Dell's old-time "American" values questioned neither the state of American society nor the place of individuals within it. Dell acted *in loco parentis* to inculcate appropriate values in America's children: anticommunism, corporatism, consumption, domesticity, middle-class aspirations, and foreign policy assumptions based on the benevolent supremacy of the United States.[50]

BEYOND COMICS

In addition to comic books, radio, and television shows, hundreds of licensed Lone Ranger products encouraged children to act out imaginary scenarios. Games and play sets provided interactive sites where children could engage in active role-playing that normalized the unequal relationships inherent in benevolent supremacy. By its twentieth anniversary, Trendle's company signed more than 60 license agreements to merchandise hundreds of products. The *Detroit Free Press* reported in 1950 that "[t]he number of manufactured articles bearing The Lone Ranger imprimatur has what appears to be endless bounds. It now includes clothing, games, toys, cutlery, displays, innumerable novelty items, school pencils, pens and bags, shoes, books, raincoats, musical instruments, candy, chains, badges, buttons, molds, and so on."[51]

In the early 1970s, Marx Toys created 11 "adventure toy" sets to correspond with particular episodes of *The Lone Ranger*.[52] The "Adventure of the Tribal Powwow" set (1970) included the comic book along with a headdress, tribal mask, shakers, tomahawk, leather bag, and beaded bracelet. "Adventure of the Hidden Silver Mine" came with the comic book, a pick and shovel, dynamite, mining cars, and loads of silver pellets. Finally, "Adventure of the Hopi Medicine Man" included the comic book, feathered wings and mask, and a small totem.[53] These games were accompanied by specific scripts in the form of the comic book, and many children would have seen the televised episode. Provided with specific props, they were encouraged to re-enact a prewritten script with which they were already familiar. The accessories in "The Tribal Powwow" and "The Hopi Medicine Man," for example, encouraged children to "play Indian." But these sets also offered endless possibilities for imaginative play. Children could recreate the stories with their own variations or simply ignore the scripts to create entirely original adventures of their own (Figure 1.1).

A board game with less creative flexibility, Milton Bradley's 1966 "The Lone Ranger" board game (intended for ages 5–12) encouraged players to

Figure 1.1 Children's toys, like The Lone Ranger play sets of the early 1970s, provided scripted play as well as opportunities for children to invent their own narratives. The small figure of Tonto, beads, tribal mask, totem, and feathered headdress, however, conflated Native cultures into a stereotype and encouraged children to "play Indian." Courtesy of the Autry Museum of the American West.

take on the roles of imperiled stagecoach travelers en route to an American military fort. Along the way, the players encounter dangers in the form of injured horses, attacking mountain lions, outlaws, stampeding cattle, snakes, rock slides, broken wagon wheels, and, finally, a band of marauding Indians. When the player landed on a yellow "danger" circle, he or she had to spin the specified character—the Lone Ranger, Tonto, the Lone Ranger and Tonto, or Taka—in order to be "rescued." The first player to reach the safety of the US military fort won. The game created clear zones of safety and danger; areas beyond the walled-off protection of the US military were dangerous, unstable, and vulnerable to any number of threats (Figure 1.2). Players achieved security only within the confines of American protection, and only representatives of American power

Figure 1.2 This Milton Bradley Lone Ranger board game (1966) created a "safe zone" behind the walls of a US fort. Beyond those walls, beyond the protection of the US government, travelers were vulnerable to a variety of threats and dangers. Courtesy of the Autry Museum of the American West.

could rescue threatened players. The board game echoed the themes of American foreign policy during the Cold War, promising protection to nations and peoples who accepted the authority of the United States and its war against communist expansion.

The Lone Ranger was just one of many juvenile Westerns published during the Cold War that created and sustained images of "frontiers" as wild, dangerous, and unpredictable spaces where violent colonial contests took place. These texts, programs, and games suggested to viewers and players the importance of the nation and individual Americans in modernizing and stabilizing frontiers, whether in the Old West or in contemporary postcolonial nations. Children's popular culture, both scripted and unscripted, in comic books, board games, radio, and television shows, provided an arena in which historical "frontier" dramas could be endlessly repeated and solved through a relationship of benevolent supremacy, in which the United States offered protection in return for a nation's dependency.

COLD WAR COMICS IN THE SOVIET UNION

In the Soviet Union, which lacked a strong comics tradition, state-sponsored children's magazines and school primers accomplished the same goal as commercial American comics: entertainment bolstered by a sense of national purpose. In the postwar years, the children's magazine *Veselie Kartinki* (*Merry Pictures*) offered the comic series *The Incredible Adventures of the Famed Traveler Petia Ryzhik and His Loyal Friends Mik and Muk* featuring young Petia, the "Russian Tintin," and his friends (who) "travel all over the world [and to the moon], encountering class foes [usually Americans] and friends [Third World peoples]." Much like *The Lone Ranger* narratives, Petia's stories "always ended with the vanquishing of the former, though never in any overly violent way."[54] Despite the obvious ideological differences, comics in both the United States and the USSR sought to inculcate a sense of national identity and purpose and to teach children their roles and responsibilities in a new global struggle.

In contrast to the multiple areas of child socialization in the United States (comics, television, radio, toys, and games), children's socialization in Soviet society, Felicity O'Dell argues, was far more monolithic. "In a pluralistic society," she wrote,

> the demands made on a child are both fewer in number and more various. One set of values is taught to him in school, another at home, another on television, another at Scout meetings, another in his comics, and these different sets of values are often, at least in part, contradictory. . . . [T]he demands which socialization makes on the Soviet child in his monistic society are as unified as possible. The values and norms fostered by schools, television, Pioneer meetings, and children's magazines are the same. It is hoped that those taught at home also coincide.[55]

In the United States, the job of inculcating nationalism was left primarily to the schools and the free market, but the Soviet government took matters into its own hands.

The Soviet Union simply had no parallel to the hundreds of American commercial comic books circulating in the postwar period. Comics were banned by the Bolsheviks for their "bourgeois" Western origins after the adoption of Socialist Realism as official culture in 1934. Despite occasional appearances in children's magazines—like *Murzilka, Veselie kartinki, Chizh i ezh*—the form largely remained "underground" until the *perestroika* era. José Alaniz argues that, under Stalin and later during the Thaw, Western-style comics had little chance of developing in such a hostile environment. "If anything," he argues, "prejudice against American mass culture deepened" during the 1950s and 1960s. Despite the long-standing suspicion and derision of the comic form, however, Soviet children were exposed to didactic *komics* in state-sponsored children's magazines. Alaniz describes several of Ivan Semenov's 1960s Petia Ryzhik comic strips, perhaps the most comparable popular cultural form to American comics. In 1956, Semenov co-founded the children's magazine *Veselie Kartinki* (*Merry Pictures*), a monthly humor magazine for preschoolers and first-graders that featured

stories, amusing adventures, riddles, and games. Unlike many of his con-
temporaries, Semenov used word balloons and sound effects in his work,
devices that were considered American. But the narratives certainly were
not. In one 1964 episode, Petia and his dogs Mik and Muk explore a cave
in which they find a dragon, among other remarkable discoveries. The
happy ending includes the dragon finding "free housing and 'three meals
a day' at the zoo," demonstrating the "Soviet values of teamwork, fearless-
ness, embrace of the other, and a benevolent state providing for the needs
of all." Another episode depicts Petia constructing a kite that transports
him to an "imperialist colony in Africa." There he wreaks havoc at a military base where the soldiers wear helmets emblazoned with dollar signs,
and he befriends several local boys. When a wicked man brandishing a
whip and wearing a cowboy hat demands that Petia "stop interfering with
the 'black-skins' work," Petia ties the kite string to the plantation owner's
belt, and he is carried off "somewhere to the sea." Petia and the villagers
celebrate by teaching one another their native dances.[56]

By employing the symbol of the American cowboy—his hat—the comic
clearly constructs an American enemy—greedy, racist, imperialistic, and
militaristic—as antithetical to the Russian hero. Unlike in the United
States, Soviet children's literature and Soviet culture more generally positioned the child as the central actor and hero. From a young age, children
were taught to advance the socialist cause; books and magazines depicted
children performing patriotic duties such as attending parades or Young
Pioneer meetings, serving as spies during World War II, and working on
collective farms. Russian comics functioned ideologically by constructing an "us versus them" mentality in a more straightforward manner than
the Lone Ranger, which didn't clearly define a Soviet enemy but rather
elevated "American" values such as justice and freedom. As this analysis makes clear, however, the two were not so different. Far from simple
"entertainment," clashes between the Lone Ranger and frontier outlaws
re-enacted national myths that pitted American justice against the forces
of destruction. Although formulaic, young viewers repeatedly experienced the champion of democracy triumphing over evil. And, of course,
The Lone Ranger was but one in a multitude of explicitly anticommunist

comics, such as *Captain America*, which clearly defined the "red menace" as the primary public threat.

The Soviet historian Catriona Kelly has argued that Stalin's death in March 1953 did not create a marked or immediate change in the ideological content of children's literature. Although Stalin's image was purged from public sites and textbooks by the early 1960s, the vacuum was filled with images of cosmonauts, World War II heroes, and a resurrection of the Lenin cult. In children's culture, *skazka*—fairy tales—remained the central genre, and Korney Chukovsky and Samuil Marshak "rose to an unassailable authority as 'founding fathers' of Russian children's literature."[57]

State-sponsored children's magazines, and the stories, poems, and occasional *komics* in them, display how the Soviet Union actively cultivated a national mythology during the Cold War, much as *The Lone Ranger* comic books and television shows did in the United States. Drawing on both national histories and contemporary rivalry with the United States, Soviet narratives suggested to children the roles they and their nation should play in the postwar world. Although obviously not state-sponsored and enforced in the same way, American commercial comic strips such as *The Lone Ranger* functioned in similar ways, drawing on heroic American narratives and the civil religion of westward expansion and applying those lessons to modern political situations. The Lone Ranger glorified the "American way of life," democracy, and freedom just as stories of the Russian Civil War and the Communist Revolution mythologized the Soviet past for children in the 1950s and beyond.[58]

THE LONE RANGER'S PEACE PATROL, 1958–1960

Although popular culture in the United States was left to the private market, the federal government both recognized and manipulated the ideological links between foreign policy objectives and the national mythology represented by the Lone Ranger. Beginning in 1958, the Treasury Department specifically targeted American children to help fund Cold War military imperatives because "peace costs money."[59] In an effort to expand the

Treasury Department's savings stamps program, the Lone Ranger personally invited young Americans to join his Peace Patrol, "a nationwide organization of boys and girls who buy United States School Savings Stamps and
Savings Bonds to help build the economic and military strength required to
preserve our freedom and insure the peace."[60] Children's nickels and dimes
helped to fund Eisenhower's policy of deterrence through massive retali-
ation, which guaranteed peace by enlarging the nation's nuclear arsenal.
While children read *Lone Ranger* comic books or watched his adventures
on television, their school teachers encouraged them to participate in the
Savings Stamps program, with a little help from the Masked Man himself.
Americans, mostly children, bought $20 million worth of stamps in 1957.
As one Treasury official noted, 7 million American children attended public schools, 4 million babies were born every year, and "no American has a
greater stake in peace than the *young* American."[61]

The Treasury Department kicked off the Peace Patrol campaign in
June 1958 with a two-day program featuring the Lone Ranger's appearance before "a mammoth youth rally" of more than 6,000 children on
the grounds of the Washington Monument. Sixty children were singled
out for recognition as "outstanding . . . volunteer salesmen." Throughout
the fall, Clayton Moore visited 30 cities to promote the program; advertisers on more than 160 television stations plugged the program during
The Lone Ranger show, and Jack Wrather's Lone Ranger Corporation distributed more than 50,000 Peace Patrol posters, millions of membership
cards, and an eight-minute film for unrestricted use by local television
stations and schools. Radio and television spots targeted children with
messages to "go into partnership with Uncle Sam," and "It's smart to save!"
In a comic strip created especially for the Boy Scouts of America (BSA)'s
Boys' Life magazine, the Lone Ranger encouraged Scouts to embark on
a mission of "thrift and patriotism" by investing in savings stamps and
joining his Peace Patrol. Treasury Department ads encouraged mothers to
teach their children "the value of thrift" and to help their "ranger get a real
start in life." Other ads directed children and their parents to inquire about
the program at school or their local post office.[62] The Lone Ranger asked
American schoolchildren—7 million and growing in 1958—to "LEARN

because knowledge and understanding will keep peace in the world, and SAVE because buying US Saving Stamps and Bonds will help keep our country strong."[63]

Public schools participated in the Saving Stamps program in a variety of ways. The *Merritt Point Chimes*, a Maryland elementary school news-letter, featured a message from the principal encouraging students to save their money to buy Savings Stamps. At least two elementary schools used the program to teach thrift and finance. Sixth-graders at the Fulton and Marshall Schools in Dubuque, Iowa, took turns serving as record-keepers and cashiers for younger students who purchased Savings Stamps.[64] Ad Council campaigns targeted teachers with ads such as "Peace Power . . . In Your Classroom," which enlisted teachers to encourage their students to buy Savings Stamps.[65] School and PTA administrators encouraged the program as well. The President of the American Association of School Administrators linked thrift to national identity: "Our nation developed and grew to maturity on the savings of our forefathers, and the practice of thrift is deeply ingrained in our heritage and traditions." Similarly, the President of the National Congress of Parents and Teachers affirmed, "Thrift is a quality necessary in our economic system and appropriate to our way of life. A citizen of the United States, through savings, expresses faith in his own future and that of his country."[66] By all accounts, the Peace Patrol was a smashing success and continued into the 1959–1960 aca-demic year with visits by the Lone Ranger to another ten American cities, the national School Administrator's conference in Atlantic City, and an appearance on "Lassie" to induct the first (and only) canine member of the Peace Patrol.

How should historians interpret the decisions of an estimated 4 million young people who opted to join the Peace Patrol, "a vast peace time army on a mission of thrift and patriotism," during the 1958–59 school year? Perhaps some children joined simply for the coveted membership card from the Lone Ranger, while older or more politically aware youth did so to demonstrate their patriotism and awareness of the need to maintain the peace. Perhaps others were just saving money for the future. The badges, oaths, advertisements and film, and patriotic pageants surely clarified the ideological connotations of the Lone Ranger's sponsorship: service to community, voting, respect for law and order, preservation of heritage, and freedom of speech. Some young people recognized the global implications of the Lone Ranger, who "kept the peace" on unstable frontiers, made the West (and the world) safe for white settlers, and brought law and order to the uncivilized. Did young Americans see themselves and their country as a global peacekeeper through the doctrines of benevolent supremacy and military preparedness? The Soviet Union's representation of American capitalism in a cowboy hat lends credence to the theory that foreign children would have recognized the Ranger as a representative of the United States. Without a doubt, millions of American children loved the Lone Ranger, and he did in fact inspire them. Clayton Moore's daughter Dawn affirmed the Ranger's importance to children, remembering in a 2016 interview, "I still get letters from policemen, firemen, and teachers who say they chose a career in service because of him."[67] For American youth, the imaginative world of the Lone Ranger and other Western heroes that dominated screens big and small throughout the Cold War functioned as a tool, a means through which they could make sense of the Cold War and their place in it.

CONCLUSION

Although it is tempting to dismiss children's popular culture as frivolous, Western heroes like the Lone Ranger offered young people an accessible and concrete way to make sense of their environments, to distinguish right from wrong, and to position themselves in a complicated world. The American cowboy represented law and order, God and country, economic development, and security in seemingly timeless narratives with little historical context. Such timeless lessons and moral virtues, learned through popular culture, were reinforced in numerous ways. The Lone Ranger's Peace Patrol was just one component of the Treasury Department's Peace Power Program, designed to remind Americans young and old that peace was not free. On the contrary, maintaining world peace depended on the

ability of the United States to maintain a "deterrent of massive retalia-
tory power."[68] Other federal programs, such as the Department of Justice's
awards, the Young American Medal for Bravery, and the Young American
Medal for Service, reinforced the Ranger's messages. Created in 1950, the
Medal for Bravery was awarded to a youth under age 18 who "exhibited
exceptional courage, attended by extraordinary decisiveness, presence of
mind, and unusual swiftness of action, regardless of his or her own personal safety, in an effort to save or in saving the life of any person or persons in actual imminent danger." The description could be taken from one
of George Trendle's Lone Ranger scripts. The Young American Medal for
Service recognized a young person who exhibited outstanding "character
and service" of a public nature. The President of the United States awarded
the medals to two young Americans each year.[69]

The multiple sites of engagement, various media forms, and political–
civic connections between the Lone Ranger and children's play during the
Cold War years create a complex and fruitful area of study. Offering scripted
play through radio, television, comic books, and board games as well as
unstructured play opportunities through merchandised toys like masks and
holster sets, the Lone Ranger and Tonto created an imaginative world in
which children could negotiate many possible narratives. Of course, George
Trendle, Fran Stryker, MGM film producer Jack Chertok, and director
George B. Seitz Jr. meant to limit and structure these interpretations, creating a particular story, a version of American history and heritage that
aligned with Cold War national security goals. The federal government and
Hollywood mobilized this national narrative in order to influence young
Americans to actively participate in national defense initiatives, and millions did. Working through children's popular culture, the federal government prepared American children to fund, and fight, the Cold War.

NOTES

1. Margaret Peacock, *Innocent Weapons*.
2. The 2013 film, directed by Gore Verbinski, was panned by critics for a variety of
    reasons, but the foremost criticism among fans was the failure of the Lone Ranger

to match his historical character—he is a bumbling, comic figure; fails to bring the villains to justice; and even curses.

3. Stanley Corkin, *Cowboys as Cold Warriors: The Western and US History* (Philadelphia: Temple University Press, 2004): 5, 20–24.

4. Melani McAlister, *Epic Encounters,* 43–83.

5. Steven Mintz, *Huck's Raft: A History of American Childhood* (Cambridge: Harvard University Press, 2004): 264.

6. *Life* magazine (February 1, 1943): 37–40.

7. Gerard C. Raiti, "The Disappearance of Disney Animated Propaganda: A Globalization Perspective," *Animation* 2.2 (2007): 156–157.

8. Matthew J. Costello, *Secret Identity Crisis: Comic Books and the Unmasking of Cold War America* (Continuum, 2009): 5.

9. Bradford W. Wright, *Comic Book Nation: The Transformation of Youth Culture in America* (Baltimore: Johns Hopkins University Press, 2001): 31.

10. Sanderson Vanderbilt, "The Comics," *Yank: The Army Weekly* (November 23, 1945), cited in Wright, *Comic Book Nation* (2001): 57.

11. "Children Abroad to Get No Comics," *New York Times* (November 8, 1945): 19.

12. Francis J. Bassett, "Comic Books for Germany: Protest Voiced over Giving Wrong Concept of Our Democracy," *New York Times* (November 11, 1948): 26. The ECA was created by the Economic Recovery Act of April 1948 to administer postwar American aid to Western Europe; it was widely known as the agency that administered the Marshall Plan.

13. "Russian Says Comic Books 'Fascisize' US Children," *New York Times* (October 16, 1949): 33.

14. Levine and Gordon, *Tales of Wo-Chi-Ca,* 106–107.

15. Wright, *Comic Book Nation* (2001): 75; William Savage, Jr. *Commies, Cowboys, and Jungle Queens: Comic Books and America* (Hanover NH: Wesleyan University Press, 1990): 74.

16. "US to Use Cartoon Books to Tell Asia Our Story," *New York Times* (December 20, 1949): 25. *A Picture Story of the United States* was translated into 11 languages and distributed by the USIS between November 1953 and November 1956. National Archives and Records Administration, RG 306, Press and Publication Service/ Publications Division, Master File Copies of Pamphlets and Leaflets, 1953–1983, Container 18.

17. USIA, *A Picture Story of the United States* (1953): 47. Container 18, RG 306, Press and Publication Service/Publications Division, Master File Copies of Pamphlets and Leaflets, 1953–1983, USIA, NARA, College Park, MD.

18. "How America Grew . . . The Communist Experiment," *Boys' Life* (October 1957): C7.

19. Howard Chudacoff, *Children at Play: An American History* (New York: New York University Press, 2007): 3; Brian Sutton-Smith, *Toys as Culture* (New York: Gardner Press, 1986): 247.

20. Donald D. Markstein, Toonpedia, http://www.toonopedia.com/dell.htm

21. Michael Barrier, *Funnybooks: The Improbable Glories of the Best American Comic Books* (Berkeley: University of California Press, 2014): 293.

22. David Wilson Parker, *A Descriptive Analysis of the Lone Ranger as Popular Art* (PhD diss., Northwestern University, ProQuest, UMI Dissertations Publishing, 1955): 126–128.

23. Chadwick Allen, "Hero with Two Faces: The Lone Ranger as Treaty Discourse," *American Literature* 68.3 (September 1996): 618–619.

24. Corkin, *Cowboys as Cold Warriors*, 2.

25. Fred Zinnemann's 1952 film *High Noon*, an allegory that criticizes blacklisting and McCarthyism, is the exception that proves the rule. John Wayne refused the part of sheriff Will Kane and, in a 1971 interview in *Playboy* magazine, called *High Noon* "the most un-American thing I've ever seen in my life." The Motion Picture Alliance for the Preservation of American Ideals was founded by Hollywood conservatives to protect the film industry from communist infiltration. The organization cooperated fully in the HUAC investigations.

26. Quoted in Shane Maddock, "Defending the American Way and Containing the Atom," in Mariner, Rosemary B., and G. Kurt Piehler, eds. *The Atomic Bomb and American Society: New Perspectives* (Knoxville: University of Tennessee Press, 2009): 125.

27. "The Lone Ranger Standards and Backgrounds," Quoted in Parker *A Descriptive Analysis of the Lone Ranger* (1955): 213.

28. Wright, *Comic Book Nation*, 103, 187.

29. Parker, *A Descriptive Analysis of the Lone Ranger*, 184–185.

30. Peter C. Rollins and John E. O'Connor, eds. *Hollywood's West: The American Frontier in Film, Television, and History* (Lexington: University of Kentucky Press, 2009).

31. Quoted in Parker, *A Descriptive Analysis of the Lone Ranger*, 210.

32. Michael Ray Fitzgerald, "The White Savior and His Junior Partner: The Lone Ranger and Tonto on Cold War Television," *Journal of Popular Culture* 46.1 (2013): 79–108.

33. Ariel Dorfman, *The Empire's Old Clothes: What the Lone Ranger, Babar, and Other Heroes Do to Our Minds* (Durham: Duke University Press, 2010): 68–69.

34. Fitzgerald, "The White Savior and His Junior Partner," 89.

35. Allen, "Hero with Two Faces," 610.

36. Corkin, *Cowboys as Cold Warriors*, 10.

37. Allen, "Hero with Two Faces," 609–638.

38. "The Lone Ranger and the Tunnel Builders," 1.23 (May 1950), New York: Dell Publishing.

39. Chris York, "Beyond the Frontier: *Turok, Son of Stone* and the Native American in Cold War America," in Chris York and Rafiel York, eds. *Comic Books and the Cold War, 1946–1962* (London: McFarland and Company, Inc., 2012): 180–181, 183.

40. "When a Fellow's Seventeen," in Maureen Daly, *Profile of Youth* (Philadelphia and New York: J. B. Lippincott Company, 1951): 35.

41. Quoted in Parker, *A Descriptive Analysis of the Lone Ranger*, 202.

42. Parker, *A Descriptive Analysis of the Lone Ranger*, 206–207.

43. "The Lone Ranger and the Legion of the Black Arrow," No. 2, March/April 1948.

44. Stephen J. Whitfield, *The Culture of the Cold War* (Baltimore: Johns Hopkins University Press, 1991): 45–69.

45. "The Lone Ranger and the Clever Impostors" and "The Lone Ranger and the Gold Mine Episode," script by Fran Striker, art by Charles Flanders, Dell Publishing, No. 4 (July–August 1948).

46. Quoted in Parker, *A Descriptive Analysis of the Lone Ranger*, 212.

47. Elaine Tyler May, *Homeward Bound: American Families in the Cold War* (New York: Basic Books, 2008): 24–29; McAlister, *Epic Encounters* (2005): 199–200, 207–209.

48. *The Lone Ranger*, 1.82 (April 1955). Inside cover.

49. R. W. Stewart, "The Lone Ranger," *New York Times* (August 1, 1948): X7.

50. Wright, *Comic Book Nation,* 199. Wright argues that Dell declined in the 1960s for two reasons. First, in 1961, Dell raised its prices from 10 to 15 cents, and its sales dropped nearly 75% over the next few years. Second, comic books like Dell's that affirmed all the basic and bland assumptions of the Cold War consensus fell behind the times and failed to speak to the social and emotional disorientation of young people. See pgs. 187–189, 200–201. See also Jean-Paul Gabilliet, *Of Comics and Men: A Cultural History of American Comic Books* (Jackson: University Press of Mississippi, 2010): 55.

51. *Detroit Free Press* (February 19, 1950), cited in Parker, *A Descriptive Analysis of the Lone Ranger* (1955): 127.

52. Marx was the largest toy manufacturer in the United States by 1955, the year *Time* magazine proclaimed Louis Marx "the Toy King." Marx created numerous boxed playsets throughout the 1950s and 1960s, including many Western-themed sets for Roy Rogers, Davy Crockett, Gunsmoke, and many others.

53. All of these toys, as well as a complete run of *The Lone Ranger* comic books, are housed in the collection of the Autry Museum of the American West, Los Angeles, California.

54. José Alaniz, *Komiks: Comic Art in Russia* (Jackson: University Press of Mississippi, 2010): 65.

55. Felicity O'Dell, *Socialisation Through Children's Literature: The Soviet Example* (Cambridge: Cambridge University Press, 1978): 49.

56. Alaniz, *Komiks*, 65–66.

57. Catriona Kelly, *Children's World: Growing Up in Russia, 1890–1991* (New Haven: Yale University Press, 2007): 135.

58. Julie K. deGraffenried, *Sacrificing Childhood: Children and the Soviet State in the Great Patriotic War* (Lawrence: University Press of Kansas, 2014): 104–131.

59. Advertisement, "Peace Power in Your Classroom," RG 56, General Records of the US Treasury Dept., Records of the Savings Bond Division, Series: Historical Files of the Office of the National Director, 1941–1969, Container 1, File: Lone Ranger—Promotion Kits, NARA.

60. Program, Advertising Club Luncheon, June 17, 1958; RG 56, General Records of the US Treasury Dept., Records of the Savings Bond Division, Series: Historical Files of the Office of the National Director, 1941–1969, Container 1, File: Lone

Ranger Promotion (6/16–17/58). Folder: Lone Ranger Agenda—June 16–17, 1958 (Includes speech material for events), NARA.

61. "Mr. Stiles' Talk, Washington Advertising Club Luncheon," June 17, 1958. Emphasis in the original.

62. The comic, drawn by cartoonist Tom Gill, ran in the November 1958 issue of *Boys' Life*, which had a circulation of 1.6 million. Record Group 56: General Records of the Department of the Treasury, 1775–2005; Records of the Savings Bond Division; Series: Historical Files of the Office of the National Director, 1941–1969; Container 1; File: Lone Ranger—Promotion Kits, NARA.

63. Uppercase in the original. Pledge on Peace Patrol membership cards, RG 56, Records of the US Treasury Dept., Records of the Savings Bond Division, Series: Historical Files of the Office of the National Director, 1941–1969, Container 1, File: Lone Ranger—Promotion Kits. Caps in original.

64. The Lou Smith Organization, no date, 2 pgs.; *Merritt Point Chimes*, December 1958; "Lone Rangers Helps Students Learn a Lesson in Finance," Dubuque, Iowa *Telegraph-Herald* (November 9, 1958); RG 56, Container 14, Envelope: Lone Ranger Peace Patrol Clippings.

65. Advertisement, "Peace Power in Your Classroom," RG 56, General Records of the US Treasury Dept., Records of the Savings Bond Division, Series: Historical Files of the Office of the National Director, 1941–1969, Container 1, File: Lone Ranger—Promotion Kits, NARA.

66. "Roving Ambassador of Good Will for United States School Savings Program," RG 56, General Records of the US Treasury Dept., Records of the Savings Bond Division, Series: Historical Files of the Office of the National Director, 1941–1969; Container 3; Folder: A&P—11—Special Events and Promotions, Lone Ranger Peace Patrol—1959, NARA.

67. Nick Thomas, "A Daughter Remembers the Lone Ranger," *The Spectrum* (September 26, 2016).

68. John Foster Dulles, "The Evolution of Foreign Policy," Before the Council of Foreign Relations, New York, NY, *Department of State, Press Release No. 81* (January 12, 1954).

69. https://www.law.cornell.edu/cfr/text/28/50.22

2

A Small Paintbrush in the Hands of a Small Child

*Children's Art and Cultural Diplomacy
During the Cold War*

If children's popular culture has been largely overlooked by Cold War historians, the same cannot be said of American high culture. Historians have written extensively about the cultural Cold War—the use of the visual arts, music, literature, film, and dance by both the United States and the Soviet Union to demonstrate the superiority of each nation's political, economic, and cultural systems. More recently, historians have begun to explore how ordinary people, including children and their representatives, engaged with the Cold War on local and personal levels.[1] This chapter explores the intersection of these two questions, asking how and why children's art became a powerful weapon in the arsenal of the cultural Cold War and exploring how American children functioned as cultural ambassadors through art programs. The assumed innocence of children's art became a vital tool in negotiating questions of American national identity and America's "fight for peace" during the 1950s and 1960s. Childhood innocence came to represent national innocence, a propaganda message sent abroad and reinforced at home.

As Karen Dubinsky has argued, children are generally not considered to
be political citizens, but they are ubiquitous political *subjects* in the iconography of nation states, political parties, and social movements. Children
are typically depicted as defenseless, in need of a strong protector. Their
vulnerability authorizes an adult viewer to act to change or maintain particular power relations.[2] The particular case of children's art after World
War II shares some interpretive similarities with US-sponsored international humanitarian aid, much of which originated during and after
World War I. As noted by Julia Irwin, the ostensible goal of humanitarian
aid was to improve the lives of people suffering in the aftermath of war,
but the reality was far more complex. Like humanitarian aid, children's art
exchanges functioned on multiple levels simultaneously: as propaganda
and public relations, a tool of statecraft, and a means of citizen education.[3] But peace activists and educators also encouraged children's cultural
diplomacy through the visual arts as a means of achieving "world friendship" and avoiding another war.

After both world wars, US children participated in countless cultural
diplomacy projects, but few originated from their own initiative. The vast
majority of child-centered projects were adult-initiated, organized, and
led; they mobilized images of childhood vulnerability while simultaneously relying on children's volunteer labor. The term "voluntold" describes
the subtle coercion at the heart of children's "voluntary" work.[4] Faced with
the requests or suggestions of adult authority figures, children may have
felt they had little choice but to participate, and the overwhelming pressure to demonstrate one's patriotism during the Cold War would have
made refusal unlikely. Keeping in mind this element of subtle coercion,
children participated in numerous projects dedicated to cultivating international understanding and world friendship during the postwar decades.
Interest groups as politically diverse as the Women's International League
for Peace and Freedom (WILPF), art educators, Girl and Boy Scouts, the
Junior League, and the State Department all considered art exchanges to
be promising diplomatic efforts. In the United States, numerous organizations sprung up to promote peace and international understanding
through children and their art, sometimes independently and sometimes

as part of pen pal or other already established programs. Although the adult leaders of these organizations did not always operate on the same political assumptions or have the same goals, they did share some basic beliefs about the political utility of childhood innocence and the power of art to achieve diplomatic goals. Art for World Friendship (AWF), an art exchange program sponsored by the WILPF, provides a case study into how children themselves—even those guided with suggestions and otherwise "voluntold"—conceptualized world peace during the Cold War and their role in achieving it. This chapter considers how ideas about childhood and cultural diplomacy animated art exchange projects, how art exchange programs both challenged and meshed with dominant Cold War conceptions of nationhood and democracy, and how various interest groups employed childhood vulnerability to negotiate Cold War political issues through art.

Recent scholarship on postwar childhood makes the case that children were vital participants in international Cold War politics on both sides of the Iron Curtain. Child refugees shaped international politics and United Nations policies, adopted and sponsored children were seen as intermediaries among nations and as tools to establish positive international relationships, and American children's participation in charitable activities was understood as crucial for forging relationships with potential allies. American children were encouraged to think of themselves as "little diplomats" representing the United States when they traveled abroad, exchanged pictures with new friends, corresponded with pen pals, or collected pennies for UNICEF. In the Soviet Union, the appearance of a happy childhood was central to the success of the Soviet project. The common refrain "Thank you, Comrade Stalin, for a happy childhood" attributed both physical and emotional well-being to the beneficence of the Soviet state. In return, grateful Soviet children functioned as ambassadors, carrying the socialist message to far-flung parts of the Soviet Union, and to allied nations such as China and Cuba, through youth festivals and state-sponsored tourism.[5]

The home front was the most important battlefield during the Cold War for American youth. The nuclear threat brought American women and children into Cold War politics with an unprecedented sense of urgency. These usually protected groups became suddenly vulnerable to atomic attacks in their homes, neighborhoods, and schools, while grocery shopping, practicing "duck-and-cover" drills, or stocking a family fallout shelter. Communist subversion threatened to infiltrate Hollywood films and television shows as well as school textbooks. Women and children, therefore, had important roles to play in the fight against communism. Typically excluded from high international political debates, many women activists like Maude Muller, the founder of AWF, influenced youth behind the scenes through cultural projects, in peace organizations such as the WILPF, and in public schools and local voluntary organizations. Cold War politics necessitated new approaches to old problems and, in the process, created strange bedfellows of women's peace groups and federal propaganda agencies.

WORLD PEACE AND THE INNOCENCE OF CHILDREN

Mrs. Frederick Muller, a retired schoolteacher, peace activist, arts patron, and Pennsylvania housewife was among the 1,000 delegates who attended America's First National Conference on UNESCO in March 1947. As President of the Media, Pennsylvania, branch of the WILPF, Muller represented the organization at UNESCO's Philadelphia meeting, 12 days after President Truman announced his policy of containing the Soviet Union and the threat of global communism. Conference participants were asked to consider how UNESCO and interested national organizations could work toward to the goal of international peace in the midst of global tensions. Of 14 sessions, Muller attended "The Contribution of the Creative Arts to UNESCO," where she heard a proposal to encourage world peace through a global exchange of professional art. Why, she wondered, wouldn't *children* be the ideal participants for such an exchange? Since children were innocent of prejudice, naturally expressive, and open to new ideas, Muller believed they would be better able to communicate freely with other children around the world. Their communication would translate

into understanding and friendship among peoples and nations, the building blocks of peace. Muller returned to her Drexel Hill home and launched
AWF, a child-to-child art exchange program. Twenty-one years later, in
1968, AWF had grown into an international organization that exchanged
millions of paintings and drawings among children from 77 nations and
distributed exhibitions of child art around the world.[6]

As the example of AWF indicates, foreign policy, international aid, and
ideological mobilization occurred on many levels during the Cold War.
American citizens were encouraged to participate personally in national
defense through organizations to which they already belonged, to assist
local preparedness efforts, and to use their professional skills for the good
of the nation. For Americans, the Cold War did not take place primarily on foreign battlefields, but more often in a daily battle for hearts and
minds, both at home and abroad. "Ideas . . . will win, not dollars," wrote
Supreme Court Justice William O. Douglas in 1951. Goodwill among people was of primary importance in the Cold War battle for the allegiance
of other nations. "Neither wealth nor might will determine the outcome
of the struggles," he wrote after a 1950 visit to India. "They will turn on
emotional factors too subtle to measure. Political alliances of an enduring
nature will be built not on the power of guns or dollars, but on affection."
Children were crucial in creating such international bonds of affection.[7]

In this ongoing battle for hearts and minds, Soviet and American
children were both political activists and potential victims. This dual
role originated, as Dominique Marshall and others have argued, in the
aftermath of World War I. The American Relief Administration (ARA)
focused on children because they were considered especially vulnerable,
psychologically victimized by war, and politically appealing to donors.
Depictions of suffering children were prominent in ARA publications
as they could "represent the endangered innocence of whole nations."[8]
After World War II, foreign aid agencies such as UNICEF focused on
children in part because their vulnerability and innocence made children the least controversial beneficiaries of international aid. Few could
deny aid to the child refugees and orphans of postwar Europe and Asia,
and UNICEF's focus on children protected the organization from falling

victim to power struggles within the United Nations. As Sian Roberts demonstrated, intersecting networks of peace activists, religious groups, arts educators, and women's organizations launched the first child art humanitarian projects in the aftermath of World War I.[9] Those networks remained in place following World War II. Nancy Babb, for example, was a Quaker field representative for the Red Cross and a relief worker in Russia from 1917 to the mid-1920s. On her return to the United States in 1928, Babb became active in a number of women's organizations, including the WILPF. She established the National Circulating Library of Student's Peace Posters (NCLSPP), an organization that sponsored antiwar poster contests for youth from 1935 to 1940.[10] In 1938, Maude Muller served as a hostess for one of these NCLSPP poster exhibits in Philadelphia.[11] Perhaps that experience convinced her that children could most effectively publicize the devastating impact of war on future generations.

Similarly, during the Spanish Civil War, children were encouraged to remember and recreate their experiences of evacuation and war through visual art. In 1937–1938, Spain's Ministry of Public Education asked children to produce pictures that recalled their lives before and during the war and to imagine their postwar lives. Quaker volunteers collected more than 2,000 of these drawings, exhibited and sold them abroad, and used the proceeds to publicize the plight of orphans and refugees, evacuate endangered children, and provide assistance to already established youth refugee colonies.[12] In 1938, the American Friends Service Committee published 60 children's drawings in a book titled *And They Still Draw Pictures!* with an introduction by Aldous Huxley. Drawing on popular theories of primitivism, Huxley claimed that young children, "all unwittingly, of course, and by instinct, display a "sure sense of colour [sic], a feeling for form, a remarkable capacity for decorative invention, artistic resourcefulness, and power of expression and execution."[13] Most postwar children's art programs retained echoes of aesthetic primitivism—the idea that the untutored could most directly and immediately represent life and raw experience. Art educators considered such immediacy and lack of pretense in representing the supposedly "universal" conditions of childhood conducive to developing world understanding among children from different nations and cultures.

The Cold War did not require fundraising or child welfare campaigns in the direct sense engendered by earlier wartime emergencies. As the refugee and food crises following World War II began to ease, peace activists shifted from using art to raise awareness or funds to using art to foster peace and deter nuclear war. Undergirding these efforts was a romantic notion of childhood such as that expressed by children's author Harry Behn, "Especially is this the dominion of childhood, that worldwide nation without boundaries or wars."[14] Despite the obvious fallacy of this statement—most children had experienced war in some form—the notion of childhood innocence continued to provide some justification for using children and their art for political purposes. The presence of nuclear weapons and rising tensions between the United States and the Soviet Union required the intensification of interwar peace and education efforts to prevent a catastrophic third world war. Maude Muller therefore positioned AWF as an "apolitical" WILPF program, intended to foster international friendship and creativity among the world's children.

AWF perpetuated early twentieth-century peace efforts in other ways as well. In the 1920s, patriot groups red-baited the WILPF and other peace organizations; in the late 1940s, the American Legion and the Daughters of the American Revolution labeled the WILPF a communist front organization, and the FBI conducted investigations. In another example of the chilling effects of the Red Scare, Muller steered clear of potentially problematic allies. In November 1955, the president of the American–Russian Institute in San Francisco contacted Muller, proposing a cooperative effort in children's art exchanges. WILPF discovered that the organization was on the Attorney General's list of subversive organizations and was "one of the favorite targets of investigating committees." Muller replied to the Institute's representative that although she wished they could work together, "in the present state of the world it would be wiser for us to make our USSR contact through the USSR embassy."[15] In the 1950s, the pink-tinged WILPF rejected cooperation with the blacklisted American–Russian Institute to avoid political problems. But the WILPF also saw children themselves as an effective way to deflect accusations of communist infiltration. Although adult art was often criticized as propaganda, politically innocent and naïve children seemed incapable of explicitly political intent.[16] Childhood innocence implied a lack of politics, allowing the WILPF to deflect accusations of leftist intentions.

Second, just as in the post–World War I years, Cold War–era peace efforts mobilized largely female philanthropic, activist, and volunteer communities. The Child Welfare Committee of the League of Nations was established as a result of pressure from international women's associations who believed that maternal instinct could overcome nationalism: "The interest of each mother in her own child must be built up [into] an interest in the mother and child of all other countries, and in this way, we can join together to build up the welfare of the whole world."[17] Tarah Brookfield has demonstrated that Canadian female peace activists claimed the authority to intervene in traditionally male political domains through their status as mothers or potential mothers, and she often described their work in maternalist language. Maude Muller referred to herself as a "housewife" even as she corresponded with the Soviet consulate and gave interviews to the US State Department. She saw her work with AWF in the tradition of female responsibility for children extending from the local to the global, as necessitated by the threat of the Cold War. Finally, AWF replicated earlier strategies of peace organizations. In 1953, AWF sold for $1 notepaper decorated with original linocuts by Dutch children and donated the profits to Dutch relief efforts for children. The Dorr Foundation contributed 100 copies of photographer Nell Dorr's 1954 book of "visual poetry," *Mother and Child*, for inclusion in AWF packages.[18] Dorr's work tends toward an unabashedly sentimental and universalist depiction of the mother–child relationship. By 1957, AWF included packages of flower seeds with their shipments of child art to all parts of the world to symbolize the power of art to sow the seeds of peace. In all of these ways, AWF perpetuated the work of post–World War I peace activists.

Maude Muller's living room served as the international office of AWF for more than two decades. Beginning as a small, local WILPF project, the staff consisted of Muller and a few part-time volunteers who corresponded with teachers, youth leaders, and government officials; maintained records and budgets; arranged local exhibitions, mainly in department stores; and shipped artwork around the globe. Over time, as AWF attracted national and international attention, Muller articulated the basic philosophy of the project, which was rooted in the WILPF and a global women's peace network. During these initial years, Muller's reports to WILPF, letters to foreign embassies, and requests to educational organizations for participation explained AWF and its larger goals. As she wrote in 1950, AWF was an "exchange of drawings, not in any way a contest but a means of communication to learn to know and understand one another. We believe that world peace will be greatly strengthened and furthered by friendship among children. Children are not prejudiced and are not particularly interested in politics, but they are interested in what children of other countries do at home, in school or on the playground." Muller rhetorically removed children from the political realm even as she engaged them in an explicitly political project. Muller and AWF articulated a common conception of children as innocent, vulnerable, and apolitical, even though AWF was rooted in a political organization, WILPF, with a political goal.[19]

During AWF's first year in operation, 14 countries agreed to participate in the art exchange program. By 1952, more than 30 nations and 40 US states were actively involved in art exchanges through AWF, amounting to about 25,000 pictures. Muller stated in a 1952 report, "This year due to articles and to active cooperation by the Voice of America, the rate of exchange is being promoted so rapidly that the half million mark appears attainable. By the end of 1953 it is estimated that at least 2 million children will have exchanged drawings!"[20] "The work of AWF," Muller wrote the following year, "results in intangibles—friendship, understanding, a climate where peace may grow." In 1954, she explained, "Art as a creative activity helps not only the individual child, but bridges the distance between different customs and different cultures. It will help towards developing one world."[21] The perceived innocence of children allowed several incompatible ideas to co-exist: Muller heralded children's art as a means toward building a broad internationalism even as Cold Warriors envisioned children's art as a way to depict American superiority. The US State Department actively promoted AWF through the Voice of America, even as the FBI investigated the WILPF as a communist front organization.[22]

Changing conceptions of childhood in the postwar years shaped many American art exchange programs. Throughout the 1950s, Muller's reports and letters reflect the increasingly prevalent idea of children as a separate and special age group, even as the international movement from child-saving to child-rights challenged those distinctions. Muller asserted in a 1953 report, "everywhere it seems to be recognized that children are the connective links—they are not only representatives of their own nation but always they are the envoys of a great and conciliatory world. Now that they are being recognized more and more as individuals in their own right rather than small adults, their power is even greater." Children's power lay in their perceived difference from adults, their lack of prejudice, their innocence. Particularly in the postwar United States, where the nuclear family and the protected status of white childhood reached new heights during the Baby Boom, children were seen as endangered and in need of protection. They were also envisioned as cultural ambassadors and representatives of democratic capitalism. In their study of how nongovernmental organizations (NGOs) have framed images of children, Ali, James, and Vultee argue that "needy" children typically are depicted as either passive recipients or as evidence of an organization's success. During the Cold War, photographs of isolated, passive, and deprived children throughout the developing world were contrasted with images of healthy, active American children, often depicted in a secure, familial setting. Images of American children, particularly in their role as saviors to the world's less fortunate, were explicitly political; they suggested that the United States was able to protect not only its own children, but the future well-being of the world through democratic capitalism. Images of healthy, cared-for American children implied that the rest of the world should emulate the American way.[23]

THE UNIVERSALITY OF ART

The world wars of the twentieth century made child welfare an international political, social, and cultural issue. In 1924, the League of Nations adopted the Geneva Declaration, affirming the principle that "mankind owes to the Child the best that it has to give." This historic document recognized for the first time the existence of rights specific to children and adult responsibilities towards children, including providing the means for spiritual and material development, relief in times of distress, and protection from exploitation. In the aftermath of World War II, the UN reaffirmed and expanded the Geneva Declaration. Addressing the incredible physical destruction and deprivation throughout Europe and Asia were immediate postwar priorities. But, as many soon realized, the devastation was not limited to physical ruin. UNESCO Director-General Jaime Torres Bodet explained in 1949, "The havoc wrought by the war in people's minds, and especially in children's minds, is even more serious than the material destruction. The problem of the re-education of child victims of the war is one of those to which UNESCO intends to devote closest concern." UNESCO aimed to "restore to young people whose minds are obsessed by so much violence and poisoned by so much hatred . . . the desire to reconstruct and to share the experience of human fellowship." To this end, UNESCO organized youth camps, created the International Federation of Children's Communities to coordinate the activities of the hundreds of children's homes and children's villages that arose after World War II to meet the needs of millions of displaced or orphaned children, and offered teacher training courses on international understanding, which became, through cultural and educational exchange, UNESCO's prime objective. And art, as both therapy and diplomacy, was one means of achieving it.[24]

The use of children's art for political purposes during the postwar years is exceptional only as a matter of degree. By the late 1940s, children's art had been used for 30 years to raise funds and awareness for child welfare. Rooted in the rise of the avant-garde at the turn of the twentieth century, artists and educators valued both primitive and children's art for their access to "the innocent eye." Charles Baudelaire's famous dictum, "Genius is nothing more nor less than childhood recaptured at will" elevated spontaneity, creativity, imagination, experience, and raw perception as the goals of artistic expression. The second key factor in the use of children's art for political purposes lies in the rise of progressive art education, which paralleled the rise of modern art. Since the 1930s, art education had undergone significant revision. Gone were the days of imitation and coerced copying of masterpieces. The progressive education movement had taken firm root among art educators, who encouraged children to develop at their own pace, explore a variety of materials and methods, and favor process over product. John Dewey's 1932 book, *Art as Experience*, summed up the progressive argument that art should be removed from its elitist pedestal and reincorporated into daily life, beginning with early childhood education. The dislocations of World War II and the global concern for children's mental and emotional recovery renewed interest in the benefits of creative activity.[25]

Judging by the contents of their professional journal, *Art Education*, American art educators were committed to UNESCO's program of educational and cultural exchange and equally convinced that the arts would help achieve these goals. In 1946, the National Art Education Association (NAEA) partnered with the American Junior Red Cross to launch the International School Art Program (ISAP). The goal: to provide an opportunity for students to "contribute to world peace through understanding." Though they embodied the same general purpose, the differences between this program and AWF are instructive. The ISAP intended to "arouse in the young people of the world a friendly interest in each other's way of life" and to "encourage our students to use first-hand experiences as material for art expression." Open to students in grades 7 through 12, the art work was expected to "represent the best creative work in our schools." The National Chairman of ISAP, Rosemary Beymer, emphasized the self-conscious portrayal of "our school and community life" in work that would travel abroad. Committees of art educators screened the submissions and selected those that would successfully "interpret American life to youth of other lands." Work that failed to depict appropriate subject matter, that was "weak or timid," or "stereotyped and trite" would be rejected. Like the AWF, the ISAP suggested appropriate subject matter, including Our Cafeteria Crowds, My First Date, Our Family at Ease, My Own Room, Our Street on a Lazy Afternoon, After the Big Snow, Shopping at Christmas Time, and My Summer Job in a Factory, among others. Students were asked to depict daily events in their lives and subjects or experiences that might interest their peers in other countries. By creating art that depicted how Americans "feel, think, and see" and that gives a "straight-forward interpretation of contemporary life," teenagers were acting as "real ambassadors."[26]

It was in this context of universal childhood that Muller could claim the universality of art as a language of peace and international friendship among the world's children. In AWF correspondence and public relations literature, she regularly quoted from well-known art educators such as Victor D'Amico, the Director of Education at the Museum of Modern Art (MoMA), and Edwin Ziegfeld, the President of International Society for Education Through Art (ISEA). In 1957 Muller explained that art was a "natural bond between children" that transcended differences of "race, language, creed or education." Through an exchange of children's art, AWF hoped to create "a climate where the seeds of peace could grow and prosper—to lift the world with loving kindness." Muller rejected any suggestions of art competitions for fear they would destroy the creativity and spontaneity that made child art so valuable. As a "universal language," art made both children and adults "more aware of their oneness with all mankind." In 1958, Muller wrote of yet another more personal benefit of participation in AWF for individual children: "When conformity seems the great virtue of the day it is most important that the growing child . . . be given the opportunity to express himself creatively." AWF reflected current understandings of both childhood and progressive art education.[27]

Victor D'Amico, the Director of Education at the MoMA from 1937 to 1969 and editor of *Art Education Today*, was at the forefront of art education from the late 1930s through the postwar years; he wrote prolifically about the benefits of art education at all stages of human development, but he focused on children. Under D'Amico's guidance, in 1942, the MoMA launched the Children's Carnival of Modern Art, which was based on "specific principles of child psychology and according to particular theories about creative growth," including the importance of a visually appealing environment and the value of play in creative learning. The installation consisted of two distinct spaces. One area of toys, paintings, and sculpture by modern artists encouraged interaction, intimacy, and tactile experiences. Children between the ages of four and eight were encouraged to play with plastic mobiles, a slide machine of paintings from the Museum's collection, and a color player with a keyboard and foot pedals that projected colored abstract patterns on a screen. The second area was a workshop with paints, easels, paper, and work tables where children could "follow the inspiration received from seeing artists' work by creating his own ideas." For one hour, 40 children used the materials while five art teachers shared innovative techniques. The Carnival traveled to the International Trade Fairs in Milan and Barcelona in 1957, to the American Pavilion at the Brussels World's Fair in 1958, and to India in 1962 to demonstrate "American methods of art education." The project was bound up with international politics and a demonstration of American cultural superiority rooted in artistic freedom. As quoted by D'Amico, one Italian journalist enthused, "What better way is there of strengthening a feeling of brotherhood among nations than to develop the creative abilities of children?"[28]

D'Amico was also among the founders of the Committee on Art in American Education and Society in 1943, a group dedicated to "promot[ing] the creative arts during the war period, to mak[ing] them function in the changing contemporary world, and to plan[ning] for their increased importance and usefulness in the reconstruction to come."[29] D'Amico also presided over the creation of the War Veterans' Art Center in 1944 and its transformation into the People's Art Center in 1948.[30] He urged public recognition of art as a valuable tool for the emotional and mental growth of children and as a release from daily tensions for adults who increasingly looked to the arts as a leisure activity. In the early 1950s, the MoMA's People's Art Center offered 77 classes for a range of ages in a variety of media. The educational guidelines of the center forged a middle path between "rule and imitation" (traditional) on the one hand and "not teaching at all" (progressive) on the other. D'Amico's philosophy was grounded in a "totally new concept of education based on knowledge of the child's creative and psychological growth and on mastery of teaching techniques needed for their development."[31]

Postwar progressive art educators were profoundly influenced by British art educator Herbert Read's *Education Through Art* (1946), a landmark study on the theory and practice of art education that remains a classic in the field. A veteran of World War I, Read became a pacifist, poet, and art critic. He was instrumental in UNESCO's art education program and a catalyst in the field of child art. Read called for a thorough revision of education, placing art at the center of the curriculum, not as a subject to master, but as a method for acquiring knowledge, developing morality and a sense of community, and, most importantly, achieving self-actualization and individual freedom.[32] The language of progressive art education, with its emphasis on personal creativity, independence, and self-actualization became an ideological tool in the cultural Cold War. Western democracies pointed to intellectual freedom as a necessity for the healthy development of children, art, and society in general while noting the lack of personal freedom among Soviet artists. Jazz, abstract expressionism, and child art shared particular characteristics—spontaneity, freedom, experimentation—that served as the antithesis to the regimentation imposed on Soviet children and artists. Like modern artists, child artists were given free rein for personal expression.

As Cold War imperatives turned artistic freedom into a crucial component of democracy, progressive art educators adopted Cold War language to argue for the importance of their work. Since the "promotion of understanding" was generally considered "the most important objective in today's world," wrote the superintendent of Chicago Public Schools in 1950, the arts had to be used to their fullest capacity to develop a universal means of expression. Art encouraged American children to freely express their personalities and learn to appreciate the free expression of others, thereby better preparing them to live in a democratic society. Art education in particular was "geared to the basic principle of developing respect for the individual personality," a necessity for democratic living. The universal languages of the arts encouraged the "mutuality of feeling, interest in cooperation and assistance" that promoted world understanding and "advanced the cause of democracy world-wide." Such optimism translated into passionate support for UNESCO's guiding purpose: increasing international understanding through education and cultural and scientific exchanges. Progressive art educators around the world took an active interest in using the arts to further world understanding. At UNESCO's first general conferences in 1946 and 1947, they adopted resolutions to investigate potential roles for art education. In 1948, a committee was formed with this goal. Art educators at the 1950 White House Conference lent official recognition to the importance of the arts in a democracy. As "natural outlets for emotional experiences," they argued, "the arts contributed to mental health, the growth of individual self-reliance and freedom, a sense of community and cooperation, and a means of counteracting materialism."[33]

The rising interest in child art was not limited to the United States. On the contrary, America lagged behind Europe in terms of professional and museum interest in childhood art, according to a November 1947 article, "Child Art in Paris" by Marion B. Cothren in *The Horn Book*, a magazine devoted to children's literature. According to Cothren, "exhibitions of children's paintings have been increasing at an amazing rate, especially in the postwar years, and France has been in the vanguard." A recent show, *The Liberation of Paris*, featured 1,000 paintings by the children of Brazil, Chile, Peru, Paraguay, Uruguay, Bolivia, Argentina, Ecuador, and Venezuela. Another exhibition at the usually staid École des Beaux Arts featured 500 paintings by Norwegian children depicting their national day of liberation. For several weeks, the Musée Pedagogique de L'État exhibited the work of Swiss, Finn, Austrian, Czech, Polish, and British children as well as fifty "most interesting" paintings from China, some of which were in the "conservative, meticulous manner of old Chinese paintings," but "more were alive with the spirit of Young China." The largest exhibition of the year, held in the Musée de Luxembourg, featured 2,000 paintings by children from 40 different nations (neither Germany nor Japan was invited, and the Soviet Union declined to submit any paintings), selected from 20,000 works submitted to L'Union des Arts Plastiques. "The United States," Cothren pointedly stated, "was represented by 40 and France by 400." Clearly, Americans were falling behind. Cothren attributed French superiority to the ongoing public commitment, even during the war years, to instructing French children in art. She cited the example of Monsieur Paillard, a color manufacturer, who had for the previous 12 years sponsored painting competitions for French children, 60 of whom won awards distributed by professional art critics.[34] Art education in the United States, Cothren noted, did not measure up to other nations' standards.

CHILDREN'S ART AND THE CULTURAL COLD WAR

Art, as it turned out, was a particularly effective means not only for developing a healthy personality, self-reliance, and independence, but also for spreading democracy around the world. During the Cold War, federal propaganda machines in the State Department and the US Information Agency (USIA) selectively made use of existing networks among art educators and peace organizations to improve the image of the United States abroad. AWF, Junior League art exchanges, and scrapbooks created by Girl Scout troops all were touted by the federal government at excellent examples of person-to-person diplomacy that would advance the cause of world peace and friendship.

As the concept of child welfare expanded after World War II to include not only physical well-being, but mental and emotional health as well, children's art became politically important. In government circles, child welfare concerns were couched in the language of the Cold War. From the 1950 White House Conference on Children and Youth to President Eisenhower's Council on Youth Fitness and his 1957 People-to-People Program, child welfare and children were deeply enmeshed in the Cold War. If "American ideology" was to win the "great struggle" for global supremacy, Eisenhower announced in 1957, thousands of "independent private groups and millions of individual Americans . . . men, women, and children" had to establish "person-to-person communication in foreign lands."[35] The structure of AWF and other art exchange programs meshed precisely with the federal government's emphasis on personal, citizen-initiated diplomatic efforts that could refute accusations of propaganda while simultaneously relaying the government's propaganda messages both at home and abroad. Children's art communicated the abundance of the US economy, the cared-for nature of American children, and the national emphasis on "culture."

In 1950, thousands of child welfare professionals gathered for fifth White House Conference on Children and Youth to discuss "A Healthy Personality for Every Child." From the outset, the conference goal of "promoting good human relations through building in children full mental, emotional and spiritual health" linked the well-being of American children to foreign diplomacy. Addressing the conference, President Truman placed child welfare in the context of a global struggle against communism. "I believe," he said, "the single most important things our young people will need to meet this critical challenge in the years ahead is moral strength—strength of character." Children had to be taught "the value of free institutions and the values on which they rest. . . . Nothing will have a greater effect on the world struggle against Communism than spelling out the ways in which our young people can better understand our democratic institutions, and why we must fight, when necessary, to defend our democratic institutions, our belief in the rights of the individual, and our fundamental belief in God." Inculcating a strong sense of democratic citizenship was essential, and at an earlier age than ever before. Rather than insulating American children from "the uncertainties of the world," Truman urged conference participants to prepare them to meet the world armed with strength of character, self-reliance, and independence. The arts, and their therapeutic benefits, became one way to achieve these goals for American youth.[36]

As Frances Stoner, Serge Guilbaut, Kenneth Osgood, and other scholars have demonstrated, the USIA, the State Department, and the Central Intelligence Agency (CIA) had already established the cultural realm as a legitimate arena in which to fight the Cold War. Abstract Expressionist paintings and jazz musicians had been touring Europe with the gospel of democracy since the end of World War II. In this context, AWF became a noteworthy weapon in America's cultural arsenal. Although AWF firmly disavowed any explicitly political goal beyond working toward world friendship through individual children, the organization had grown so rapidly by mid-1953 that it attracted the attention of the US State Department. In June 1953, the State Department sent "two young men" to Philadelphia to interview Muller for their journal, *Free World*. The resulting story, "A World Fellowship of Young Artists," described AWF as a program "designed to illustrate American Efforts (*sic*) and ideals looking toward a world of peace and friendship." The international press service translated the story into 11 languages in 77 countries. Whether Maude Muller and the WILPF would have agreed to participate in the State Department's cultural Cold War is a different matter.[37] Child art, however, fit the Cold War imperatives of peace organizations, art educators, *and* Cold Warriors within the US government.

The connections between international politics and children's art were formally recognized in the summer of 1951, when art educators from around the world met in Bristol, England, for UNESCO's three-week seminar, The Visual Arts in General Education. The American delegate, Edwin Ziegfeld, a well-known art educator from Teacher's College at Columbia University, later remembered how surprised his colleagues were by the quality of American children's art. Surely, they insisted, he brought a "highly selective" display. Surely these examples weren't typical of American schoolchildren. Their disbelief stemmed from the widespread perception that Americans were interested "only in bathtubs, motor cars, and refrigerators." Soviet propaganda commonly depicted the United States as a cultural wasteland dominated by materialism, an accusation that the State Department and USIA were eager to disprove. Children's art became another tool in the battle for cultural supremacy during the Cold War.

The International Society for Education through Art (InSEA) was born from the 1951 UNESCO conference and formally came into being in July 1954 with the adoption of its constitution, which states:

International co-operation and the better understanding between peoples would be furthered by a more completely integrated design

and permanent structure for the diffusion of beliefs and practices
concerning education through art, so that the right of man [sic]
'freely to participate in the cultural life of the community, to enjoy
the arts' and to create beauty for himself in reciprocal relationship
with his environment, would become a living reality.[38]

InSEA created a large exhibition of children's art that traveled internationally, distributed sets of color transparencies of children's art, assembled
bibliographies of art education materials, and compiled an international
listing of available programs and materials. At InSEA's Second General
Assembly at The Hague in 1957, the organization worked with the
Municipal Museum to stage "the largest and most important exhibition"
of paintings and drawings by adolescents "that the world has ever seen."
InSEA was in the vanguard of organizations that promoted international
understanding through children's art.[39]

AWF and InSEA were but two of a multitude of art exchange programs that had arisen since the end of the war. In an effort to coordinate
these programs, the US Office of Education and the NAEA convened a
three-day conference on the International Exchange of Children's Art in
1959. More than 30 participants representing schools, museums, NGOs,
and government agencies met to consider problems and possibilities
for future development. Of particular interest are the conference delib-
erations on the question of why international exchanges of children's art
would lead to tolerance and peace. In addition, the participants provided
details about their programs and attempted to come to consensus on
questions of competitions, quality control, standardization, and facilita-
tion of exchanges.

The organizations involved—the International School Art Program,
AWF, the Silvermine Guild School Art Program, the Biennial International
Children's Art Exhibition, President Eisenhower's People-to-People
Program, the Junior Red Cross art exchange program, UNESCO, *School
Arts* magazine, and the NAEA—participated directly or indirectly in chil-
dren's international art exchanges during the Cold War. Although they
differed in both philosophy and methods, each operated under certain

assumptions about children, art, and cultural diplomacy. InSEA director Edwin Ziegfeld discussed his role in working with The Hague's exhibition of children's art; both the exhibition and slides of the work circulated internationally. Victor D'Amico spoke of the Children's Carnival of Modern Art and its popularity at international fairs in 1957 and the Brussels World's Fair in 1958. The International School Art Program, cosponsored by the American Junior Red Cross and the NAEA, was more interested in "recruiting interested young artists" to put "creative talent to a social use in a very definite framework." The Red Cross handled the organizational side of the program, while the NAEA created screening committees to "select material for shipment abroad." The Silvermine Guild School began its exchange program in 1953 with children in Osaka, Japan, and hosted an annual Children's Art Festival, featuring work from a different country each year. Since 1954, the University of Nebraska sponsored a Biennial International Children's Art Exhibition, which then traveled to public and private schools in Nebraska as well as to colleges and universities throughout the United States and Canada. The coordinator of the project spoke forcefully for the creation of a central agency to screen all child art sent from the United States "to insure that this work represents the philosophy of art educators in our country."[40]

Despite their differences, all the participants explained their confidence in the efficacy of art exchange. They agreed that children's art "is an instinctive form of human expression," that could express "in an unspoiled way" a picture of a child's culture and show the "common ground between children around the world." Specifically, art exchanges could strengthen international understanding by acquainting other nations with the "ideals, interests, and values" of American children, informing other countries of American values, "focus[ing] attention on the purposes and values of education in other countries," displaying "evidence of American interest" in the cultures of other nations, and, finally, by providing a "stimulating experience" for American children.[41] Dr. Kenneth Winebrenner, a lifelong art educator and the editor of *School Arts* magazine wrote, "We believe that the exchange of children's art work between different countries can be an effective instrument for peace and world understanding, and that a small paint brush in the hands of a small child might conceivably have greater influence . . . than purely political and military considerations." It is worth noting that, by 1959, the intellectual exchange seemed to be directed from the United States to other nations. That is, art exchange organizations found it necessary and important to explain America to other nations, rather than engaging in mutual learning.

The USIA considered these private organizations crucial for improving the image of America abroad. Communist propaganda routinely charged that America was a cultural wasteland of mass-produced gadgetry. To combat such accusations, the State Department sent abroad the best American artists and musicians. The USIA, however, also focused its attention on grassroots cultural activities and accomplishments. Both bureaucracies saw the value in AWF, which "proved" that American children learned not only about the free enterprise system but also about the fundamentals of art and creativity.

In an effort to deflect accusations of propaganda, the State Department and the USIA did not openly support most American cultural efforts, particularly grassroots organizations. However, they did publicize organizations through "news stories" that in effect functioned as propaganda. The State Department's *Free World* and the Voice of America (transferred to the USIA in 1953) carried stories about AWF and numerous other art exchange projects around the world. The US Department of Education, the National Association of Art, the US National Commission for UNESCO, and the 1960 White House Conference on Children and Youth all invited Muller to attend. An unofficial ambassador herself, Muller spent three months visiting Holland, Denmark, England, and Ireland in 1954, making contacts for AWF. The idea of children's cultural exchange meshed well with official ideologies of cultural freedom and truth-telling, as well as progressive efforts toward world peace.

The impact of international politics, although muted, is clear in AWF correspondence with representatives of the Soviet Union and Eastern Bloc nations. Muller initiated contact with Mrs. N. Khimatch, the Cultural Attaché at the Soviet Embassy, in May 1952; their correspondence continued until Muller's poor health forced AWF to close in 1968. Americans were very interested in Soviet children's art, but, to Muller's continual frustration, the Soviet government resisted participating in direct child-to-child exchange. Instead, they sent only organized exhibitions of child art to tour US cities. Muller appreciated the value of such exhibitions and in fact created traveling exhibitions from AWF collections, but she considered spontaneous expression and personal contact more important than the quality of the art. Nevertheless, the Brooklyn Museum hosted an exhibit of Soviet children's art in February 1962, which then travelled to Minneapolis and Washington. In May 1964, 96 pictures by Soviet children arrived in Washington, DC and traveled to Philadelphia; Orange, Texas; Detroit; Chicago; and Denver. Although the subject matter adhered to AWF suggestions of daily scenes of play, work, and celebration, the highly accomplished work obviously had been selected for its artistic quality. From November 1964 through at least November 1965, an exhibition of American children's art toured the Soviet Union, showing in Moscow, Minsk, and Brest to "great interest."[42] By 1966 and throughout 1967, however, Muller lamented, "cultural exchanges in various fields have practically come to a stop because of the US war in Vietnam."

After 1961, AWF made inroads in the developing world by working with Peace Corps volunteers. From 1964 through 1967, Muller received numerous letters from Peace Corps volunteers in Africa requesting paper, crayons, and reproductions of artwork. AWF sent these, along with requests for completed pictures from African children to share with American youth. Through such partnerships, AWF "followed the flag" and represented the United States as a cultural ambassador throughout the world well into the 1960s.

As AWF expanded, America's racial politics became a major foreign and domestic policy issue in the 1950s and 1960s, especially as Soviet propaganda emphasized racism and legal discrimination against African-Americans. Here, too, children's art was understood as a way to counteract negative publicity. AWF did not actively engage in civil rights issues, but, as the program expanded to Southern states, some teachers discovered that interracial projects "held out hope to overcome racial barriers." In

1959, the new Director of the Community Art Center at the Museum of Fine Arts in Little Rock, Arkansas wrote, "It would be especially good to have something from much maligned but wonderful Little Rock—perhaps a joint group of drawings by colored and white children. This is just my idea," she cautioned, "and would have to be approved by our Board, of course, with the controversy drawn as it is at this time." Writing shortly after the "Lost Year," when Governor Orval Faubus closed all four of the city's high schools in an effort to prevent racial integration, the community center director hoped to improve her city's image by using children's art and its perceived lack of racism. The peace movement, art educators, the State Department, and local teachers interested in civil rights seemed to embrace the idea that children's art could simultaneously rise above politics while achieving political goals.[43]

WORLD FRIENDSHIP THROUGH THE EYES OF CHILDREN

Given the powerful interests involved in using children's art to advocate for particular political agendas, one might ask what images of American culture, ideals, and values actually emerged from the millions of pictures children were encouraged to paint and draw at school, in Scout meetings, and at church. If childhood represents a moment of innocence and purity in an otherwise corrupt world, what of children's art? Scholars of the cultural Cold War have shown that the CIA and the State Department fostered a particular interpretation of American culture as fundamentally free.[44] As the argument went, jazz and abstract expressionism were not state-sponsored or ideologically driven arts, but the artist's unfettered personal expression, the essence of American values distilled into cultural form. Children's art was even less structured by professional standards or political motives; childhood innocence translated into political and ideological innocence. Their political naiveté meant they were the ultimate truth-tellers. Children's art expressed "universal" emotions and experiences— tolerance, love for parents and friends, fascination with nature, the exuberance of play and fun. Yet, even as art exchange organizations talked about universal values, the federal government saw the exchanges as a way for foreign children to see how American children lived and, through them, the promises of American democratic capitalism. In practice then, AWF meshed with the federal government's desire to promote a favorable view of the United States through person-to-person cultural diplomacy.

The art collected and distributed by AWF offers a rare opportunity to recover the perspectives, experiences, and agency of American children through their depictions of "daily life." AWF did not have any requirements per se, other than size limits (pictures could not exceed 12 by 18 inches) and a ban on depictions of war, "except where they represent typical scenes in the life of the child." However, AWF guidelines did suggest that children draw "themselves, doing familiar things, working, playing in places familiar to them, such as at home, at school, in their backyards, on their street, in the park or playground. We like to see the house they live in, the kind of clothes they wear, the games they play (individually or in a group), the toys they play with, perhaps what their parents do. In other words we want them to tell in pictures what is typical of their everyday lives." Muller's description is remarkably similar to what Dwight Eisenhower suggested to Congress in 1947. Advocating a comprehensive cultural information program that could be "readily comprehended by the (foreign) people," Eisenhower recommended topics including "ice boxes, radios, cars, how much Americans had to eat, what they wear, when they go to sports spectacles, and what they have available in the way of art galleries." In 1954, Eisenhower requested emergency appropriations to fund cultural exchange programs and trade fair presentations, citing the essential need to "demonstrate the superiority of the products and cultural values of our system of free enterprise." Since Stalin's death, the Soviet Union had devoted unprecedented attention and resources to trade fairs and cultural tours. This "thaw" was taken by the Eisenhower administration as a threat to American cultural hegemony and American leadership abroad, one that demanded an American response.[45] Children's art provided a "non-political" response to the Soviet cultural offensive.

Given AWF guidelines and the notion of "voluntold" labor, what did children choose to draw or paint to represent "typical life?" How did they express the ideals, interests, and values of the United States? What does the ideology of freedom look like through the eyes of a child? A selection of artwork by American children depicts a range of topics, but almost all project the images of childhood innocence that AWF, the State Department, and USIA hoped to see. Among them are landscape scenes, such as Mount Rushmore, or a long, empty highway through the Nevada desert as remembered by a sixth-grade California boy on a road trip to visit his grandparents in Kansas. The size, scale, and wide open spaces of the West clearly impressed him. Denver children painted pictures of children skiing down a snow-covered mountain and swimming in a pool under the watchful eye of a lifeguard in an impossibly high chair. There are drawings of children on swings in school playgrounds; children building snowmen, ice skating, and having snowball fights; there is a cross-section view of a house that would surely have pleased any USIA administrator for its innocent depiction of a comfortable three-story home, with a television (Figure 2.1). A series of drawings, "People Who Help Us," a theme likely supplied by a teacher, depicts a fire fighter, police officer, and doctor, but also a singing cowboy who "helps us have fun." Such images may have humanized Americans to a foreign audience and softened the image of the nation, as State Department bureaucrats hoped, and the fact that the artists were children and that the sponsoring organization was an international peace group defused possible charges of propaganda. These images also served as evidence that the United States valued creativity and imagination as well as business and Hollywood movies.

Few AWF pictures depict any sort of difficulty or conflict. America's racial situation goes unnoticed except in one woodcut of a black boy and a white boy shaking hands (Figure 2.2). There couldn't have been a better picture from the State Department's perspective to represent race relations. The United States may have its problems, the official line went, but democratic institutions were gradually correcting the regional mistakes of the past in a constant march toward progress.[46] Poverty, too, is invisible, except in one picture by a 17-year-old student at Chicago's DuSable High School. Built in 1935, the school was gradually surrounded by the Robert Taylor Homes, a public housing project that became notorious for drug

Figure 2.1 Nine-year-old Donna Wyatt of Burlington, Massachusetts, depicted this cross-section of a home's interior. By its very ordinariness, the comforts and relative luxuries of this single-family home, innocently depicted by a child, served as ideal propaganda. The US State Department valued voluntary world friendship programs because children seemed to unknowingly prove the superior quality of life made possible by democratic capitalism. Courtesy of Swarthmore College Peace Collection, Art for World Friendship Records.

problems and gang violence. Up to 80% of DuSable's students lived in the projects. This boy's depiction of his surroundings included a brick wall tagged with graffiti, a broken window, and an overflowing trashcan. These two images are the exception to the general rule of pleasant, descriptive pictures of "typical" life in the United States.

Some children looked beyond their immediate surroundings and daily lives to depict images of "America" in a larger context. One boy depicted "The US on the Moon," complete with fantastic robots, aliens, and rocket launchers. Another boy drew a rocket launch. Another child chose Ford's

Figure 2.2 Fifteen-year-old George Wilson of Chicago drew this hopeful vision of American race relations, depicting young people in a Northern city progressing beyond the racism of the Southern past to forge interracial friendships. Courtesy of Swarthmore College Peace Collection, Art for World Friendship Records.

River Rouge plant as the subject of his drawing. If left completely to their own devices, however, it is impossible to know if the resulting images would have had common themes or not. From the USIA point of view, however, American children were very effective diplomats. Their depictions of healthy, happy children in a modern country where everyone could afford a home and a car; where science, technology, and art were national priorities; and where problems like racism were gradually disappearing, seemingly proved the superiority of the American way of life.

AWF and Gimbel Brothers department store sponsored an annual essay competition for Philadelphia-area children who participated in exchanges. Like the art itself, the essays were determined in part by adult instruction, but children were given wide latitude for self-expression within a set of guidelines. Children were asked to respond to one of the following open-ended but leading questions:

- What do I think of the pictures exhibited in the Gallery?
- Which works impress me most?
- Do I want to know the children of other lands?
- Have I something to give to them?
- Have they something to give to me?
- Should I serve the world I live in as well as my own country?
- Can the children of the world play a part in establishing Universal Peace?

The surviving essays show that young children had already been exposed to American propaganda. One 12-year-old boy thought that if children in "red China and Communist-controlled Russia" were taught the truth about the rest of the world, especially America, they wouldn't grow up to hate and distrust other nations. He suggested that if children in those nations played "sports and games" like American children, they would "have respect and understanding for the people of other countries." An 11-year-old girl felt sure that pictures could contribute to world peace because American children could "thank God we are the lucky ones to live in the United States," where we need not fear that "any passing plane is coming from an enemy country" or that "someone may come and take our parents away from us." Although we cannot know what pictures this child saw, we can be sure she did not see depictions of threatening enemy planes or parents being dragged from their children. One can only surmise that she received such ideas from other sources, such as the American media; anticommunist popular culture like comic books, movies, and television; or from the adults in her life. On the other hand, the girl continued, the pictures sent from American children to other nations would show "the freedom of our America and what a wonderful place we live in." Their pictures would provide hope that "someday their country would be a free, peace-loving place." Other children wrote of the United States' responsibility to assume a leadership role in the world "because of our freedom and democracy." One boy wrote that the United States should "give the children of the world money, clothes, and food, also idea's (*sic*) of freedom" rather than ammunition.[47] As these examples demonstrate, sixth-grade children were far from apolitical; they had a clear sense of national superiority and of their responsibilities as citizens and cultural diplomats.

The children's comments are all the more interesting because their authors had received drawings from children in other parts of the world. The AWF archives has collected dozens of drawings, paintings, and collages from children in Samoa, Australia, Denmark, the Netherlands, Japan, Sweden, and the Soviet Union, among other nations. These children showed what daily life was like for them, including scenes of nature and leisure activities, school and play, city scenes and architecture, cosmonauts and family pets. Figures 2.3 and 2.4 are examples of artwork from

Figure 2.3 This work by a fourteen-year-old Soviet youth shows two children engaged in a leisure activity that may have been familiar to some American children, as well as comfortable homes that may have surprised American viewers. Courtesy of Swarthmore College Peace Collection, Art for World Friendship Records.

Figure 2.4 Thirteen-year-old Raev of Odessa seems to have been as fascinated by Russian space travel and cosmonauts as many American children who drew pictures of US rockets on the moon. Children of both nations were encouraged to imagine space as another frontier where their nations competed for dominance. Courtesy of Swarthmore College Peace Collection, Art for World Friendship Records.

the Soviet Union that American children received from an AWF exchange. In comparison to submissions by children from other nations, the Soviet artwork seems far more polished and well-executed, as if only the most talented students were permitted to represent their nation.

CONCLUSION

Like the many art exchange programs that arose in the post–World War II decades, AWF highlights the fact that children, *because* they were children, were considered crucial actors in national and international Cold

War politics. Educators, government officials, peace activists, and leaders of NGOs from across the political spectrum believed that children
could and should help to foster international understanding of the United
States in an increasingly dangerous world.[48] Implicit in postwar youth art
exchange programs is a belief in the political and cultural innocence of
children, coupled with the explicit politicization of childhood innocence.
If, on the one hand, children were potential victims of nuclear warfare,
they also functioned as cultural diplomats and potential agents of international political change. Maude Muller and WILPF hoped that the shared
joys and experiences of universal childhood could overcome political tensions to achieve "world friendship," while State Department bureaucrats
saw in children's drawings "innocent" propaganda that proved American
superiority to young people around the world. These twin ideas, childhood as an innocent and universal stage of life, coupled with the use of
children's culture as "nonpolitical" propaganda, informed the many art
and cultural exchange programs of the postwar years. As we will see in
the following chapter, the US and Soviet governments also used children's
books as weapons in the cultural Cold War.

NOTES

1. Marilyn Holt, *Cold War Kids: Politics and Childhood in Postwar America* (Lawrence:
    University Press of Kansas, 2014).
2. Karen Dubinsky, "Children, Ideology, and Iconography: How Babies Rule the
    World," *The Journal of the History of Childhood and Youth* 5.1 (Winter 2012): 7–9.
3. Julia F. Irwin, "Taming Total War: Great War-Era American Humanitarianism and
    its Legacies," *Diplomatic History* 38.4 (2014): 763.
4. Sarah Glassford, " 'Voluntold': Child Labour in the Canadian Red Cross, 1899–
    1970." Unpublished conference paper presented at the Eighth Biennial Society for
    the History of Children and Youth, Vancouver, British Columbia, June 25, 2015.
5. Kelly, *Children's World: Growing Up in Russia, 1890–1991*; Peacock, *Innocent Weapons*;
    Sara Fieldston, "Little Cold Warriors: Child Sponsorship and International Affairs,"
    Diplomatic History 38.2 (2014): 240–250; Gleb Tsipursky, " 'Active and Conscious
    Builders of Communism': State Sponsored Tourism for Soviet Adolescents in the
    Early Cold War 1945–53," *Journal of Social History* 48.1 (2014): 20–46.
6. Carl E. Guthe and Marian W. Smith, "The First National Conference on UNESCO,"
    American Anthropologist, New Series, 49.4, Part 1 (October–December 1947): 681–685.

7. William O. Douglas, *Strange Lands and Friendly People* (New York: Harper, 1951): 296, 321, 326.

8. Dominique Marshall, "Humanitarian Sympathy for Children in Times of War and the History of Children's Rights, 1919–1959," in James Marten, ed., *Children and War: A Historical Anthology* (New York: New York University Press, 2002): 185–187.

9. Sian Roberts, "Exhibiting Children at Risk: Child Art, International Exhibitions, and Save the Children Fund in Vienna, 1919–1923," *Paedagogica Historica* 45 (April 2009): 171–190.

10. National Circulating Library of Students' Peace Posters Collected Records (CDG-A), Swarthmore College Peace Collection, hereafter SCPC.

11. "Local Women Active in Poster Exhibit" (March 10, 1938) Clipping in Art for World Friendship Records (DG 066c), Box 1, Series A: Personal Papers of Maude Muller, Folder: Maude Muller Biographical Material, Swarthmore College Peace Collection, hereafter AWF SCPC.

12. *Children's Drawings of the Spanish Civil War,* https://exhibitions.cul.columbia.edu/exhibits/show/children

13. Alduous Huxley, *They Still Draw Pictures!* (New York: The Spanish Child Welfare Association of America, 1938): 4–6.

14. Harry Behn, "The Golden Age," *Hornbook Magazine* (April 1960): 113.

15. Correspondence between Maude Muller and Mr. Holland Roberts (November 28, 1955), AWF SCPC, Box 11, Series C: Correspondence—US, Folder: USSR, 1964–68.

16. Tarah Brookfield, *Cold War Comforts: Canadian Women, Child Safety, and Global Insecurity* (Waterloo, ON: Wilfrid Laurier University Press, 2012): 5–7, 122.

17. Quoted in Marshall, "Humanitarian Sympathy for Children," 192.

18. Muller, AWF Report to WILPF, pencil dated 1953 in top right corner, AWF SCPC, Box 3, Series B: Administrative Files, Folder: Administrative Reports (1 of 3).

19. Muller, AWF Report to WILPF, May 1950, AWF SCPC, Box 3, Series B: Administrative Files, Folder: Administrative Reports (1 of 3).

20. Muller, "AWF History," April 4, 1952; AWF SCPC, Box 3, Series B: Administrative Files Folder: Administrative Reports (1 of 3).

21. Muller, Report to WILPF, January 1953–1954, AWF SCPC, Box 3, Series B: Administrative Files, Folder: Administrative Reports (1 of 3), SCPC.

22. Muller's reference to "one world" was not uncommon among WILPF activists and refers to varying levels of political commitment to the ideas summed up in Wendell Wilkie's 1943 book *One World*, which rejected nationalism in its call for an internationalist post–World War II global order, an idea that disgusted and alarmed many conservatives.

23. Muller, Report to WILPF, 1953, AWF SCPC, Box 3, Series B: Administrative Files, Folder: Administrative Reports (1 of 3); "Strike a Pose: Comparing Associated Press and UNICEF Visual Representations of the Children of Darfur," *African Conflict and Peacebuilding Review* 1.3 (2013): 1–26; Jo Boyden, "Childhood and the Policy Makers: A Comparative Perspective on the Globalization of Childhood," in Allison James and Alan Prout, eds. *Constructing and Reconstructing Childhood: Contemporary Issues in the Sociological Study of Childhood* (New York: Falmer, 1990): 184–215.

24. UNESCO, "50 Years for Education," (UNESCO, 1997): 40–45, 107–108.

25. Mayo Bryce and Ralph Beelke, *Report of Conference on International Exchange of Children's Art* (Washington, DC: US Department of Health, Education, and Welfare, 1959): 2; Victoria Grieve, *The Federal Art Project and the Creation of Middlebrow Culture* (Champaign: University of Illinois Press, 2009): 11–36.

26. Rosemary Beymer, "How You May Participate 1950–1951: The International School Art Program," *Art Education* (November–December 1950): 9–11; Rosemary Beymer, Felicia Beverly, and Livingston Blair, "International School Art Program," *Art Education* (November 1952): 8–9.

27. Muller, "Art for World Friendship Report, December 31, 1956–December 31, 1957"; Muller, AWF, October 1958. AWF SCPC, Box 3, Series B: Administrative Files, Folder: Administrative Reports (2 of 3).

28. Radio interview with Victor D'Amico, WNYC, December 1949. Accessed at http://www.wnyc.org/story/childrens-carnival-at-moma/; Victor D'Amico, "Creative Art for Children, Young People, Adults, Schools," *The Bulletin of the Museum of Modern Art* 19 (Autumn 1951): 12; Mayo Bryce and Ralph Beelke, *Report of Conference on International Exchange of Children's Art* (Washington DC: US Department of Health, Education, and Welfare, Office of Education, 1959): 4–5.

29. Announcement of the Committee on Art in American Education and Society, *Art Education Today* (1943): 68, cited in Kerry Freedman, "Art Education and Changing Political Agendas: An Analysis of Curriculum Concerns of the 1940s and 1950s," *Studies in Art Education* 29.1 (Autumn 1987): 20–21.

30. Laurel Humble, "Response and Responsibility: The War Veterans' Art Center at the Museum of Modern Art, 1944–48" (2016). *CUNY Academic Works.*

31. D'Amico, "Creative Art for Children, Young People, Adults, Schools," 7.

32. John S. Keel, "Herbert Read on Education Through Art," *Journal of Aesthetic Education* 3.4 (October 1969): 47–58.

33. Herold Hunt, "The Arts: Promoters of Understanding," *Art Education* (September–October 1950): 2–5. "Aesthetic Experience and Artistic Expression," Summaries of Work Group Opinions, *Proceedings of the Mid-Century White House Conference on Children and Youth*," ed. Edward A. Richards (Raleigh: Health Publications Institute, Inc., 1950): 215–217.

34. Marion B. Cothren, "Child Art in Paris," *The Horn Book* (November 1947): 411–418.

35. Press Release regarding June 12 White House Conference on People-to-People Partnership (May 31, 1956), DDE's Records as President, Official File, Box 764, 325 (2), Eisenhower Archive and Presidential Library, Abilene KS.

36. Katharine Lenroot, "Today's Promise—Tomorrow's Action," 93; Harry S. Truman, "Report to the Nation," 50–52, both in *Proceedings of the Mid-Century White House Conference on Children and Youth*," ed. Edward A. Richards (Raleigh: Health Publications Institute, Inc., 1950).

37. See Stonor Saunders, *The Cultural Cold War*; Guibaut, *How New York Stole the Idea of Modern Art*; Osgood, *Total Cold War*; Caute, *The Dancer Defects*; Krenn *Fall-out Shelters for the Human Spirit*; Stephen A. Crist, "Jazz as Democracy? Dave Brubeck and Cold War Politics," *The Journal of Musicology* 26 (2009): 133–174; Von Eschen, *Satchmo Blows Up the World*; Graham Carr, "Diplomatic Notes: American

Musicians and Cold War Politics in the Near and Middle East, 1954–60," *Popular Music History* 1 (2004): 37–63; Ingrid Monson, *Freedom Sounds: Civil Rights Call Out to Jazz and Africa* (New York: Oxford University Press, 2007); Maude Muller, Report by Mrs. Frederick W. Muller, International Chairman, AWF Committee, WILPF: January 1953–1954, AWF (DG066), Box 3, Series B, Folder: Administrative Reports (1 of 3), SCPC.

38. Preamble to the Constitution of the International Society for Education Through Art (InSEA) ratified at the First General Assembly, UNESCO, Paris, in July 1954.

39. Bryce and Beelke, *Report of Conference on International Exchange of Children's Art,* 2–3, "Art Teachers Meet," *New York Times* (August 20, 1957): 29.

40. Bryce and Beelke, *Report of Conference on International Exchange of Children's Art,* 6–10.

41. Bryce and Beelke, *Report of Conference on International Exchange of Children's Art,* 23–24.

42. Letter from T. Setunskaja to Mme. Muller (November 11, 1965), Box 11 of 44, Series C: Correspondence—US, Folder: USSR, 1964–68, AWF, SCPC.

43. Muller, Art for World Friendship Report (June 1959), Box 3, Series B, Folder: Administrative Reports (2 of 3), AWF, SCPC; Anne Holliday Webb to Mrs. Lucius Cole (December 18, 1959), Box 11, Series C, Folder: Arkansas, 1955–66, AWF, SCPC.

44. Stonor Saunders, *The Cultural Cold War*; Crist, "Jazz as Democracy?," 133–174.

45. "Rules for 'Art for Friendship' Exhibition Exchange," Box 4. Folder: Exhibits: General (1 of 2), AWF, SCPC; Quoted in Osgood, *Total Cold War*, 216–218.

46. Mary Dudziak, *Cold War Civil Rights: Race and the Image of American Democracy* (Princeton: Princeton University Press, 2011): 48–50.

47. Art for World Friendship Collection (DG066), Box 3 of 44, Series B: Administrative Files, Folder: Essay Contest, 1954, AWF, SCPC.

48. Janet Neuman, Fundraising letter (October 23, 1950), AWF (DG066), Box 6 of 44. Series B: Administrative Files, Folder: Public Relations correspondence of Janet Neuman, 1950–51, AWF, SCPC; "Trick or Treat for UNICEF," *Social Service Review* 29 (September 1955): 296.

3

The Accidental Political Advantages of a Nonpolitical Book Program

Franklin Publications and Juvenile Books Abroad

Addressing the American Booksellers Association in 1942, President Franklin Roosevelt said, "No man and no force can take from the world the books that embody man's eternal fight against tyranny. In this war, we know, books are weapons."[1] Throughout World War II, the US government, American publishers, librarians, and citizens took this idea seriously, contrasting Hitler's book burnings to the intellectual freedom in the United States, sending books to servicemen abroad, and replenishing the libraries of war-torn Europe.[2] In the early years of the Cold War, books and the principles they represented once again were called into ideological service. The US government devoted substantial energy and funds to using books as weapons against the Soviet Union in the cultural Cold War. State Department bureaucrats and US congressmen debated which books best represented the United States, which books should fill the shelves of US Information Service (USIS) libraries abroad, and which books and authors should be banned. Juvenile literature, like children's art, was considered less ideological than adult literature, more a reflection of the supposedly universal childhood traits of innocence, purity, and tolerance. Children's books could transcend their material reality in print and paper to embody principles and values beyond mere words on a page. They could change hearts and minds, represent intellectual freedom, cultural maturity, the values of a beneficent nation, and simultaneously influence the opinions of young people in both the United States and abroad. While recent scholarship has expanded our knowledge about the ideological uses of print culture during the Cold War, most scholars have largely neglected a key target audience of both public and private international book programs—young people.[3]

Americans across the political spectrum who engaged in literary diplomacy shared enormous faith in the power of books to sway readers' opinions about the United States in some fundamental way, either for good or for ill. Organizations as diverse as *Hornbook*, a children's literary magazine, and the US State Department politicized books by using them to promote "American" values such as freedom and democracy. UNESCO and CARE promoted international understanding and friendship through the written word. The Junior Literary Guild and the American Library Association's Division of Libraries for Children and Young People had differing ideas about what constituted the "right book" for young people, but mainly because these programs shared the idea that reading was crucial for preparing young people for citizenship. Should they be world citizens or national citizens first? The State Department's international cultural programs and Soviet propagandists in the late 1940s specifically targeted young people and students through print as future opinion-makers and national leaders. Cold Warriors in both nations used libraries, books, and print as powerful weapons, particularly targeting young leaders in developing nations. What work did children's books do that made them such powerful weapons in Cold War cultural and diplomatic battles?[4] This chapter explores the workings of Franklin Books Program, Inc., a gray propaganda program that operated at the nexus of US public–private cultural diplomacy, to answer that question.

LITERARY STRATEGIES IN THE CULTURAL COLD WAR

The State Department's International Information Administration (IIA) funded the creation of a nonprofit corporation in June 1952 to translate American books into foreign languages for publication and distribution abroad, initially in the Middle East. Datus C. Smith, Jr., the former president of the Association of American University Presses and the director of Princeton University Press since 1942, agreed to direct the new organization. Smith's extensive professional connections linked Franklin Books to prestigious university and commercial publishers who were concerned primarily with fostering education, literacy, and the growth of publishing industries in developing countries. They tended to view books as a means for strengthening international understanding and expanding American overseas markets rather than as a weapon to fight the Soviet propaganda machine. The founders named the organization for America's first book publisher, Benjamin Franklin.[5]

The strategists in the IIA (reorganized and renamed the US Information Agency [USIA] in 1953), however, had somewhat different, although not incompatible, priorities. The US government understood Franklin's official purpose, as stated in its certificate of incorporation, to

> publish and disseminate the printed word to the peoples of the world outside the United States, to stimulate interest in and promote the freedom, dignity and welfare of mankind; and to convey to them the knowledge and information relating to the people of the United States; and to stimulate interest in the history, government, culture, economy, technology, science and learning of the people of the United States.[6]

Theirs was an explicitly one-way intellectual street. American books were to be translated into Persian to explain American exceptionalism to Iranians. USIA officials did not consider reverse translation—that is, translating Iranian classics into English for American readers—because they were not interested in "international understanding" or intellectual exchange. When George Brett, the president of Macmillan, Inc. and the director of Eisenhower's People-to-People Book Committee, asked Malcolm Johnson of D. Van Nostrand, Co. to serve on Franklin's Board of Directors, Brett urged him to do so in order to "combat the influence which the Soviets are exerting on the backward countries of the world by . . . spreading . . . Soviet ideology in book form." Eventually, Franklin would "combat Communism" on a "global basis," but they began "in the so-called Arabic countries."[7] For USIA administrators, anticommunism trumped the bookmen's literacy and economic development goals. In 1952, the different priorities of the two organizations overlapped sufficiently to make the relationship work, at least for a time.

The differences between the two organizations, however, eventually became more problematic as the Cold War evolved between 1945 and 1965. The USIA sponsored its own Books in Translation program, which translated about 700 titles per year in 44 different languages, amounting to 3 million books annually. By 1956, the USIA operated 160 information centers and libraries in 67 nations with holdings of more than 2.6 million books that circulated among 46 million users.[8] In contrast to Franklin Books, USIA officials selected books for translation based strictly on foreign policy imperatives: to promote the interests of the United States and to endorse or highlight anticommunism, American internationalism, consumer products, the peaceful uses of science, and education.[9] The USIA did not focus on juvenile books. Following Senator Joseph McCarthy's 1953 investigations of overseas USIS libraries, the selection criteria became even more stringent. McCarthy advocated banning books by "controversial" authors such as Howard Fast, overturning an earlier State Department directive that instructed overseas librarians to judge books by their content.[10] Under McCarthy's rule, Fast's *Thomas Paine*, which showed the United States in a positive light, would have been banned from USIS reading rooms. The American Library Association (ALA) mounted the successful Freedom to Read campaign against McCarthy's attacks on intellectual freedom, and acceptable content, not authors, remained the overriding litmus test for USIA-approved texts.[11] As a speaker at Dartmouth College's graduation ceremony in June 1953, President Eisenhower urged the graduates, "Don't join the book burners. . . . Don't be afraid to go in your library and read every book as long as that document does not offend our own ideas of decency." It was Eisenhower's first public condemnation of McCarthyism.[12]

Despite their differing priorities, however, both groups agreed on two key points: books were powerful and legitimate weapons in the Cold War, and children were especially important targets. As a foreign policy tool, Franklin Books did not stray far from the USIA's policies of thematic inclusion and exclusion. In other words, Franklin's title choices emphasized the vitality of the American democratic process, federal government activism, US–Third World educational and cultural exchange, American artistic and technological innovation, and cooperation across racial, ethnic, economic, and national lines. Franklin followed the federal government's lead in generally ignoring or attempting to downplay less flattering aspects of the contemporary United States, such as anticommunist investigations, poverty, racism, and labor problems.[13]

Although USIS overseas libraries and State Department translations were widely used and read, locals recognized these resources as US propaganda. Realizing the value of unattributed, grassroots, and locally produced pro-American media, in the early 1950s, the US government turned increasingly to the use of gray propaganda. Radio Free Europe (RFE) and the Congress for Cultural Freedom are the best-known examples of seemingly independent but secretly financed CIA efforts, but Franklin Publications operated in a similar manner. Franklin's origins in the State Department were not publicized; the USIA brand did not appear on any Franklin publications, and its funding source remained veiled. Both USIA and Franklin administrators believed it unwise to publicly identify Franklin with the US government for fear of losing credibility among target populations. An undated document presumably written by the State Department, "Covert Support of Book Publishing," outlined Franklin's basic operating plans. The author acknowledged that "technical books" might not "convey psychological messages," but they were necessary lest "all books appearing under the imprint . . . be considered propaganda vehicles." Stimulating "natives" to "tell [their] own people how democracy helps them and conversely how communism enslaves them" would be "most effective in a propaganda sense."[14] But Datus Smith went further, insisting that Franklin rise above the short-term needs of Cold War politics, refrain completely from distributing American propaganda, and take a longer view of the potential benefits of a book program for fostering genuine and positive relationships between the US and Middle Eastern nations. Most importantly, Smith was adamant that local needs and suggestions drive the program, rather than book lists provided by the US government. This proved to be the most distinctive characteristic of Franklin Books, and, although agreed upon in principle, the extent of local control became a persistent, and eventually decisive, source of tension between the USIA and Franklin.

As early as 1953, disagreement erupted between Franklin and the USIA over the agency's insistence that it maintain final approval over title selection. Franklin resisted the USIA's attempts to apply the same standards to Franklin's publications as it applied to its own translation program, believing that a blatantly political approach would limit their flexibility in working with foreign advisors and publishers. The USIA and Franklin exchanged a flurry of letters, which resulted in the USIA backing down, for the time being. However, Franklin's initial focus on Arab nations of the Middle East, a region of primary strategic importance in the Cold War, prompted the USIA to insist that Franklin publications meet the following "program objectives":

- Minimizing the difficulty of Arab–Western collaboration by reducing Arab ignorance and resentment of the West
- Helping Arabs achieve a sound and comprehensive world picture in which they may play a respected role
- Aiding Arabs in acquisition of insights into the character of responsible government; of public, social, and economic policy; and of economic organization
- Emphasizing the central themes of Western thought from Plato onward, with special emphasis on those most eloquently stating the Western ideals of the dignity and freedom of individual men[15]

Although Franklin's administrators may have had less overtly paternalistic and manipulative intentions than the USIA, their organization remained deeply enmeshed in Cold War politics. The strategic importance of the Middle East to US foreign policy was a key factor in the creation of Franklin Books. Since Truman's recognition of Israel in 1947, anti-American sentiment had been on the rise in the region, making it an increasingly hot spot in the Cold War as the United States and the Soviet Union vied for influence there. In 1951, US ambassadors met in Istanbul to evaluate the USIA's program achievements and needs. Subsequently, USIS posts in the region increased the production of posters, pamphlets, and film screenings, and, shortly afterward, the USIA launched Franklin Publications to provide translations of American books. In June 1953, Franklin opened its first field office in Cairo; by late 1956, the Soviets had established the Dal-al-Fikr publishing house there. When the USSR established an embassy in Djakarta in 1954, Franklin opened a field office there to combat Soviet influence. Furthermore, the USIA asked Franklin to facilitate the US government's attempt to "de-emphasize the Egyptian position of Arab-bloc leadership" when Nasser formed a closer relationship with the Soviet Union in 1956. How could a book translation organization accomplish this? Instead of asking Egyptian ministers to write introductions for Franklin publications, for example, they might invite a Syrian or Iraqi politician or intellectual to do so instead. In this way, Franklin could help "other Arab countries to achieve a better sense of their own importance." If non-Egyptians were unavailable, the State Department advised Franklin to "occasionally drop an introduction altogether, even at the cost of sales." Also as a result of rising Egyptian nationalism, Franklin opened a Baghdad office to balance Arab power in the Middle East.[16] In short, Cold War politics, not local publishing conditions and literacy needs, often played a direct role in Franklin's growth and operations (Figure 3.1).

Regardless of its role in advancing American foreign policy, Franklin was unique among government-sponsored cultural projects in the extent to which Franklin administrators formed genuine partnerships with host communities. In addition to choosing titles, locals staffed Franklin's field offices and translated, edited, published, and sold their books. Franklin

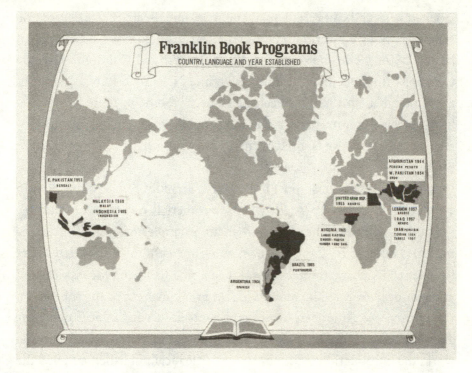

Figure 3.1 Between 1954 and 1965, Franklin Books expanded from the Middle East to Asia and Latin America, reflecting the Cold War priorities of the US government. Franklin Book Programs, Manuscripts Division, Department of Rare Books and Special Collections, Princeton University Library.

could not impose a book title on a local office, but the New York office could propose alternatives for out-of-date or "low quality" books. In cases where local advisors lacked adequate information to make selections, Franklin relied on American specialists to suggest titles. In the juvenile field, for example, Franklin received "a couple hundred" title selections from people "competent to express an opinion." From these, Datus Smith selected a list of 70, which he submitted to Constance Stone, the former USIS librarian in Baghdad, and a librarian in the Children's Department of the Washington DC Public Library, for review.[17] For recommendations in juvenile science books, Franklin called on James Newman, the book editor for *Scientific American*; Constance Stone; Avis Zebker of the Brooklyn Public Library; Elizabeth Gurney of the American News Company; Jane

Hockett, the USIS librarian in Damascus; and Beatrice Hurley of the NYU School of Education.[18] Franklin also consulted book lists supplied by the USIA, *Library Journal*, the ALA's *Booklist* and Children's List, the Children's Book Council, the Brooklyn and New York Public Libraries, and Columbia University's Teacher's College.[19] Some of these lists would likely exclude controversial authors or content and emphasize the pro-American perspective favored by the USIA, while others might emphasize literary quality.

Based on its relationship with the USIA, Franklin reserved the right to veto a title suggested by local advisors, but there is no evidence that they ever did so. On the other hand, there are examples of Franklin defending titles rejected by the USIA or making the case for books that failed to meet USIA program objectives. Once a title had been locally selected and approved by Franklin and the USIA, Franklin secured the translation rights from the American owner and contracted with a local publisher and translator. Franklin paid for the translation, any special editorial work, the introduction, and the artwork. The local publisher supplied the paper (unless it was hard to secure, in which case Franklin would provide it), printing, binding, and all other normal publishing expenses. The publisher also paid Franklin 10% of the local selling price, which was intentionally inexpensive but not free, since locals associated free books with propaganda.[20] Sarah Knowles Bolton's *Lives of Poor Boys*, for example, retailed in Cairo for $4.20, but the Franklin edition cost only 23 cents.[21] After publication, Franklin made wholesaler arrangements and assisted with promotion and advertising efforts.

Given its unique position, Franklin administrators carefully protected the organization's local reputation, even when this meant straining relations with its sponsor, the USIA. Title selection remained the main source of conflict, but early correspondence between George Brett, the head of Macmillan and one of the chief initiators of Franklin, and Datus Smith reveals disagreement concerning Franklin's target audience as well. Brett wrote that, given the aim of the USIA to improve public opinion of the United States abroad, Franklin should publish books aimed at the "man in the street." Smith, however, fearing accusations of cultural imperialism

and anti-American backlash, believed the wiser course was to first target intellectuals and "opinion makers" in each country. For their part, the
USIA wanted to see literature that highlighted the benefits of democratic
capitalism versus communism. But Smith argued, "Our goal is targeting
literate people not the masses because they are the influential people who
are the best target for an operation of this sort."[22] Their exchange reveals
another persistent struggle at the heart of the Franklin enterprise, as well as
Cold War cultural propaganda more generally. The USIA aimed to change
hearts and minds through direct propaganda to a mainstream audience,
but USIA-sponsored intellectuals tended to have a longer view and a sub-
tler approach. Franklin operated on the principle that an educated population that enjoyed positive relationships with US-supported institutions
and that did not appear to have ulterior motives would be stronger allies
in the long term. Smith's memos and reports repeatedly tout "the political
benefits of a non-political book program" to justify Franklin's title selections, target audiences, and juvenile book projects to the USIA.

FRANKLIN'S "NONPOLITICAL" TRANSLATIONS

In April 1953, Franklin signed its first contract with a Cairo publisher
for Edward R. Murrow's *This I Believe*. Franklin's adaptation featured an
image of Egyptian Prime Minister Muhammad Naguib on the cover and
biographies of 25 prominent Arabs alongside those of 25 distinguished
Americans. A product of Cold War anxieties, Murrow's popular radio
show of the same name first aired in 1951, with the following introduction:

> We hardly need to be reminded that we are living in an age of con-
> fusion. A lot of us have traded in our beliefs for bitterness and cyni-
> cism, or for a heavy package of despair, or even a quivering portion
> of hysteria. Opinions can be picked up cheap in the marketplace,
> while such commodities as courage and fortitude and faith are in
> alarmingly short supply. Around us all . . . there is an enveloping
> cloud of fear. It has become more difficult than ever to distinguish

black from white, good from evil, right from wrong. What truths can a human being afford to furnish the cluttered nervous room of his mind with when he has no real idea how long a lease he has on the future.[23]

The US government aired Murrow's show over the Voice of America network, and the State Department offered a print version to 97 allied nations. *This I Believe* became Franklin's most popular Arabic-language book, selling out on its first day, and selling an estimated 30,000 copies in six months.

Sarah K. Bolton's book for young readers, *Lives of Poor Boys Who Became Famous*, adapted by Franklin into Persian, was a close second. First published in 1885, Bolton's 28 biographies demonstrated that poverty was not a barrier to success, but "develops ambition and nerves people to action." Like Franklin's adaptation of *This I Believe*, Bolton's book included both Muslim and American rags-to-riches stories. Both books met the USIA program objective of "explaining" the American political and economic system in a positive light, as well as Franklin's goal of cultivating international understanding by highlighting common values. Like children's art, books can be interpreted on many levels. Bolton's biography of the merchant George Peabody could teach young readers two very different stories. On one hand, Peabody's parents were too poor to pay for his education, so he went to work at age 11 and was left completely destitute at age 15 when his father died. He was rescued from poverty by a generous uncle and, according to Bolton, by his own good habits and hard work. Readers could take away the message that American children were deprived of education, sent to work at a young age, and that orphans were left without security. On the other hand, they could learn Bolton's intended message—that in the United States, hard work could overcome poverty and that one's future success was not limited by family position or immutable class status. Was his story about hardship and struggle, or about the individualism and opportunity available only in the United States? This flexibility allowed a variety of interested groups concerned with literary diplomacy to see in the same books their preferred lessons.[24]

Every US public diplomacy organization eventually had to confront the issue of American racial segregation and discrimination and how to provide the best possible interpretation for foreign audiences. As scholars like Mary Dudziak have argued, American race relations were a critical foreign policy issue for the United States during the Cold War.[25] The USSR routinely publicized racial problems in the United States, and people in the developing world were curious about the political and economic realities for African-Americans. In September 1954, an Egyptian reader wrote to Franklin's Cairo office suggesting that they publish Richard Wright's *Outsider* and other books. This raised a thorny problem for Franklin because Wright was under FBI surveillance at the time, and the USIA did not consider him an "acceptable" representative of American race relations for foreign consumption. Datus Smith wrote to Franklin Steiner at the USIA for guidance on Wright and three other titles, asking for "good ways to meet the problem." "Is there any Wright which is usable?" he asked. In other words, what titles did the USIA use to present America's "racial situation" in a positive light to foreigners? Steiner suggested Ruby BerkEley Goodwin's *It's Good to Be Black* (1953). The USIA review described the book as "the true picture of a mixed American community living, working and playing together without race problems." In a more revealing internal memo, Datus Smith indicated that the book failed to tackle America's race problem at all and that the author in fact seemed "to be unaware that the problem exists."[26] Such were the limitations of a publicly funded Cold War propaganda program.

SCHOOL TEXTBOOKS AND SUPPLEMENTAL READERS

Children's books played an important role in American foreign policy during World War II and continued to do so as cultural diplomacy became more important in the postwar period. USIA translations and private book programs distributed millions of American books abroad. Initially, however, school textbooks remained off limits. Foreign involvement in education was considered politically sensitive and likely to arouse resentment among locals who harbored both "healthy local pride and fanatical xenophobia."[27] The US government avoided direct intervention in foreign schools through textbook publication, a policy that Franklin expected to follow. Over time, however, private publishing companies such as Silver Burdett, at the request of a Pakistani school district, produced "more than a dozen strikingly handsome graded texts . . . using local artists and writers." Because the texts were published in the United States, however, they aroused bitter opposition among local publishing companies. Franklin's bookmen saw the Silver Burdett textbook project as proof of the "advantages of American–local cooperation" for "a particular reason in a particular country," but still they hesitated to institute a general textbook program.[28] Circumstances on the ground soon changed their approach, however.

If fear of anti-American backlash initially discouraged Franklin's participation in the juvenile textbook market, the demands of local advisors increasingly drew the organization into the field. In its early years, Franklin's administrators considered it "dangerous if not fatal to undertake publication of school textbooks in most countries of the Arab-Asian area." After only two years in operation, however, by mid-1954, the overwhelming demand for children's books—fiction, nonfiction, supplemental readers, and school textbooks—overcame their initial reservations. "In every Arab-Asian country," Franklin reported, the lack of literature for children resulted in eagerness for both translations and the publication of local stories. Given the demand, Franklin predicted, "the publications would undoubtedly carry themselves commercially" and "would revolutionize the character of juvenile publishing in the country concerned without need for further additional foreign help."[29] Franklin administrators were intrigued and excited by the possibility of fostering publishing industries in developing nations, not in spreading the gospel of American democracy.

The demand from local organizations, governments, and educators overwhelmed Franklin's reluctance to enter the juvenile field, first in the Middle East and eventually in Asia, Africa, and Latin America. By September 1954, Franklin's juvenile and young adult fiction lists included

Louisa May Alcott's *Little Women* (which sold out its first two print runs of 5,100 and 4,900; see Figure 3.2); Esther Forbes's patriotic tale of colonial history, *Johnny Tremain* (released by Disney films in 1957); Robert Lawson's 1948 *Robbut*; Hardie Gramatky's classic 1939 picture book *Little Toot*, about the lazy tug that didn't want to tug; Katharine Ann Porter's *Pale Horse, Pale Rider*; and *Pictures to Grow Up With* by Katharine Gibson. The *New York Times* described Gibson's 1942 picture book: "A volume to be treasured at any time, the appearance of this one now is an affirmation of one of the principles for which we are fighting, for this is a war to preserve culture as well as political ideals, and now more than ever do we need to know and appreciate our heritage of art."[30] Lauded as a weapon of war and a means of preserving American culture in 1942, Gibson's book

Figure 3.2 Franklin translated American classics into Arabic, including Louisa May Alcott's *Little Women*. Franklin Book Programs, Manuscripts Division, Department of Rare Books and Special Collections, Princeton University Library.

was re-released to fight a new enemy in 1954. The Franklin editions of the Porter and Gibson books sold out their first 20,000 print runs in Arabic.[31] Juvenile titles, it turned out, were among Franklin's most in-demand translations.

Franklin's most popular nonfiction juveniles included Bolton's *Lives of Girls Who Became Famous* and *Lives of Poor Boys Who Became Famous*, as well as *Mama's Bank Account*, the feel-good bestseller published by Katharine Forbes in 1943 about a working-class Norwegian immigrant family trying to achieve the American Dream in early twentieth-century San Francisco. The book touches on themes crucial to Cold War Americanism: class fluidity, assimilation, hard work, the primacy of the nuclear family, and women's domestic roles. It is not surprising, therefore, that the book inspired a play (1944), film (1948), musical (1979), and the long-running TV show, "I Remember Mama" (1949–57).[32]

Despite the popularity of juvenile fiction, according to Franklin, "The most popular category of books chosen for publication is popular science—especially science for young people," which accounted for a remarkable 25% of total Franklin publications.[33] Franklin's most requested juvenile science titles included Bertha Parker's *Basic Science* series, Jeanne Bendick's *All Around You*, and Richard Bishop's *Stepping Stones to Light*. In 1958, two of Franklin's juvenile science titles—Munro Leaf's *Health Can Be Fun* and Bertha Parker's *Sound*—won first and second prize, respectively, at East Pakistan's Book Exhibition. Parker's *Basic Science Series* had been nominated by *Sukhan*, a magazine "comparable to the *Saturday Review* but *Harper*-ish too," for the best Persian children's book the previous year.[34] Franklin's January 9, 1957, annual report listed 17 juvenile science titles; by 1965, Franklin had published 27 titles from Parker's *Basic Science Series* alone in 113 foreign-language editions (Figure 3.3).[35]

Although juvenile science books seemed "a far cry from political ideology," science was politicized throughout the Cold War. The geopolitical conflicts of the twentieth century led to a dramatic expansion in federal support for scientific and technological developments in atomic weapons and the arms race, space exploration, and communications technologies. American politicians and educators issued routine warnings that the

Figure 3.3 Franklin Books showcased their Juvenile Science books in translation at the Cairo Exhibition in April 1958. Like children's art, juvenile science books were considered "apolitical." Franklin Book Programs, Manuscripts Division, Department of Rare Books and Special Collections, Princeton University Library.

United States was losing the "technological race" with the Soviet Union. A 1951 *Life* magazine article, "The Golden Youth of Communism," warned that the Soviet government was actively cultivating "an elite generation" of scientists, while the United States suffered a shortage of scientists and engineers.[36] Datus Smith argued that juvenile science books exemplified the "accidental political advantages of a non-political book program." The Urdu edition of Margaret Hyde's *Atoms Today and Tomorrow* (1955), for example, included an introduction by Pakistan's Atomic Energy Commission chairman who stated, "Only the countries of the West . . . have turned their attention toward the constructive uses of atomic energy." Smith suggested that juvenile books on atomic science, such as John Lewellen's *Mighty Atom* (1955), Waldemar Kaempffert's *Many Uses of the Atom* (1956), and

Martin Mann's *Peacetime Uses of Atomic Energy* (1957) would have been considered propaganda had they been distributed by the USIA. As the products of local publishers, however, education ministries, teachers, and parents viewed them as educational texts fit for school use.[37] Furthermore, children's science books were among the "strongest deterrents to the 'pie in the sky' philosophy on which Communism feeds and flourishes."[38] Although Smith conceded that "the precise . . . degree of impact can never be scientifically determined," he insisted that it was important "that attractive children's books mirroring the American way of life have filled a need which otherwise would be filled by Communist Line material."[39]

Despite Franklin's initial reluctance to becoming involved in school textbook publishing for fear of inciting local accusations of "imperialist poisoning of the minds of children," local needs were so acute that Franklin's supplemental books frequently made their way into local universities as "textbooks," and noneducational texts filled the need for supplemental reading materials in school libraries. Smith reported, "School libraries have been virtually unknown in the past, but there is a rapidly growing awareness of the need for supplementary material, both in general school collections and for purchase by parents and children. Up to very recently, the educational book which is not a textbook—one of the finest products of US juvenile publishing—has been non-existent in most countries of the Middle East, but the translation of such American books into local languages is now being urged and encouraged by various ministries of education."[40] Smith wrote of the Middle East in 1955, "With only a few noteworthy exceptions, there is a dearth of school textbooks . . . and those that are available are poorly printed, unimaginatively written and designed, and in general are based upon no recognizable principles of pedagogy."[41] By 1956, the Egyptian Ministry of Education had placed every Franklin juvenile publication on its list of approved books for school library use.[42] In 1957, Franklin launched textbook programs in Afghanistan and Iran at the request of the Ministries of Education in those nations. Franklin advisors improved content, supplied new design and artwork or trained local graphic designers to do so, and produced the textbooks. By the end of the 1950s, Iranian, Afghani, and Pakistani

elementary schoolchildren were using Franklin textbooks in their class-
rooms. By 1960, ten of Franklin's "rapid readers" were approved for school
use in East Pakistan: Wilfrid Bronson's 1948 *Pinto's Journey*, Buchheimer's
Let's Go to the Library, Alice Dalgleish's *The Courage of Sarah Noble*, James
Daugherty's 1938 picture book *Andy and the Lion*, Madge and Morrill
Haines's 1955 *The Wright Brothers: The First to Fly*, four books from Munro
Leaf's *Can Be Fun* series (Geography, History, Health, and Safety), and
Samuel Nisenson's *100 Minute Biographies*.[43] Although not explicitly ideo-
logical, these books reflected positively on the United States, highlighted
American accomplishments, and described American history from a
triumphant but sympathetic perspective. By the end of its first decade,
Franklin's presence in juvenile educational publishing, both textbooks and
supplemental readers, was well-established in the Middle East.

Middle Eastern nations suggested particular educational texts as well.
In 1952, Iraq's Ministry of Education requested picture geographies of the
world and of Iraq, as well as an atlas of Iraq, for the primary grades.[44]
Franklin's most ambitious project was the translation and adaptation of
the Viking-Columbia Encyclopedia into Arabic in 1953. Seven months
of travel throughout the Middle East; interviews with scholars, teachers,
librarians, and publishers; and consultations with "several hundred knowl-
edgeable Arabs" about the most immediate literary needs of the region led
Franklin to the conclusion that an Arab-language general reference book
would most benefit local populations. Native consultants agreed that targeting a literacy level at the "top grades of secondary school" would reach
the widest audience. If aimed at younger readers, the encyclopedia would
be useless for adults, while a scholarly reference would be inaccessible to
the general public.[45]

Over the course of its 25 years in operation, Franklin's Tehran office, the
organization's largest, published 800 titles. As seen in Table 3.1, children's
books accounted for 18% of *all* books published in Persian, just barely second to literature. Juvenile science books like Bertha Parker's series and
Elsa Jane Werner's *Golden Geography: A Child's Introduction to the World*,
which had been adopted for fifth-grade use in 1958, are included in this
number.[46]

Table 3.1 Books published by Franklin Books in Persian, 1953–1977

Category of Publication	Percentage of Franklin's Persian Publications
Literature (fiction, essays, verse±)	19
Children's books	18
History	17
Science (nonjuvenile; including medicine)	15
Psychology and education	12
Persian and Islamic studies	9
Philosophy	7
Art	3

Charles Griffith reported a similar situation throughout Asia. Burma, a nonaligned nation with a relatively high literacy rate (40%) and established commercial bookstores, had no tradition of juvenile publishing. The US government supplied the Burma Translation Society with a modern printing plant that produced editions of 30,000, two-thirds of which the government appropriated for school use; the remainder went to the bookstore trade. The USIS sponsored the only public library in Rangoon; its children's section was a "noteworthy contribution" to the community. Private US textbook publishers "generously sent samples" to the Society, and Bertha Parker's elementary science series was widely distributed to public schools. Despite this progress, Griffith reported in 1955, "Throughout Asia, there are very few books for children. These peoples are universally fascinated with our juveniles and want translations." Griffith listed juveniles and school textbooks among the top five priorities for Burma, with similar needs in Thailand, Malaya, Singapore, and the Philippines.[47] Inspired by Franklin's success in the Middle East, the USIA commissioned Franklin to study the possibility of producing school textbooks for overseas Chinese communities as an alternative to widely available and low-priced Communist books.[48] Although this project never materialized, both Franklin and the US government eagerly responded to local demands for translations of educational books for children, including "nonpolitical" school textbooks.

CONFLICT WITH THE USIA AND THE USSR

Despite the prevalence of children's books on Franklin's list and the organization's venture into the textbook market, conflict arose not with local populations or pro-communist agitators, as Franklin initially feared, but with the USIA. In March 1955, B. Franklin Steiner, the chief of the Translation Division of the USIA, informed Datus Smith that USIA would no longer approve translation of Leonard Weisgard's *Silly Willy Nilly* in Urdu or Persian, not because of political concerns, but because they considered it "a marginal work in both text and illustration." Smith's response highlights one of the distinctions he saw between propaganda and effective cultural relations. The Weisgard book, a simple story of a baby elephant who forgets his mother's rules until he learns them the hard way, and Robert Lawson's *Robbut: A Tale of Tales*, were crucial, according to Smith because they aroused support for Franklin among *adults* interested in juvenile literature and children's education more generally. If Franklin published only children's books that functioned as political propaganda, Smith argued, they would alienate their most ardent supporters.[49] Similarly, the importance of Franklin's science books for children lay less in their promotion of American scientific advances than in their association of the United States with progress, the peaceful uses of science, and the broad diffusion of knowledge.[50] In short, Smith argued, "nonpolitical" children's books were in fact political, and their publication reaped significant goodwill for the United States.

These fundamental conflicts over the meaning of propaganda guaranteed that funding would remain a constant source of concern for Franklin. President Kennedy appointed Edward Murrow as Director of the USIA in March 1961, and, by 1962, the issue of local control came to a head. The USIA informed Franklin that "This agency cannot subscribe to a stated policy which, in effect, delegates to foreign nationals, i.e. Franklin branch managers, the authority to determine how Agency funds are to be expended." Murrow suggested that the USIA would contract with Franklin to publish a set list of 50 books chosen by the branch managers from a list preselected and approved by the USIA. Any other titles would have to be supported using "funds from other sources."[51]

If Franklin and the USIA did not always see eye to eye on appropriate titles, authors, and audiences, how did the two groups assess Franklin's impact and accomplishments? Franklin's annual reports described their accomplishments to their sponsor, the US government, and did so with considerable attention to Franklin's translations of educational and juvenile titles. Datus Smith regularly noted the high local demand for children's books all around the world and assured the USIA that the Ministries of Education in Egypt, Iran, Afghanistan, West and East Pakistan, Thailand, Malay, and Indonesia consistently requested Franklin-produced school textbooks and supplemental books for school library use. Franklin also received substantial orders for educational juvenile books from Kuwait, Bahrein, Libya, Tunisia, Jordan, Saudi Arabia, and Sudan.[52] By June 1954, Franklin had published 132 titles in Persian, Urdu, Turkish, and Indonesian. By the end of 1957, Franklin had contracted with the Iranian and Afghan governments to publish a three-year supply of texts for elementary and secondary grades, thereby preventing the entry of Russian books into schools there. Franklin's textbook in Afghanistan had replaced a Soviet early reader that was "devoid of propaganda . . . but the illustrations show a landlord supervising the beating of a peasant, a money-lender cheating a peasant, etc."[53] By the end of 1959, Franklin had published more than 15.6 million textbooks in Iran and Afghanistan and launched new textbook programs in Indonesia and Malaya. Franklin's field offices in Tehran and Tabriz, Iran; Lahore, Pakistan; Dacca, Bangladesh; Djakarta, Indonesia; Kuala Lumpur, Malaysia; Beirut, Lebanon; and Baghdad, Iraq had published more than 630 titles.[54] All of these facts and figures, particularly Franklin's success with school textbooks, buttressed the State Department's program goals of challenging communism and reaching one of their main target audiences—youth. They simultaneously fulfilled

Franklin's goals of meeting local needs, developing markets abroad, and fostering international understanding. Cold War politics were not black and white; liberal cultural programs were coopted to meet conservative foreign policy goals.

In addition to publication data, Franklin administrators cited Soviet reactions to demonstrate Franklin's successful operations. In the early 1950s, the Soviets established a translation program in Cairo that published "literary classics" devoid of direct propaganda and a "book agency" in East Pakistan. Shortly after, anti-Franklin press campaigns surfaced in Beirut, Cairo, Baghdad, and Medina, charging that Franklin books had swept Arab publications from the bookstores and had infiltrated schools to poison young minds.[55] Anti-American attacks by both Arab nationalists and Soviets writers surfaced in 1954, 1960, and 1967. An article covering the proceedings of the 1953 Nation's Conference in Beirut reported that some conference participants had registered complaints against the "bribery" of the Fulbright Program and Franklin's cheap books, which were intended to "kill Arab writers and authors."[56] Attacks against Franklin resumed in July 1960, with an article titled "Intellectual Aggression." Franklin was not mentioned by name, but the author criticized both the Eastern and Western blocs for publishing "a variety of books of excellent make-up and cheap in price . . . to influence the minds and hearts of our young men for the interest of the bloc to which they belong."[57] The author accused both the United States and the USSR of "Intellectual Aggression." As late as 1967, a lengthy article using the language of Soviet communism rather than Arab nationalism attacked American publishing and Franklin in particular.

As noted by the Arab author just mentioned, US and Soviet literary diplomacy strategies probably looked remarkably similar to locals. The USSR created its own distribution network of communist publishing houses and bookshops in India, as well as regular retail bookshops, libraries, book fairs and displays, newsstands, street hawkers, bookmobiles, and communist front organizations, in particular, the Indo-Soviet Cultural Society and other cultural exchange and friendship societies. Mezhdunarodnaya Kniga (the International Book Company) was the

Soviet export firm for books, newspapers, and other printed matter, and it supplied a major Indian firm, the Hindustan Publishing Company in Delhi. As with Franklin Books, the Hindustan Publishing Company sold their books below cost, including "very attractive and astonishingly cheap children's books of good quality" and textbooks for Indian primary and high schools, and it distributed some books for free or at prices below the cost of manufacturing.[58] In 1956, the USSR invited 38 Indian (11 Hindi, 9 Bengali, 7 Urdu, 6 Tamil, and 5 Telugu) translators and 7 announcers to visit the USSR to work with the Foreign Languages Publishing House and Radio Moscow, paying the equivalent of about $1,000 per month stipend. The following year, the Moscow Foreign Languages Publishing House translated 62 titles into Hindi, 39 into Bengali, and 34 into Urdu, for a total of 2.88 million books. Titles included books about the Soviet Union, especially about its economic and scientific successes; Russian classics; fiction; books for children; and a Russian grammar in Hindi.[59] Franklin also supplemented its translation program with training programs for foreign publishers. For example, in July 1964, Franklin brought two managers from their local offices in Nigeria to the Brooklyn Public Library specifically to study "school books, children's books, children's libraries, school libraries, and books for the undereducated."[60] In other words, the "independent" Franklin Books shared some striking similarities with the Soviet Union's state-sponsored literary diplomacy organizations.

CHILDREN'S BOOKS IN AN ERA OF CHANGING COLD WAR IMPERATIVES

By the end of its first decade of operations, Franklin had gained, for the most part, official respect in the countries where it operated, surviving a total of 21 changes of government. Franklin's administrators prided themselves on refraining from involvement in national or international politics, although they received funds and support from the US and foreign governments. As Smith reported to Tom Wilson, the director of Harvard University Press and a Franklin board member, in 1962, the "political news" from Iran was good: "Our friend Asadollah Alam . . . is the new Prime Minister [and] . . . the new Minister of Education, Parviz Khanlari, is one of Franklin's firmest friends and supporters. He has translated several books for us and he was the author of the two elementary school history books."[61] Franklin's program had fostered intellectual development, boosted local economies, and assisted fledgling book industries in the developing world.

Despite these successes and continued expansion into the mid-1960s, the priorities of the incoming Kennedy administration and evolving Cold War imperatives reduced Franklin's budget and challenged their operations. The State Department cut Franklin's budget nearly in half in 1959. By 1962, the US government had channeled $4.6 million to Franklin. "Other donors," including "foreign governments, the Shah and Princess Ashraf in Iran, the League of Arab States, and the Ford Foundation" had provided another $4.8 million. With federal funding in decline, Franklin began to seek financial support from large corporations and foundations with a vested interest in economic development. In a 1962 letter to IBM, for example, Franklin's Vice President Harold N. Munger, Jr. emphasized the importance of education and literacy to industrial development and a qualified workforce.[62] At the same time, Franklin redirected its activities toward educational programming and professional development. Their educational initiatives included developing libraries and literacy campaigns, producing encyclopedias and dictionaries, and publishing textbooks—activities that targeted young and/or beginning readers. Franklin sponsored training seminars in book publishing and writers' workshops, technical assistance programs for printers, publishers, and book sellers, and offered extended visits to the US for publishing professionals that included workshops with librarians and tours of publishing houses.

The 1960s marked Franklin's most active period in juvenile publishing and a new direction for Franklin Books in general. In October 1961, the Council on Books in Wartime, a nonprofit founded during World War II to use books as "weapons in the war of ideas," closed its doors. Franklin representatives petitioned the Council to assign its residual funds to Franklin for three main activities: payment of translation rights, training for foreign publishers, and creating collections of American books for foreign use, specifically textbooks and children's books "in nearly every country where Franklin works."[63] In December 1961, Franklin proposed expanding to Malaya, citing a list from that nation's Ministry of Education prioritizing "translated American books for young people," including "children's stories, folklore and fables, biographies of world figures, popular science, the history of mankind, discovery, nature study, great philosophers and thinkers, and general reading as a supplement to textbooks." The Malay government "from the Prime Minister down" was determined to create "a wide selection of good books in the national language for both educational and recreational reading."[64]

In the mid-1960s, Franklin expanded to South America (Argentina in 1964; Brazil in 1965) and Africa (Nigeria in 1965) and proposed three new programs, "Books for the Children of Latin America," a supplementary books program for children in Philippine vernaculars, and a Children's Book Foundation. These programs demonstrate the changing nature of Cold War imperatives. Children's book programs meshed easily with the idealistic rhetoric of international development prevalent in 1960s. None of the proposals cited the need to spread democracy or combat Soviet influence; instead, they focused on economic development and the needs of children in developing nations.[65] In 1965, Eugene Black, the former president of the World Bank and a former Franklin board member, suggested that "ventures such as the Franklin undertaking are the most effective foreign economic assistance this nation can offer" because "they aim chiefly at aiding a foreign country's economic development—not at preventing communism or winning friends for the United States."[66] An article about Franklin in *The Saturday Review* noted, "The book has become a more potent device than the bomb." By 1965, it went without saying that political benefits would accrue from foreign aid programs. As economic development trumped anticommunism as the most effective argument for international book programs, the private sector rather than the US government assumed responsibility for them. Regardless of the method, however, foreign youth remained among the primary targets of American assistance.

Even as Franklin's advertising reflected the changing nature of its programming from Cold War cultural diplomacy to economic development, children remained central. A 1970 Franklin advertisement titled "BUY THE WORLD A BOOK: ONLY 1½¢ A WORD" relied on familiar visual tropes to appeal to the American public. Although the ad doesn't focus specifically on books for children, the central image features a young, barefoot boy crouching on the ground, outdoors, engrossed in a book. By 1970, Franklin had archived dozens of images of well-dressed Iranian children reading in bookstores and libraries, diligently working at their desks in schools, reading at the 1958 Franklin Book Exhibit in Cairo, or buying books at the 1967 Children's Book Exhibit in Dacca, East Pakistan. Franklin's choice of image, however, reflected and reinforced American expectations of what "Third World children" looked like: always poor, always in need, always the objects of American benevolence. The text assured American readers that "thousands of children in the far-flung corners of this earth . . . smile knowingly when they hear the name Franklin," not because they are familiar with Benjamin Franklin, but with the organization named for him. The full-page ad ran in *Time*, *Sports Illustrated*, and *Africa Reports*, indicating an intended audience that encompassed the general public as well as readers with more specialized business and economic interests. The ad reminded the (male) reader that one day "his own child will ask him if he did anything great." If he supported Franklin, he would be able to say, "I helped save a mind. I bought the world a book" (see Figure 3.4).[67]

By the end of the 1960s, however, Franklin was struggling to justify its existence in the context of a changing Cold War. With a thaw in US–Soviet relations and the decline of aggressive cultural diplomacy, Franklin seemed increasingly irrelevant, and expensive. Franklin Publications changed its title to Franklin Book Programs in 1964, to emphasize the organization's nonprofit status and to deflect the impression that Franklin competed with local publishers. This shift also reflected dwindling federal financial support. The US and foreign governments were losing interest in subsidizing Cold War-style translation programs, and, by 1967, Franklin's financial situation was unsustainable. Before he retired that year, Datus

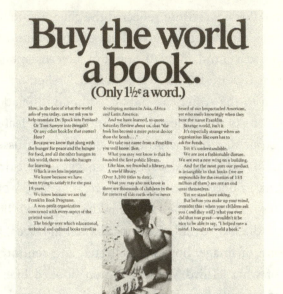

Figure 3.4 Franklin's choice of image in their "Buy the World a Book" ad campaign reflected and reinforced American expectations of what "Third World children" looked like: always poor, always in need, always the objects of American benevolence. Franklin Book Programs, Manuscripts Division, Department of Rare Books and Special Collections, Princeton University Library.

Smith reduced staff levels in all Franklin offices, eliminated marginal but relatively costly programs, confined the translation program to donor-supported titles, and established stricter budgetary controls. Smith's successor, John Kyle, stated in a November 1968 memo to the board of directors that although the translated book program had assisted local publishers, it had not revolutionized indigenous publishing industries, nor was it a significant factor in educational and economic development. In short, Franklin was a relatively low-volume, high-cost program that required a burdensome subsidy.

In 1971, Franklin established two task forces: one to consider a merger and the other to review its programs, fundraising activities, and viability.

The first task force recommended that Franklin remain independent if it could possibly do so while the other task force recommended that "Franklin's role be expanded worldwide, it become an aggressive seeker of funds, and become a representative of a broad section of the American business and professional community in developing education, which is the key to the improvement of the quality of life in developing countries." For the next seven years, Franklin struggled to pursue the latter goals. In 1972, the Children's Book Council of Iran named four Franklin titles (*Charlotte's Web*, *The Family Under the Bridge*, *Island of the Blue Dolphin*, and *Pippi Longstocking*) as among the six "Best Books of the Year." In addition to publishing hundreds of juvenile titles, Franklin supported an Iranian children's magazine called *PAIR*, similar to the *Weekly Reader*, that boasted a bi-weekly circulation of 7.5 million in a country with a population of only 30 million people. As late as December 1976, Franklin's Cairo operation was reprinting 45 children's books and requesting more titles, particularly nonfiction books. Despite these continuing achievements, in June 1978, the board of directors voted to dissolve the corporation, asserting that Franklin's original mission had been achieved.[68]

CONCLUSION

Franklin Book Program's juvenile publishing operations from 1952 through 1970 highlight the ideological importance of children in Cold War American cultural diplomacy and the tensions in the US public–private approach to propaganda efforts. Founded by literary men but funded by the federal government, Franklin always struggled to satisfy the needs of two very different audiences: the USIA and foreign reading publics. Was Franklin a nonpolitical book program meant to stimulate local publishing industries, aid education, and create goodwill in the developing world? Or was it, as the State Department expected, meant to function as a more traditional gray propaganda program that improved America's reputation by highlighting its strengths and downplaying its weaknesses to an international audience? For a time, those goals overlapped sufficiently and

Franklin was able to stimulate the development of school libraries by providing books to fill their shelves; publish virtually all of Iran's elementary
school textbooks, and more in Afghanistan and Pakistan; and highlight
American literary classics and scientific achievements. Even then, Ruby
Berkely Goodwin's representation of American race relations trumped
Richard Wright's. As far as the US government was concerned, Franklin
successfully carried out diplomatic objectives as long as it fulfilled particular policy imperatives that highlighted the positive aspects of American
ideology. The men who ran Franklin, however, had a different conception
of propaganda, one that highlighted the "nonpolitical" aspects of foreign
relations, many of which directly related to children. The State Department
prioritized showcasing American strengths to foreign youth; Franklin saw
the long-term benefits of creating a literate population friendly to the
United States. Both sides of the debate, however, saw the value of reaching
out to foreign youth through books, which, like art, seemed to transcend
the written word and to represent abstract ideals of freedom and democracy. In the end, Franklin Books was a product of the Cold War; when the
Cold War thawed, Franklin was no longer relevant to American foreign
policy.

NOTES

1. Franklin D. Roosevelt, "Weapons for Man's Freedom," *ALA Bulletin* 36 (1942): 582.
2. John B. Hench, *Books as Weapons: Propaganda, Publishing, and the Battle for Global Markets in the Era of World War II* (Ithaca, NY: Cornell University Press, 2010).
3. Greg Barnhisel, "Cold Warriors of the Book: American Book Programs in the 1950s," *Book History* 13 (2010): 185–217. An exception is Christine Jenkins, "International Harmony: Threat or Menace? US Youth Services Librarians and Cold War Censorship, 1946–1955," *Libraries & Culture* 36.1 (2001): 116–130.
4. Christine Jenkins, "ALA Youth Services Librarians and the CARE-UNESCO Children's Book Fund: Selecting the 'Right Book' for Children in Cold War America, 1950–1958," *Libraries & Culture* 31.1 (Winter 1996): 209–234; Anne Morey, "The Junior Literary Guild and the Child Reader as Citizen," *The Lion and the Unicorn* 38.3 (September 2014): 279–302.
5. Franklin Book Programs Finding Aid, Princeton University Library, http://find-ingaids.princeton.edu/names/167703189. Early board members consisted of repre-sentatives from McGraw-Hill, Macmillan, Houghton Mifflin, Malcolm Johnson,

Donald Cameron, Silver Burdett, Harvard University Press, Random House, D. Van Nostrand, W. W. Norton, Harper and Brothers, Cornell University Press, W. B. Saunders, and the Book of the Month Club.

6. Franklin Book Programs Finding Aid, Princeton University Library, http://findin-gaids.princeton.edu/names/167703189.

7. Letter from George Brett to Malcolm Johnson (May 21, 1952), General Correspondence; December1951–May 1952; Franklin Book Programs Records, Box 18, Folder 1–2; Public Policy Papers, Department of Rare Books and Special Collections, Princeton University Library. (Hereafter FBPA.)

8. Peter S. Jennison, "How American Books Reach Readers Abroad," *Library Trends* 5.1 (July 1956): 9–10. Jennison was the Assistant Managing Director of the American Book Publishers Council, Inc.

9. Amanda Laugesen, "Books for the World: American Book Programs in the Developing World, 1948–1968," in Greg Barnhisel and Catherine Turner, eds. *Pressing the Fight: Print, Propaganda, and the Cold War* (Amherst: University of Massachusetts Press, 2010): 130.

10. Fast served a three-month prison sentence in 1950 for contempt of Congress, for refusing to provide a list of communist associates.

11. Louise Robbins, "The Overseas Library Controversy and the Freedom to Read: US Librarians and Publishers Confront Joseph McCarthy," *Libraries & Culture* 36.1 (2001): 27–39.

12. Dwight D. Eisenhower, "Remarks at the Dartmouth College Commencement Exercises," Dartmouth NH, June 14, 1953.

13. Nick Natanson, "Old Frontiers, New Frontiers: Reassessing USIA and State Department Photography of the Cold War Era," paper delivered at The Power of Free Inquiry and Cold War International History Conference, National Archives, College Park, MD, September 25–26, 1998. Available at http://www.archives.gov/research/foreign-policy/coldwar/conference/natanson.html.

14. "Covert Support of Book Publishing and Export House" (November 15, 1951), Box 18, Folder 2, FBPA.

15. See http://findingaids.princeton.edu/collections/MC057#description.

16. Classified letter from Malcolm Johnson to Datus Smith (May 31, 1956), 2 pgs., Box 65, Folder 16: USIA Administrative Policy, Suez, FBPA.

17. Letter from Datus Smith to Dan Lacy (January 4, 1952), Box 10, Folder 12, FBPA.

18. Annual Report (August 15, 1954): 3, Box 16, Folder 1, FBPA.

19. Box 16, Folder 10, p. 4, FBPA.

20. "Covert Support of Book Publishing and Export House," 1–1, Box 18, Folder 1, FBPA.

21. Annual Report (August 15, 1954), Box 16, Folder 1, FBPA.

22. Letter from Datus Smith to George Brett (January 21, 1953), Box 7, Folder 6, FBPA.

23. Transcript available at: http://www.npr.org/thisibelieve/murrow_transcript.html.

24. Projects for Future Development (August 15, 1954): 27–28, Box 16, Folder 1, FBPA; Sarah K. Bolton, *Lives of Poor Boys Who Became Famous* (Boston: Norwood Press, 1885): 5.

25. Dudziak, *Cold War Civil Rights*.

26. Letter from Datus Smith to Franklin Steiner (September 21, 1954); Letter from Franklin Steiner to Datus Smith with enclosed report (September 28, 1954); Typed memo by Datus Smith (September 29, 1954), Box 71, Folder 8, FBPA.

27. Annual Report (August 15, 1954): 29, Box 16, Folder 1, FBPA.

28. "Project 29: Textbooks," Annual Report (August 15, 1954), Box 16, Folder 1, FBPA.

29. 1954 Annual Report, 27, Box 16, Folder 1, FBPA.

30. Ellen Lewis Buell, *New York Times* (May 10, 1942): BR8.

31. Franklin Publications, "Sales Figures: Arabic" (January 1957), Box 15, Folder 9, FBPA.

32. A 2012 reviewer on goodreads.com described the book, "These are the kind of good quality people that make America what it is today. Good parents raising kids with values."

33. "How Franklin Book Programs Works – Some Highlights," 2, Box 29, Folder 12, FBPA.

34. Franklin Fact Sheets (January 8, 1958), "Prizes in East Pakistan," Box 29, Folder 12, FBPA; Letter from Donald S. Cameron to Thomas J. Wilson (February 14, 1958), Box 15, Folder 1, FBPA.

35. John Tebbel, "A Strong and Steady Light," *The Saturday Review* (March 13, 1965): 150.

36. Edward Clark, "Exclusive Report on a Growing Army of Soviet Scientists: The Golden Youth of Communism," *Life* (March 5, 1956): 31–36.

37. Franklin Fact Sheets, "Accidental Political Advantages of a Non-Political Book Program" (December 30, 1957), Box 29, Folder 12, FBPA.

38. Special Memo B (March 7, 1955), Box 71, Folder 8, FBPA.

39. Franklin Publications, Report, "Impact on Local Countries" (January 7, 1957): 1, Box 15, Folder 9, FBPA.

40. Datus Smith, "American Books in the Middle East," 5, Box 38, Folder 2, FBPA.

41. Datus C. Smith, "American Books in the Middle East," presented at the American Books Abroad conference, Princeton, NJ (September 1955). Published in Dan Lacy, Charles G. Bolté, and Peter S. Jennison, eds. "American Books Abroad," *Library Trends* 5.1 (July 1956): 49.

42. Franklin Fact Sheets (January 13, 1958): 4, Box 29, Folder 12, FBPA.

43. Franklin Publications, Inc. Newsletter (April 15, 1960): 3, Box 39, Folder 2, FBPA.

44. Letter from Charles E. Griffith to Franklin Publications (October 30, 1952): 2, FBPA.

45. Franklin Publications, Encyclopedia Project (July 6, 1953): 3, Box 92, Folder 2, FBPA.

46. Franklin Publications, Inc. Newsletter (January 15, 1959): 3, Box 39, Folder 2, FBPA; Encyclopedia Iranica, http://www.iranicaonline.org/articles/franklin-book-program

47. Charles Griffith, "American Books in Southeast Asia," presented at the American Books Abroad conference, Princeton, NJ (September 1955). Published in Lacy, Bolté, and Jennison, eds. "American Books Abroad," 123–125. Griffith was referring to the Bertha M. Parker's *Basic Science Series*, which was awarded "Best Children's Book Published in Persian" in 1957 by *Sukhan*, an Iranian literary magazine.

48. Charles Griffith, Francis R. St. John, and Datus Smith, "The Overseas Chinese: Report and Recommendations" (February 6, 1954), Box 88, Folder 2—China, FBPA.

49. Special Memo A, "Children's Stories" (March 7, 1955), Box 71, Folder 8, FBPA.

50. Correspondence between B. Franklin Steiner and Datus Smith (March 7, 1955), Special Memo B, "Children's Science Books," Box 71, File 8, FBPA.

51. Letter from Edward R. Murrow to Thomas Wilson (March 22, 1962), Box 15, Folder 1, FBPA.

52. Franklin Publications, Inc. Memoranda (January 10, 1957), Box 15, Folder 9. FBPA.

53. Franklin Fact Sheets, "Textbooks" (December 30, 1957), Box 29, Folder 12, FBPA.

54. Franklin Publications (August 28, 1956): 1; Dix, William; 1956–1977; Franklin Book Programs Records, Box 8, Folder 1–2; Public Policy Papers, Department of Rare Books and Special Collections, Princeton University Library.

55. Franklin Fact Sheets, "Communist Reaction" (December 27, 1957), Box 29, Folder 12, FBPA.

56. Letter from Hassan G. Aroussy to Datus Smith (January 13, 1954), Box 92, Folder 9, FBPA.

57. Saleh Gawdat, "Intellectual Aggression," *Al Kwakib* (July 1960), typescript included with a letter from Hassan Aroussy to Datus Smith (July 25, 1960), Box 92, Folder 9, FBPA.

58. Peter Sager, *Moscow's Hand in India: An Analysis of Soviet Propaganda* (Berne: Swiss Eastern Institute, 1966): 135–139.

59. Sarah Brouillette, "US–Soviet Antagonism and the 'Indirect Propaganda' of Book Schemes in India in the 1950s," *University of Toronto Quarterly* 84.4 (Fall 2015): 170–174; Evron Kirkpatrick, ed., *Year of Crisis: Communist Propaganda Activities in 1956* (New York: Macmillan, 1957): 179; Frederick C. Barghoorn, *The Soviet Cultural Offensive: The Role of Cultural Diplomacy in Soviet Foreign Policy* (Princeton: Princeton University Press, 1960): 188–189, 209–210.

60. Thomas J. Wilson to Spencer Scott, Marshall Best, and Joseph Margolis (October 5, 1961), Box 15, Folder 1, FBPA; Byron Buck to Eleanor Smith (July 8, 1964), Box 22, Folder 11, FBPA.

61. Datus Smith to Tom Wilson (July 24, 1962), Box 15, Folder 1, FBPA.

62. Harold N. Munger, Jr. to Arthur K. Watson (May 9, 1962), Box 15, Folder 1, FBPA.

63. Letter from Thomas Wilson to Spencer Scott, Marshall Best, and Joseph Margolis (October 5, 1961), Box 15, Folder 1, FBPA.

64. Supplement to Franklin Publications Proposal for Malayan Book Project (December 1961), Box 15, Folder 1, FBPA.

65. Wilbur A. Knerr, "Books for the Children of Latin America, A Plan from Franklin Book Programs, Inc." (February 2, 1965), Box 125, Folder 20; Draft, A Children's Book Foundation: A Proposal (March 10, 1966), Box 42, Folder 2: Programs and Projects, 1954–1972, FBPA.

66. Dorothy Hunt Smith, "Books for the Hungry," *Christian Science Monitor* (June 8, 1965), Box 296, Folder: Miscellaneous (2), FBPA.

67. Series 5, Photographs, Audiovisual and Oversized Photographs: Box 296, Folder: Miscellaneous, FBPA.

68. Letter from Cheryl T. Johnson to Mr. E. B. White (November 30, 1972), Box 245, Folder 7, FBPA; Letter from Kamil Farid to Byron Buck (February 13, 1977), Box 92, Folder 13: Egypt, Children's Books, 1976–77, FBPA.

4

"Your Grandchildren Will Grow Up Under Communism!"

Cold War Advertising and American Youth

If peace activists, politicians, literary men, and educators vied for authority over the meaning of childhood innocence and used children's culture to mediate Cold War political struggles, advertisers enjoyed a more unified agenda. The advances made in propaganda methods during World War II and the psychological aspects of the Cold War made advertising a key component in how it was waged at home and abroad. Under the guise of public information campaigns, domestic audiences were exposed to many of the same messages and images used in US Information Agency (USIA) propaganda for foreign audiences. The two fields shared personnel, methods, and messages and matured concurrently in the overheated consumer culture of the 1950s. A potent weapon in the Cold War, advertising relied on the notion of childhood innocence to promote Cold War containment at home and to advance a crucial pillar of US Cold War ideology abroad—the superiority of free market capitalism over communism.

This chapter explores how images of children and ideas about childhood functioned in select Advertising Council public service campaigns and consumer advertising during the 1950s. Although Americans maligned Soviet propaganda that targeted children as "brainwashing," the US government undertook propaganda campaigns and advanced similar messages in its own efforts to arouse domestic support for Cold War policies. As Margaret Peacock has argued, images of happy American and Soviet children symbolized larger sets of cultural and political values, ideals, and national goals. They offered viewers a visual shorthand for understanding what exactly was at stake in the Cold War and what benefits each nation's "way of life" offered to its youngest citizens. Although this symbolic relationship between childhood and nation had been evolving since the nineteenth century, the ideological demands of the Cold War, as well as evolving understandings of "protected childhood," required that it bear greater ideological weight. The innocence and well-being of children and youth, society's most precious resources, came to signify the moral legitimacy of each nation and necessitated the increased intervention of the state to protect and preserve that innocence.[1]

Although this chapter focuses on the ideological uses of children and childhood in the United States, it should be noted that both the USSR and the United States routinely touted the superior ability of their nation to secure the well-being of unaligned and Third World children as well. The effort to win hearts and minds included promises to provide for children's security, health, and education. In making his case for aid to Greece and Turkey in 1947, for example, President Truman noted that "eighty-five percent of the children were tubercular." Photographs in *Life* magazine depicted Berlin's children as the primary beneficiaries of the 1948–49 airlift.[2] Operation "Little Vittles" neatly symbolized the American interpretation of the struggle in postwar Europe. If Stalin was willing to starve innocent German children, the United States would shower them not only with necessities, but with luxuries as well. From September 1948 through May 1949, America's "Candy Bomber" Gail Halvorsen and 25 aircraft crews dropped 23 tons of chocolate, chewing gum, and candy over Berlin. Candy-makers throughout the United States donated to the cause, and thousands of American schoolchildren attached sweets to the miniature parachutes that rained down on the city. The Chocolate Pilot was a public relations coup abroad and captured the imaginations of Americans at home. The federal government used Operation Vittles to win friends in Germany and vilify the Soviet Union, while the US Air Force produced several films for use in American classrooms to document the success of the Marshall Plan.[3]

At the same time, Americans criticized the youth-focused efforts of the Soviet Union as particularly cynical, an obvious ploy to manipulate children's innate political innocence. The World Festivals of Youth and Students, the first held in the summer of 1947 in Prague, initially seemed cause for optimism. Students at Columbia University wrote in May,

> Fully knowing that only through the exchange of social, intellectual, and cultural ideas along with the political and scientific, we of Columbia wish to extend our best wishes and congratulations to the 140,000 student leaders, representing more than 60 nations and 45,000,000 youths, who will attend the four-week Youth Festival at Prague Czechoslovakia.[4]

Such optimism quickly soured, however, as young Americans returned from the Festival claiming that communists dominated the proceedings.[5] The 1951 festival in Berlin prompted some Americans to issue urgent calls for a wholesale response to the seeming success of the Soviet war of ideas. Likening Soviet youth groups to Hitler's *Jugend*, one writer argued that communist youth indoctrination began with literacy and succeeded because it offered useful work, a sense of belonging, large goals, and adult responsibility. Americans were still concerned in 1957, when 160 American young people attended the Moscow festival, that some "serve[d] Red purposes with folk song parodies." Fortunately, most students were not so "misguided."[6] Regardless of American criticisms, leaders of both nations recognized the crucial importance of educating young people to embrace their respective national systems.

COLD WAR PROPAGANDA AND THE AMERICAN CHILD

During World War II, many of the nation's professional ad men found work with newly created propaganda agencies at home and abroad. FDR created the Office of War Information (OWI) in 1942 to direct all overt, government-sponsored propaganda at home and abroad, including the Voice of America broadcast network.[7] The OWI created and distributed posters, booklets, photographs, radio shows, and films designed to improve morale, boost patriotism, and encourage Americans to ration commodities, donate goods, and buy war bonds. In 1943, a group of advertising and industry executives created the War Advertising Council (WAC), which they billed as a patriotic organization designed to support the war effort through voluntary donations of creative work by advertising agencies and sponsorship of public service ads by corporations. Although participation in the WAC was voluntary and uncompensated, American businesses quickly realized that they could do well by doing good. Companies were not directly compensated for donating ads, but they could deduct portions of their costs from their taxable incomes, which meant that the government might pay up to 80% of a company's advertising bills—regardless of whether they had anything to sell—which many did not, thanks to wartime rationing. Concerned that consumers would lose brand loyalty during the war, companies "donated" ads to keep corporate names in the public eye while appearing patriotic and improving public relations after the Great Depression, when many Americans lost confidence in US businesses.[8] During the war, WAC campaigns urged Americans to collect scrap and rubber, scan the skies for enemy aircraft, plant Victory Gardens, and buy war bonds. Under ad man Theodore "Ted" Repplier, who ran the organization from 1943 to 1966, the WAC perfected methods of propaganda while selling America's war aims to the public. World War II taught political leaders and advertisers that psychological warfare, propaganda, and what would later be called "cultural diplomacy" were "indispensable elements of modern warfare."[9] Ted Repplier and the Advertising Council would fight the Cold War with the techniques they had learned during World War II.

After the war, the ad men returned to a postwar economic boom and new communications technologies that provided unprecedented opportunities for the growth of American business. The WAC changed its name to the Advertising Council in 1946, but it didn't alter its tactics. Nor did the men who worked for the OWI, whose responsibilities and overseas offices were transferred to the State Department and the US Information Service (USIS) in 1945. Just as they had during the war, both organizations continued to feature children prominently in ad campaigns that sold ideological concepts through discourses emphasizing national prosperity, freedom, and security.[10] Similarly, images of happy children saturated American popular culture in the postwar period and were used to sell everything from soda pop to life insurance. During the 1950s and 1960s, advertisers learned to use audience segmentation to sell products, and television networks aired programs targeting specific audiences, including children. Popular magazines like *Life* and *Look* regularly featured articles about happy American children who enjoyed unprecedented abundance and security "under the protective umbrella of a powerful nation," and advertisers linked the Baby Boom to national prosperity and the future of the nation.[11] The advertising industry reinforced American values by equating freedom of choice with consumer options and "the good life" with the acquisition of material goods.[12]

The deeply intertwined network of government and private organizations that produced American propaganda, from Better Schools campaigns to People's Capitalism exhibits to Radio Free Europe (RFE) fundraisers, rhetorically and visually linked the well-being of American children to a domestic consensus supporting Cold War policies in the defense of childhood, family, and nation. This political consensus rested on demonstrated patriotism, militarism, consumer spending, and lack of dissent. In the economic boom of the 1950s, middle-class leisure and national abundance served as evidence of American superiority in the Cold War, as signified by the oft-cited 1959 "kitchen debate" between Vice President Richard Nixon and Soviet Premier Nikita Khrushchev. Both government propaganda and consumer advertising played on visions of idealized and threatened American children to construct markets for a vast array of consumer goods—new suburban homes, second cars, business and leisure travel, electronics, life insurance, packaged foods, and household appliances. As symbols of national innocence and as representations of the nation's future, children embodied national affluence and hinted at national vulnerability. But children were not positioned simply as symbols or passive recipients of American abundance. Both government propagandists and corporate advertisers asked children to *participate* in the Cold War and to function as living advertisements for the American way of life.

THE ADVERTISING COUNCIL

Ad Council campaigns were just one of many sources of public information that aimed to "educate" Americans about pressing social and political issues during the war years. Established in 1942 to unite corporate America behind the war effort, the WAC focused primarily on promoting the interests of US corporations, but its business and advertising members "donated" tax-deductible advertising to the war effort, a classic example of doing well by doing good, or, in today's business language, "strategic philanthropy." During the war, the Ad Council became a semi-private vehicle for public persuasion and fostered an "intimate and profitable" relationship with the federal government. In October 1945, the Advertising Council announced that it would continue operations to create "future campaigns growing out of an act of Congress and requiring public understanding or action, or problems certified in the public interest" as determined by a three-quarters vote of its Public Policy Committee.[13] Historian Robert Griffith has argued that the leaders of corporate America emerged from World War II united in their opposition to the New Deal and determined to preserve corporate autonomy. They did so through traditional means such as lobbying and campaign financing, but they also launched large-scale education programs aimed at the American public, couched in the language of Cold War fear and anxiety. William H. Whyte, Jr., the editor of *Fortune* magazine, estimated that, by 1952, American businesses spent $100 million each year to sell the idea of free enterprise to the American people.[14]

Concerned about internal subversion and vocal criticism of capitalism, as well as by polls that showed that Americans favored universal health care, full employment, and social security, business and advertising executives concluded that Americans would be more likely to support the capitalist system if they better understood how they benefitted from it. Postwar Ad Council information programs suggested to individual Americans that they could fight the Cold War by working harder, buying more, donating to UNESCO and RFE, and spending their tourist dollars abroad to reinvigorate foreign economies. In order to target and mobilize a national audience, the Council relied on images of childhood innocence and vulnerability, family unity, material comfort, economic abundance, and youth culture. Images of the threatened child encouraged parents to fear for their children's security and future and suggested ways to assuage this threat—usually through consumption. At the same time, USIA propaganda campaigns targeted foreign audiences with similar messages and images. Both domestic and foreign propaganda made ideological use of the idea of childhood as simultaneously innocent and political, vulnerable and powerful. While Truman's "Campaign of Truth" fought communist lies abroad, domestic information campaigns emphasized the "moral force" of freedom and democracy and, most importantly, the material advantages of capitalism.[15] The two campaigns discussed herein—The American Economic System and the Crusade for Freedom—targeted American children not only as abstract ideas, but as actors and participants in this ideological battle—at school and on the radio and through popular culture, parades, and "voluntold" fundraising efforts.[16] Children were central symbols *and* actors in both domestic and foreign propaganda campaigns.

The American Economic System (1948–1953)

The first of two early Cold War Ad Council campaigns demonstrates how advertisers relied on images of children to sell the Cold War to the American public. Between 1948 and 1952, General Electric, General Foods, and other large corporations "donated" $3 million in advertising revenue to explain the American Economic System *to the American people*, under the assumption that if they better understood how the economy functioned, they would work harder for its success and be less vulnerable to "disturbers and communists."[17] Corporate leaders feared that if Americans did not truly understand their economic system, they could be "misled by exaggeration of its faults" or "be made to forget its benefits" by propaganda attacks "from within and without."[18] Some worried that free enterprise was threatened less by communism than by Americans' ignorance of capitalism and their susceptibility to dangerous ideas like government regulation and socialism, which had become painfully clear in widespread public support for Roosevelt's New Deal policies before the war.[19] Although Ad Council organizers avowed their desire not to "wave the flag" or otherwise propagandize for US business interests, the Council's own researchers concluded that the campaign was successful because viewers came away from the ads with a clearer sense of the superiority of "the American way."[20] They educated the public not about capitalism, but about the superiority of capitalism.

Children as both image and audience were central to the Ad Council's explanation of why capitalism offered a better way of life than "other systems." At a meeting of the Association of National Advertisers in October 1948, the President of General Foods and Ad Council Chairman Charles Mortimer explained the strategy. Beginning in November 1948, 126 magazines with a combined circulation of 73 million readers, in addition to the Sunday newspaper inserts *American Weekly* and *Parade*, would carry the first American Economic System advertisements. Accompanying each ad would be a mail-in coupon for a special booklet created by the Ad Council, *The Miracle of America*, that explained the American economy in more detail. "We also," Mortimer noted, "hope to distribute it extensively in schools."[21] In 1951, 250 radio and television stations broadcast the Miracle of America message, in addition to the equivalent of 3,600 full-page ads in newspapers and 7,000 outdoor billboards. Requests for *The Miracle of America* arrived from 84 nations, including some in Eastern Europe, where the ad "Ivan is Watching You" was accompanied by the text, "he fears your ability to out-produce him. So let's turn out more for every hour we work. *Strength* will protect both peace and freedom." During its first year, the campaign garnered "well over two billion" radio listener impressions.[22] By 1952, the Ad Council had distributed more than 1.84 million copies of *The Miracle of America*, half to companies and a quarter "without charge to schools." Seventy-six universities had ordered the booklet "in quantity."[23] Pro-business propaganda, couched in the language of Cold War patriotism and distributed under the guise of education, targeted American schoolchildren and youth as future voters, consumers, workers, and citizens.

The American Economic System ad campaign drove home five core messages that emphasized productivity and consumption as national imperatives: (1) *consensus*: Americans agreed that the American system created a better standard of living for all, (2) *consumption*: better living standards were achieved by ever-increasing productivity and wider distribution of material benefits, (3) *collective bargaining* benefitted everyone, (4) *political and economic freedom* were interdependent, and (5) cooperation among management, labor, and the public ensured that all parties would benefit to the fullest possible degree. One typical passage reads, "Teamwork is simply working together to turn out more goods in fewer man-hours—making things at lower costs and paying higher wages to the people who make them and selling them at lower prices to the people who use them." The text is accompanied by an image of the quintessential team—an attractive, middle-class, white family of four gazing optimistically into the promised utopian future of "better housing, clothing, food, health, education . . . and ever greater opportunities for individual development."[24]

Although ads encouraged children *as individuals* to work harder and more efficiently, no matter their particular job, they were more often pictured as part of the family team. For example, another ad depicted a white family of four relaxing in a cozy, domestic setting—Dad in his slippers reading the paper, Mother sewing, junior playing with the dog, and big sister listening to records on the hi-fi—under the startlingly incongruent headline, "COMES THE REVOLUTION!" The reader is quickly reassured that in America the revolution has already been won—a historic victory unique to mankind in conquering cold, hunger, dirt, and dis-ease. Although Americans had conquered these age-old problems, the ad warns, "Right now the people of many nations are faced with a choice, between dictatorship and a free economy. And they are taking a long look at us." If Americans committed to the success of capitalism, committed to "creating more wealth for more of us and more jobs for more people, then other nations will follow *us*. If we *don't*, then they'll probably go communist or fascist."[25] With facile leaps of logic, text and image linked American domesticity, whiteness, abundance, and consumerism with national security and imagined these as threatened by foreign economic and political ideologies.

The Ad Council's strategy relied heavily on domestic images of the "typical" white, middle-class, nuclear family to motivate readers to action. As privatized units of consumption, American families were the ultimate capitalist "team." If each American family committed to the shared goal of abundance, without division or dissent, there would be no limit to the "greater things" they could "all share together." The first ad encouraged teamwork to preserve an existing reality. In these ads, family unity served as shorthand for national unity, and consensus was contained within the normative boundaries of the white, middle-class family. The second ad paired a Norman Rockwell–like image with a fear-inspiring headline to imply that white, middle-class American families were under threat, *unless. . . .* Unless Americans met the challenge of making their "free, dynamic American system run so well" that other nations chose capital-ism over communism. Both ads position the nuclear family and happy, healthy, secure, white children—the ultimate beneficiaries of national prosperity and material well-being—as the embodiment of the comfort, convenience, security, and independence that resulted from a capital-ist economy. Here, advertisers used white children to advance a vision of *imperiled* American economic and national exceptionalism and to encourage Americans to rise to the challenge of protecting their children's way of life.

The Ad Council used images of children in yet another way. Several American Economic System advertisements relied on images of vulnerable and oppressed *Soviet* children, the ultimate victims of communist lies and economic stagnation. Inspired by a news story in *Pravda* that castigated Soviet teachers for failing to instill "profound contempt" in their students for American capitalism, the ad addressed "Dear Soviet Teachers. . . ." If they wanted to raise committed communists, the ad advised, Soviet teachers should keep quiet about the advantages of the American System: unlimited opportunity, the right to change jobs as one saw fit, free enterprise, a standard of living ten times higher than that of the Soviet Union, better consumer goods, lower prices, higher wages, and shorter working hours. As the ultimate proof of capitalism's superiority, the ad argued, the American system had achieved the mass production of "the daily benefits of the automobile, telephone, radio, refrigeration, central heating, modern plumbing and better farm machinery" for the majority of its people. This "letter" was accompanied by a photograph of six Soviet schoolchildren who appeared alternately bored or anxious. The children sat crowded together in an uninviting classroom with the ever-present images of Lenin and Stalin hovering over them. Unlike American children, they were not accompanied by loving parents or caregivers, they were not embraced by domestic tranquility, security, or abundance. The students weren't engaged with or enjoying their education. Instead, the ad positioned the children as symbols of Soviet oppression, half-truths, scarcity, and insecurity; in their vulnerability, the children represented the failure of the Soviet system to care for its youngest citizens. They also represented to US viewers what might befall American children should our economy falter.[26] The first two ads depicted the safety and security that capitalism provided for cared-for white American children and families; the third depicted Soviet children as victims to arouse sympathy and fear among American audiences. The former documented the moral legitimacy of a system that cared for its children and the latter the degeneracy of a system that could not. All three ads imagined children as vulnerable and passive.

Each of these ads included a mail-in coupon for a free copy of the *Miracle of America*, a detailed booklet explaining the American Economic System. According to the pamphlet, the secret of American success was *productivity*, and the secret of continuing American success was *more productivity*. The more goods produced per hour of work, the higher the standard of living. According to the corporations that sponsored the Ad Council, constantly expanding productivity was therefore a *national necessity*. The Ad Council produced at least two versions of the pamphlet. *The Miracle of America As Discovered by One Family*, presumably the version distributed to public schools, presented its explanation of the American economy as a lesson to a son who casually asked his father, "What's our economic system, Dad?" For an explanation, the family turned to Uncle Sam, who appeared suddenly to guide the family on a highly selective tour of American economic history from the colonial era to 1948. Slavery, labor disputes, racism, and poverty—past or present—went unnoted. Progress was measured strictly by numerical comparisons. For example, in 1914, it took 41 hours to make a baby carriage; in 1948, with the benefit of modern machinery, it took only 15.5 hours. American schoolchildren learned from *The Miracle of America* that the United States was unique in human history, that production had moved gradually from independent households to factories, that political freedom fostered personal initiative and economic progress, and that only constantly expanding production could guarantee continued global American dominance. By early 1950, *Scholastic* magazine had issued 535,000 reprints of the booklet to schools.[27] Clearly, the corporations that supported the Ad Council's American Economic System campaign had much to gain from a rousing national commitment to a free enterprise system in which workers worked harder and dissented less, and business regulations were considered un-American. Through millions of "public service" advertisements, the Ad Council promoted advertising itself as responsible, civic-spirited free speech; the American economy as a uniquely productive and cooperative enterprise; and American society as dynamic, classless, and consensual.[28] Children were central to this campaign as symbols of the nation's future and as future citizens and workers themselves.

The Good Citizenship Campaign (1947–1952)

At the same time the Ad Council and corporate America sought to educate Americans about the benefits of a free market economy, the American Heritage Foundation collaborated with the Ad Council on the Good

Citizenship campaign (1947–52) to rededicate Americans in their commitment to political freedom.[29] Under the slogan "Freedom is Everybody's Job," the American Heritage campaign directly targeted youth. The first page of the 1947 pamphlet, *Good Citizen*, directly addressed "the young people of America" with a heavy responsibility: "America is banking on you to carry forward the torch of freedom and personal liberty." The booklet laid out the obligations of citizenship, including voting and volunteering in local communities and working to solve "World Problem No. 1"—finding peaceful uses for and humanitarian leadership in developing nuclear power. The anonymous narrator asked young people to commit to the "Nine Promises of a Good Citizen," including voting, jury duty, respecting the law, paying taxes, accepting wartime responsibilities, working for better public schools, improving local communities, avoiding prejudice of any kind, and teaching democracy in one's own home.[30] Only by fulfilling the duties of citizenship could young Americans protect the hard-won freedoms handed down to them by earlier generations and pass them on to their own future children and grandchildren. Children did not simply represent freedom; they were responsible for maintaining it for future generations of Americans.

In order to reinforce these lessons in citizenship, in 1952, the Freedoms Foundation at Valley Forge offered $100,000 in cash and prizes to schools whose students contributed to the understanding of the "American Way of Life."[31] Any elementary or secondary school could submit materials demonstrating their understanding of the Credo, which was visually depicted as a stout monument. The foundation stone was labeled "A Fundamental Belief in God"; above that a horizontal stone slab read, "Constitutional Government Designed to *Serve* the People"; two vertical towers rested on this slab, listing 16 individual rights; finally, on the top of the Credo, a smaller horizontal slab read, "Political and Economic Rights which Protect the Dignity and Freedom of the Individual." One hundred winning schools could select one teacher and one student for an all-expenses-paid trip to Valley Forge, Pennsylvania. The winners would receive the George Washington Honor Medal as well as the Freedoms Library, consisting of pictures, books, recordings, and films for their school. The Foundation awarded 50 additional schools the medal and library. In addition, the Freedoms Foundation offered High School Newspaper Editorial Awards to young journalists who contributed an editorial to their school newspaper that "carried out the fundamentals of the Credo."

Patriotic contests and awards were ubiquitous in the 1950s. Art contests, radio contests, essay contests—these highly publicized spectacles of young Americans functioned as both domestic and foreign propaganda. As performances for domestic audiences, the Freedoms Foundation contest winners reiterated the patriotic and economic consensus that supported the Cold War. Such contests functioned simultaneously as foreign propaganda because they were routinely "reported" by the USIA as "news" for foreign consumption. From April 1953 until May 1957, the USIA distributed monthly "youth packets" to posts around the globe. The packets consisted of compilations of news briefs and feature stories about American young people and were intended for distribution in foreign news media. For example, the USIA's April 1953 youth packet featured a story titled "US Youths 'Speak for Democracy' in Nationwide Radio Contest," which enabled the USIA to reprint four of the winning essays in their entirety and tout the purpose of the contest: "to encourage young people to think and talk positively about democracy—not disparagingly of other governments." In October of the same year, the USIA reprinted 13-year-old Robert Stiehl's prize-winning essay, "What America Means to Me." Stiehl had won a statewide essay contest sponsored by the Pennsylvania chapter of the American Veterans of World War II.[32] USIA officials chose stories for the youth packets that "show[ed] young people doing unusual, and significant things in the free world. Some will demonstrate courage or enterprise; others may illustrate youthful inventiveness, initiative or self reliance [*sic*] as opposed to the regimentation of youth in communist-dominated areas."[33] Patriotic radio, art, and essay contests functioned as global performances in which American children demonstrated their whole-hearted and "voluntary" support for the Cold War consensus.

The Crusade for Freedom (1951–1960)

Both the American and Soviet governments recognized the importance of mobilizing children and youth, at home and abroad, with Cold War propaganda. The Soviet youth newspaper *Pravda Komosol*, for example, made much of postwar layoffs of American women, reporting to its young readers in 1946, "educated girls seek any kind of work, they become housemaids and live mannequins in store windows; and that need and unemployment are driving American girls into prostitution." In the same vein, the Voice of America reported in June 1952, "Today, packs of hungry, homeless, orphaned and abandoned children still fill the railroad stations, streets, marketplaces, and slums of Russian cities. What was the effect on children of the mass seizures utilized to fill Soviet forced labor camps? How and by whom were children cared for, those whose fathers and mothers perished as victims of mass executions, as hostages, as victims of the sham courts of communism, victims of executions without trial?"[34] Domestic public information campaigns in both the Soviet Union and the United States mirrored overt propaganda sent abroad as both governments routinely accused the other of failing to care for its most vulnerable citizens.[35]

On September 4, 1950, Dwight Eisenhower, then president of Columbia University, addressed a global audience. His topic? Communist subversion and propaganda and "a campaign sponsored by private American citizens to counter the Big Lie with the Big Truth," a national battle to win the hearts and minds "of the world's multitudes." A 10-year, multimillion-dollar campaign, the Crusade for Freedom aimed to "free the minds" of millions of Eastern Europeans, particularly young people, held hostage behind the Iron Curtain. Although predicated on a lie—the Crusade was secretly managed and largely funded by the CIA, not private citizens—the Crusade raised more than $21.4 million from public and corporate contributions between 1950 and 1959 to support "truth broadcasts" over RFE and Radio Free Asia (RFA) and secured 25 million signatures in support of "freedom" for the enslaved peoples behind the Iron Curtain.[36] In comparison, known CIA funding during the same period amounted to more than $140,139,000. Founded in 1949 by former Office of Strategic

Services (OSS) intelligence officer Allan Dulles, the National Committee for a Free Europe (NCFE) launched RFE as a "private" network over which American citizens "not subject to the restrictions which hamper a government agency, could say things . . . which Voice of America, as an agency of government, was not in the position to say."[37] Abbott Washburn, a former public relations executive for General Mills, served as vice-chairman of the Crusade for Freedom, Inc. from 1950 to 1952, resigning to serve under Eisenhower as deputy director of the USIA from 1953 to 1961. Luminaries such as Eisenhower, General Lucius Clay, and media moguls Henry Luce and Cecil B. DeMille served as NCFE board members. This network of public–private organizations and administrators was a hallmark of American public diplomacy throughout the Cold War years.[38]

In July 1950, RFE built a radio transmitter in West Germany, where more than 1,000 employees directed programming from Munich; a second was installed in Portugal the following year. Intended to camouflage CIA funding for RFE, the Crusade used celebrity radio spots, outdoor advertising, posters on buses and in subway stations, rallies, and parades to encourage Americans to donate "freedom dollars," wear freedom buttons, and explain what freedom meant to them. Like youth essay and radio contests, RFE fundraising campaigns raised money while orchestrating public spectacles in which ordinary citizens repeatedly reiterated their support for the American "way of life." Their statements were in turn sent abroad through USIA propaganda channels to be published in foreign newspapers and other media outlets.

Like other propaganda campaigns, the Crusade for Freedom targeted foreign and American youth as both leaders and symbols. Among RFE's primary targets were Eastern European youths. Sports, entertainment, science, and technology programs, as well as features on youth in the West, like those highlighted in USIA youth packets, aimed to convince young listeners of the superiority of the West and the limitations of communism.[39] The CIA was also keenly aware that "literary readings [and] music programmes [sic] [were] particularly attractive to teen-age youth who tune in for the music."[40] Crusade for Freedom advertisements typically noted that communist indoctrination specifically targeted young people "who have no memories of other ways of life."[41] Crusade ads used images of foreign youth as well. One Crusade ad featured a photograph of young Karel Paces, a Czech boy rescued from a German refugee camp, broadcasting Czech folk stories to children behind the Iron Curtain via RFE. As the ad noted, native stories were "denied them by their Communist masters," but Karel was proof that "Even a Boy can fight Communism with Truth" (Figure 4.1).

In the United States, beginning on Labor Day 1950, the six-week Crusade sponsored school programs, parades, youth groups like the Boy and Girl Scouts, television shows, and radio programs to explicitly target young people with a "pageantry of patriotism," offering specific ways

Figure 4.1 The Advertising Council's Crusade for Freedom domestic information campaign mobilized children as activists and as victims of Soviet oppression. Here, a Czech refugee child, Karel Paces, reads outlawed Czech folk tales to children behind the Iron Curtain over the Radio Free Europe network. Courtesy of Ad Council Archives, University of Illinois Archives, RS 13/2/207.

they could serve their country. Children were provided the opportunity to reflect on the freedoms they enjoyed while young people in other parts of the world suffered under communism. According to Richard Cummings, the first Crusade for Freedom "truth statement" contest took place in Onondaga County, New York, in September 1950, when 300 junior and high school students submitted essays on the theme, "Why I want to participate in the Crusade for Freedom." Seven winners received a US Savings bond, and, on October 1, 1950, *The Post-Standard* published the full text of their entries and a photograph of the winners with their teachers. County Crusade leaders stated confidently, "The school essays show clearly that the challenge of positive action and reaffirmation of our American ideals of freedom have been accepted by the youngest schoolchildren."[42]

The major public component of the Freedom Crusade was the national tour of a 10-ton bronze Freedom Bell, a replica of the Liberty Bell. When the bell arrived, the host community staged public rituals that included speeches by city officials and civic leaders and much pageantry. For example, the Freedom Bell arrived in Salt Lake City, Utah, in September 1950 for a three-hour stay. The week surrounding its arrival was deemed Freedom Week in the state, with Freedom Sunday dedicated to anticommunist sermons and "School Week" dedicated to inculcating American values in students.[43] Members of the Salt Lake Jaycee auxiliary served as "Freedom Belles" at a booth in the Hotel Utah, where they collected signatures for Freedom Scrolls. Other women's groups staffed similar booths at local businesses and the state fairgrounds for the duration of Freedom Week.[44] The *Salt Lake Telegram* reported that nearly 100% of the state's junior and senior high school students and 1,800 of the University of Utah's 6,500 students had signed Freedom Scrolls during the campaign's first two weeks. By October 11, 1950, state leaders proudly announced that more than 50,000 Utahns had signed Freedom Scrolls, almost double the state's quota.[45] The scrolls, with others collected from around the nation, eventually traveled with the bell to West Berlin, where they were encased in the concrete foundation of the bell. The bell itself was installed in West Berlin's city hall on United Nation's Day, October 24, 1950. The language and rituals surrounding the Crusade for Freedom—crusade, quota, pageantry, truth statements, youth affirmations—sound to post–Cold War ears remarkably similar to the methods Soviet propaganda campaigns used to mobilize young people.[46]

The Crusade gained momentum in the early 1950s, with Henry Ford replacing Lucius Clay as chairman and Hollywood becoming an active supporter. The 1951 Crusade campaign relied on star power to attract young people. On Friday, September 28, 1951, Bing Crosby and his four sons took to the airwaves with the "Youth Crusade with the Crosbys," a half-hour radio show on NBC. Crosby asked his young listeners to sacrifice three pieces of bubble gum and donate their three pennies to buy "one brick for a new Radio Free Europe station to carry the truth behind the Iron Curtain. $100 buys a microphone." The show ran again the following day (Saturday), and again for school broadcast on "Youth Crusade Day," Wednesday, October 3, 1951. Schools across the nation aired the program, accompanied by campaigns to collect signatures for Freedom Scrolls and encourage children to wear Crusade for Freedom buttons. On February 12, 1954, in Springfield, Illinois, Boy and Girl Scouts launched 2,000 helium balloons containing an invitation for the finder to donate a "truth dollar" and 12 envelopes to distribute to other contributors. The pillow-shaped plastic bags traveled up to 700 miles at up to 30,000 feet. Springfield's was the largest of 540 similar launches in 1954.[47] *The New York Times* reported that 80,000 area Boy Scouts had been enlisted to help the program.[48] In 1955, the Crusade for Freedom's national campaign ran from February 12 to 22 (from Abraham Lincoln's to George Washington's birthday). The Civil Air Patrol, the Crusade for Freedom, and the American Legion sponsored the "Freedom Sky Drop project," in which 1,000 small airplanes flew over 200 American cities and towns, dropping packages that included replicas of the Freedom Bell medallions that had been distributed to countries behind the Iron Curtain, Freedom Scrolls for the signatures of 41 people, mailing envelopes for the submission of "Truth Dollar" contributions, and various booklets and articles that described how ordinary Americans could fight communism.

Between 1955 and 1959, the Ad Council mobilized newspaper boys by distributing campaign materials and contribution envelopes so their customers could "bring truth and eventual freedom to 70 million people who are forced to live in intellectual darkness under Communist masters." In April 1955, President Eisenhower told journalists, "I am inspired . . . that the boys of this nation will freely give of their time and energy—and their hearts—to help bring information of today's world to those whose masters provide propaganda." More than 20,000 newsboys collected $90,000 for Crusade for Freedom in 1955. The following year, newsboys who collected significant funds received the Crusade's "Award for Exceptional Service." In 1955 and 1956, four newsboys were flown to New York, where they toured RFE headquarters and broadcast "messages of hope to youngsters behind the Iron Curtain." Although it never advanced beyond the planning stages, in 1956, the Crusade explored a school citizenship project called "Freedom Crusader." The plan called for America's 25 million public school students to educate others about the Crusade by informing American schoolchildren of totalitarian practices behind the Iron Curtain, demonstrating to American youth the effectiveness of truth in the battle for men's minds, and assisting schools in their important work of building in young people a deeper appreciation and understanding of American democracy. In 1959, Utah, Montana, and Idaho school administrators encouraged public school students to participate in "Truth Broadcast" contests and placed entry cards in classrooms.[49] Richard Cummings argues that Americans in the 1950s, including children, would have been exposed constantly to Crusade for Freedom propaganda at work and school; on television and radio; through print media, billboards, and poster advertisements; and through staged and widely publicized contests and pageants.[50] Christopher Simpson points out that the $5 million spent by the CIA between 1950 and 1955 exceeded "the combined total of all the money spent on the Truman/Dewey presidential election campaign of 1948 . . . and establishes the CIA as the largest single political advertiser on the American scene during the early 1950s, rivaled only by such commercial giants as General Motors and Procter & Gamble in its domination of the airwaves."[51] In short, politically "innocent" children were mobilized to participate actively in the Crusade for Freedom.

Images of children figured prominently in Crusade for Freedom advertising, both as representations of American freedom and as victims of communist lies and propaganda. One of the most widely distributed images of the Crusade, used in newspaper releases to announce the arrival of a "Freedom Bell" in local communities, depicted a young American girl gazing up at the oversized bell, which appears to hover protectively over her. Conversely, a 1957–58 Ad Council image of "little Marinka" displayed the vulnerability of children living behind the Iron Curtain. Above the large-print caption, "Don't Let Lies Win The Battle For Her Mind!," Marinka sits in front of an open book, while a second caption, "Only With Your Help Can She Know Truth," implies that her book contains only anti-American propaganda and the "communist line." Marinka could know the truth—that Americans wanted peace—only through RFE broadcasts that penetrated the Iron Curtain. By sending their "truth dollars" to this "private organization supported by the American people," Americans would counter Soviet propaganda with the truth. Another ad distributed during the 1959 Truth Broadcast campaign depicted a young girl in a heavy coat and kerchief behind a high barbed wire fence. With the caption "Don't let her grow up without hearing the TRUTH!," the ad encouraged "freedom-loving American citizens" to submit their own "truth broadcasts." Those who submitted winning testimonies were flown to Europe to broadcast their own statement, "As an American I support Radio Free Europe because. . . ." The Ad Council distributed a print advertisement (seen in Figure 4.2) as well as a one-minute radio spot that began with a hypothetical Khrushchev proclaiming, "'Your grandchildren will grow up under Communism!' You can help make sure that this never happens. How? By fighting Communism now . . . with your own words. By writing your own Truth Broadcasts . . . to be beamed behind the Iron Curtain by Radio Free Europe."[52]

RFE benefitted from enhanced levels of prestige and visibility granted to "information" and psy-ops programs under the Eisenhower administration. Eisenhower appointed the nation's first cabinet-level propaganda advisor, Charles Douglas (known as C. D.) Jackson, who had served as deputy director of psychological warfare in the Mediterranean during World War II and headed RFE from 1951 until December 1952. At Jackson's urging, Eisenhower created the USIA in June 1953, as an independent propaganda agency with authority over all federal information operations

Figure 4.2 Although Nikita Khrushchev never actually threatened that the grandchildren of mid-century Americans would grow up under communism, the Ad Council relied on images of vulnerable children, both American and Soviet, to galvanize the American public to act. Visions of oppressed, militarized, and brainwashed Soviet children loomed large in the American imagination and led parents to fear for the future of their own children. Courtesy of Ad Council Archives, University of Illinois Archives, RS 13/2/207.

except the Fulbright program, which remained the province of the State Department. Both Eisenhower and Secretary of State John Foster Dulles considered propaganda a crucial component of American foreign policy. "I am personally convinced," the president stated in 1955, "that this is the cheapest money we can spend in the whole area of national security. This field is of vital importance in the world struggle."[53]

Classless Abundance for All

The links between the Ad Council's domestic information campaigns and foreign propaganda are equally clear in the USIA's "People's Capitalism" campaign. The idea came from Ted Repplier, the president of the Ad Council, after a 1955 tour of USIA facilities that he deemed woefully inadequate to counter Russian propaganda. In response, Repplier proposed a global propaganda effort to correct "misperceptions" of democratic capitalism and the United States by explaining American-style capitalism directly to foreign audiences. The basic argument was that Karl Marx had it wrong. Appropriating the language of communism, American propagandists argued that, in the United States, most working Americans were middle-class capitalists who enjoyed access to a vast array of new consumer goods; owned real estate, retirement plans, and cars; and enjoyed a two-week family vacation every year. Business owners recognized the wisdom of sharing the wealth among their employees, who were also their consumers. Government, business, and labor worked together to the mutual advantage of all. The USIA broadcast this message abroad through print publications, trade fairs, films, pamphlets, and posters, but the Ad Council was so impressed with its seeming success that they sought to popularize the campaign at home. "People's Capitalism" exhibits traveled the world, including a stop at Washington DC's Union Station in February 1956. The exhibit visually depicted American economic history as a steady march of progress from Spartan frontier homes on the eve of the American Revolution to the typical middle-class ranch home of the 1950s—modest but attractive and filled with the latest technology and consumer goods. The Ad Council supplied business leaders and politicians with scripts and sound bites for articles that appeared in the domestic press such as the *New York Times* and *Saturday Review*. The USIA also sponsored academic conferences to discuss the American System, making sure to record sound bites for radio shows.[54] In the case of the People's Capitalism campaign, propaganda for foreign audiences made its way directly into the American media.

For a quarter-century following World War II, Ad Council campaigns explicitly linked American political ideals with economic abundance, domestic consumption, and youth. The 1948–53 American Economic System campaign linked prosperity and political freedom to free market capitalism. From 1951 to 1960, the Crusade for Freedom mobilized millions of Americans, including children, to raise funds for RFE and to bring freedom to Eastern Europeans trapped behind the Iron Curtain. Americans fought communist "lies" with "truth dollars" generated by America's booming economy. The People's Capitalism campaign, although produced for foreign consumption, leaked into domestic "information campaigns" that emphasized widespread abundance, the idea that, in America, everyone was materially comfortable. Democratic capitalism had conquered class divisions and created a nation where American families enjoyed access to an abundance of consumer goods, inexpensive foods, and modern conveniences. Cold Warriors advocated the idea that the United States was beating the Soviet Union at its own game—providing "classless abundance for all" despite the fact that, in 1958, 31% of American households lived below the poverty level.[55] The National Association of Manufacturer's "Miracle of America" defined the United States in terms of material abundance and told Americans that their superior "standard of living and freedom are the envy of the world." Throughout the 1950s, "the language of growth, prosperity, free enterprise, and consumption increasingly supplemented the language of political liberalism and religion."[56] Images of children figured in all of these campaigns, both at home and abroad. Children and the future they represented were ultimately at stake in the struggle against communism. They were the beneficiaries of American abundance and prosperity and stood to suffer the most if that abundance declined.

SELLING TO AMERICA: CHILDREN, CONSUMER ADVERTISING, AND THE COLD WAR

Public information campaigns produced jointly by the federal government and big business were widespread throughout the 1950s, but consumer advertising, which often used similar language and images, exploded in postwar America. Throughout the period, advertising expenditures increased to unprecedented levels. The J. Walter Thompson Company (JWT), for example, saw its billings increase from $78 million in 1945 to $172 million in 1955 and $250 million by 1960. Overall, gross annual ad industry billings grew from $1.3 billion in 1950 to $6 billion in 1960. Because the 1948 Smith-Mundt Act, which authorized the State Department's public diplomacy efforts, prohibited domestic propaganda, most Americans knew little about the USIA and the messages it exported for foreign consumption. In theory, the US government did not directly propagandize its own citizens, as the Soviet Union did. Instead, the private sector, through consumer advertising, performed similar functions and delivered similar messages at home.[57] The same corporations that funded the National Association of Manufacturers "American Way" campaign in the late 1930s funded the Ad Council in the 1940s and 1950s. General Electric, General Foods, and the JWT donated funds and design services while they eagerly marketed their products to an increasingly affluent middle class. The same ad agencies that created public information campaigns through the Ad Council also supplied personnel to the USIA. Corporate advertising used the Cold War to sell products and used consumer products to sell the Cold War. And both relied on images of children and youth—usually embedded in white, middle-class families—to do so.

Advertising both reflects cultural values and normalizes particular behaviors, values, and images. Messages must be familiar enough to make sense to consumers even while they attempt to induce a certain mindset or encourage particular buying practices. For example, in the mid to late 1940s, televisions were introduced as a new technology, but, in order to make consumers comfortable with the notion of bringing them into their homes, television advertising appealed to traditional values—as a means of bringing the family together, much like the radio, or the hearth before that. Print ads embedded televisions in the middle-class home and family. DuMont promised that television owners would "get more out of life" by purchasing one of their sets. Magnavox televisions were a "gift for the whole family" at Christmas, providing "pleasure, pride and endless entertainment." Even the "severest critics"—children, of course—approved of their "Big Picture" 17-inch model, which contributed to family happiness. A 1950 Motorola ad offered parents the dubious promise of "better behavior at home and better marks in school" for children who watched television. TV would put an end to rainy day boredom and keep children out of mischief and out of mother's hair. Most ads depicted children and families gathered around the television set, emphasizing togetherness and whole-some entertainment. A few emphasized sports viewing, but none depicted a mother watching daytime television by herself. These advertisements targeted adults, but, by the early 1960s, marketers increasingly recognized the buying potential of a new, huge market—children and youth with their own disposable incomes.[58]

The postwar auto industry relied on similar strategies to sell new cars to a growing middle class. During the war, Ford ads attempted to maintain consumer demand with the promise, "There's a Ford in your future." In 1946–47, Ford promoted various features—style, safety, and efficiency—with their "Ford's out in Front!" campaign. Not until the early 1950s did ads tout fuel efficiency and quiet motors while depicting their cars embed-ded in family relationships and leisure activities. The 1951 campaign prom-ised that a Ford car would prepare young families for the years ahead; 1954 Ford station wagons promised, "there's always room for one more!"; and the 1956 ad campaign promised safety through new Lifeguard features. Like print and television ads, outdoor ads constructed a vision of post-war American abundance and consistently linked "the good life" to con-sumption within the white, middle-class family and to American political values like freedom of choice. In the 1950s, Ford's positive portrayals of an idealized (white) nuclear family enjoying their new automobile, larger homes, new consumer goods, and leisure time together replaced images of wartime scarcity and tapped the pent-up demand for consumer goods. In other words, commercial advertising reiterated many of the same mes-sages and visual tropes of the Ad Council's American Economic System and People's Capitalism campaigns. Both linked American political values with patriotic consumption.

Outdoor advertising, as a site of material culture, offers an underexam-ined way to explore how children and families functioned in Cold War ideology. Although it doesn't reveal the behavior, voices, or agency of children or families, advertising can show us something about generally agreed-upon notions of childhood and domesticity.[59] The outdoor adver-tising industry came into its own in the 1920s and 1930s, as automobile travel became more common. The Great Depression provided an early opportunity for the industry to shore up its reputation through public service advertising. In opposition to the New Deal, the National Association of Manufacturers (NAM) launched a massive public service campaign, "The American Way," from 1936 to 1938 that firmly linked the health of the free enterprise system with social welfare. Although photographers Margaret Bourke-White and Dorothea Lange famously satirized these billboards in critical photographs, corporate America argued that business, not government, provided financial security and ensured national economic health. The campaign, jointly sponsored by the US Chamber of Commerce and subsidized by the outdoor advertising industry with $1.2 million and $80,000 worth of free advertising, was meant to deflect public support for social welfare policies that had gained traction under FDR and the Democrats since 1933. Patriotic donations of advertising space during World War II further cemented the relationship between the NAM, the Outdoor Advertising Association of America (OAAA), and public service advertising. After the war's end, the shift from wartime propaganda to anticommunist, pro-business information campaigns was a seamless one as the NAM and OAAA returned to prewar messages and media.[60]

One of the oldest advertising agencies in the United States, the JWT, led the industry throughout the postwar decades. Agency records from the period reveal barely contained glee over the constantly increasing percentage of American households with unprecedented levels of disposable income and provide a window into how corporate advertisers approached the job of selling in the 1950s. Even before the end of the war, JWT Vice-President for Research Arno Johnson launched a crusade to convince Americans that patriotism demanded consumption. His 1951 speech, "Americans Must Learn to Live a Third Better," was typical of the decade and contained a message Johnson repeated in scores of trade publications and speeches from 1944 through the mid-1950s. As Johnson never tired of pointing out, Americans were four times better off in 1950 than they had been in 1940. In order to maintain their "way of life," Americans had to spend their new wealth on better living—defined by purchasing higher quality foods in larger quantities, more clothing, bigger homes, two cars, and an expanding array of consumer goods and luxury items. During the Korean War, Johnson argued that America's unmatched productive capacity could simultaneously meet the military needs of the nation while maintaining a constantly "advancing standard of living as a very effective counter-offensive against Communist propaganda."[61] America's ability to provide both guns and butter linked consumption with Cold War patriotism and seemingly proved American superiority to communism.

American children—the Baby Boom—were a key engine of this postwar consumerism. In 1946, more babies were born than in any previous year in US history—3.4 million—a 20% increase from 1945. In 1947, another 3.8 million babies were born; 3.9 million arrived in 1952; and more than 4 million were born every year from 1954 until 1964. The physical needs of these children—food, diapers, clothing, and furniture—combined with the unprecedented explosion of consumer goods meant for their entertainment produced staggering new consumer demands. Everything from Disney vacations and tourism, toys, breakfast cereal, toothpaste, televisions, appliances, cars, homes, and life insurance policies relied on images of and appeals to children and the ideals they represented: youthfulness, fun, pleasure, purity, and innocence. Advertisers soon grasped the potential of this young audience as an emerging market and began to directly target children as consumers in the mid-1950s.[62] By the end of the decade, phonographs, records, radios, magazines, clothing, and soft drinks found a receptive and increasingly affluent teen audience. But the Cold War supplied an additional rhetorical vocabulary that made American children and youth crucial signifiers of the nation: abundance, prosperity, security, the future. Corporate advertising in the postwar years routinely depicted white American children in the context of national abundance and prosperity, a clear sign of national superiority in the Cold War. Conversely, consider how humanitarian aid organizations such as CARE consistently depicted "foreign" children: in outdoor settings, barefoot, dirty, poorly clothed, hungry, always in need. In short, as the opposite of cared-for American children. Healthy, affluent children

served as a visual shorthand for the superiority of the American economic and political system.

Johnson and other business leaders were quick to link children to
national progress through consumption. Among Johnson's favorite statistics was the enormous increase in the number of American families and
children. In 1950, there were 45% more children under age 10 than there
had been in 1940, with "buying habits to form and with new and easily
moulded [sic] ideas of standards of living or goals of satisfactory achievement."[63] The mounting intensity of advertising targeting these children
reflects their growing economic and ideological importance. Between
1950 and 1964, advertisers used images of children in 11% of all ads in Look
and Life magazines.[64] In some cases, advertisers created a sense of fear
or insecurity that could be alleviated through the purchase of particular
products. Ford constantly linked family safety to their cars in outdoor and
print advertising, as did Atlas tires. Pan Am's 1955 ad, "It's nice to know
'Uncle Sam's' your skipper when you fly to faraway places" shows three
young, unaccompanied children boarding an international flight. The
children's parents are conspicuously absent, but the flight attendant and
pilot assist the children and stand in as their caretakers. Representatives of
Pan American airlines, backed by the security of the federal government
(Uncle Sam), guarantee the children's safety. The ad reassures nervous
passengers, especially parents, with the backing of US safety standards.
These advertisements linked personal and domestic security to Cold War
military policies by manipulating the desires of parents and adults to protect children, touting the government's ability to provide security for its
citizens, encouraging leisure and consumer spending, and reminding all
Americans of their responsibilities to serve as ambassadors abroad.

Travels ads often linked consumption to the priorities of Cold War
cultural diplomacy. Pan American's 1957 newspaper ad, "A tourist dollar
spent abroad is the world's busiest dollar" targeted the 1 million Americans
who were expected to fly across the Atlantic to see "the Old World" that
year. According to Pan Am, American tourist dollars would not only create memories of the "trip of a lifetime," but they would simultaneously
bolster foreign economies, decrease taxes for mutual aid, and return value

through "foreign purchases of US machinery, farm products, chemicals . . . and thousands of other US exports . . . keeping American payrolls big, and growing bigger all the time." Pan Am encouraged Americans to be "ambassadors at ease" while enjoying a two-week vacation and "making a valuable contribution to American industry and foreign economies."[65] As Pan Am passengers boarded their overseas flights, they received a passport-sized booklet titled "Make a Friend This Trip," encouraging American tourists to represent the nation "in the fundamental spirit and message of the People-to-People program." People-to-People produced millions of these booklets and made them available at "every port of debarkation" from the United States. Travel agents included copies in envelopes of traveler's checks.[66] Not to be outdone, competitor Transworld Airlines (TWA) created special Goodwill Ambassador Tours in cooperation with the People-to-People program. Travelers could choose from a number of prearranged tours that focused on education, art, religion, and agriculture and that were designed to "enable American travelers to meet and understand their counterparts overseas."[67] Corporate America sold their products by selling the Cold War.

Both propaganda for foreign consumption and domestic advertising consistently associated political democracy with the freedom to spend and the freedom to choose among a wide variety of consumer goods.[68] In 1953, Ford Motor Company's anniversary book *Ford at Fifty* foreshadowed the arguments made in the People's Capitalism campaign: class lines in the United States diminished as the middle class expanded. A high standard of living provided "the good life" for American children, who enjoyed greater material comfort than their Soviet or Third World counterparts. In a section titled "In America Workers Own the Cars," Ford told the story of a communist Minister of Production who, while showing a visiting American engineer through a plant, proudly told him that the factory was worker-owned. But the American engineer noted that the plant manager and the secret police owned the only two cars in the parking lot. When that same minister came to the United States to visit Ford's plant, he observed with disdain that Ford owned the factory and reaped all the profits. But when he saw the parking lot filled with thousands of cars, he asked incredulously, "But who owns all these cars?" "The workers own them," the American engineer explained. This anecdote, and six photographs of smiling factory workers and the River Rouge parking lot crowded with employee-owned vehicles, spoke "louder than words about the prosperity of the worker in private industry."[69]

The same could be said for the 1959 USIA-sponsored American National Exhibition at Sokolniki Park in Moscow. There, in the kitchen of a model ranch home, Vice President Nixon and Soviet Premier Khrushchev sparred over the benefits of capitalism versus communism. Nixon argued that the household appliances, televisions, and gadgets surrounding the two men demonstrated the superiority of the American system. The widespread availability of household machines freed ordinary American women from domestic drudgery and allowed them time for leisure and family; conversely, Soviet women were "free" to labor in factories while their children spent long days in childcare facilities. The USIA "People's Capitalism" exhibit (foreign propaganda), the Ad Council's "The American Economic System" (domestic information campaign), and *Ford at Fifty* (consumer advertising) worked in concert to advance the same arguments at home and abroad: the United States had achieved a classless society through widespread access to consumer products, and American children were the main beneficiaries of this high standard of living. As these many examples demonstrate, the federal government and corporate America promoted consumerism as one of the main benefits of the democratic capitalist system. Spending money was the equivalent of good citizenship.

JWT and the Ad Council worked tirelessly to convince Americans that they were living in a historic era of unprecedented economic growth and wealth. Arno Johnson's, "Memo to Americans: New Age of Promise Ahead" begins, "Since you began reading this article, a baby has been born." The single fact of population growth, he argued, meant that every facet of American business had to expand to keep up: from suburban growth, to school and home construction, to an increase in leisure and travel. Americans bought more newspapers and magazines, owned more radios, took more paid vacations, and attended more concerts than at any time in the nation's history. Furthermore, the atomic age promised to run America's trains, factories, and mines. But, he warned, "we need to press our advantage, for we cannot afford to lose it. The responsibility lies on our shoulders."[70] Patriotic citizenship required constant and increasing consumer spending to maintain economic advantage over the Soviet Union and to prove America's economic superiority to the world.

In this context of patriotic consumption, postwar American children became "icons of modern consumerism." Soft drink giants Coke and Pepsi were known for associating their products with youthfulness and fun, while health, medicine, and food were "among the first brand goods to become associated with the notion of children's 'natural' innocence."[71] Soap advertisements, for example, equated cleanliness with the innocence of children and proscribed cleanliness as part of conscientious modern parenting. Both print and outdoor advertisements offered consumerist solutions to solve the "problems" of domestic life. Ford's postwar ads suggested that their cars could ease generational tensions over the appearance, speed, and economy of the family automobile. Junior liked the speed and good looks of Ford cars, while parents appreciated their fuel economy and safety features; a Ford car had both. Likewise, both mothers and children could agree on Sunbeam bread: it was nutritious and it tasted great. Young and old, business traveler and tourist, all could enjoy a trip on Pan Am Airlines. If postwar domesticity came with its own problems, advertisers pointed out how their products could solve them.

When JWT acquired the Ford Motor Company account in 1944, they primed pent-up consumer demand with the wartime ad campaign, "There's a Ford in your future." Ford aggressively promoted the idea of the two-car family throughout the 1950s, a decade that began with 59% of American families owning one car. By the mid-1950s, automobiles surpassed packaged goods and cigarettes as the most heavily advertised consumer products.[72] In a 1956 article published in *Fortune, Western Advertising, Sales Management, Printers' Ink,* and other industry magazines, JWT praised the forward-looking executives at Ford who had created and promoted the idea of the "two-car family" to millions of Americans who hadn't yet realized that they could afford two cars. In the midst of the Baby Boom, Ford encouraged family-based consumption with the 1956 ad, "4 bedrooms, 3 baths . . . 2 Fords." Another, "Stranded in Suburbia," hinted at gender trouble. When father left for work each morning, mother was stranded all day, a virtual prisoner in her own home. "In that left-behind feeling," Ford created "a billion-dollar opportunity." JWT encouraged its account holders to follow Ford's example of creative and aggressive marketing strategies to "cut down on the time it would normally take these people to raise their living standards to the level they can now afford."[73] While the Baby Boom provided a ready strategy for marketers to inscribe their products with youthful characteristics, the Cold War context supplied a national imperative to consume.

Focusing on one consumer product, billboard ads for humble packaged bread, sheds light on advertising strategies that relied heavily on appeals to children and domesticity and reinforced Cold War cultural values such as personal and national strength, youthful innocence, purity, maternalism, and patriotism. The 1949–1950 ad campaign for Mrs. Baird's bread paired the slogan "Part of the family!" with images of children holding cuddly pets to make young mothers with growing families feel more comfortable about buying rather than baking their own bread. Another ad shows a young woman holding a loaf of homemade bread next to a package of Mrs. Baird's bread with the line, "Like you would bake it!" By 1963, text was superfluous; Baird's ads simply pictured a happy baby in a shopping cart with a loaf of bread or a freckle-faced boy in an oversized cowboy hat happily munching on a slice of bread. Butternut Bread used humor to acknowledge the Baby Boom and the importance of domestic and family life, as in the ad "2 O'Clock Feeding," showing a haggard father eating a sandwich while bottle-feeding a baby. Another features a teenage boy doing push-ups under the slogan "For that *extra* push . . . ," calling to mind Eisenhower's Presidential Council on Youth Fitness, a nationwide program developed to address concerns about the physical fitness of America's children relative to their European counterparts. Wonder Bread promised to "build health 12 ways!" Sunbeam Bread's overtly religious advertising paired the Biblical quote "Not By Bread Alone," with images of a rosy-cheeked, curly-haired blond girl kneeling in prayer, emphasizing America's Christian heritage in contrast to godless communism. Another ad, "Be Prepared With Sunbeam Energy," showed the same fresh-faced

young girl giving the Girl Scout salute. Both ads signify Cold War patriotism with calls to God and country, preparedness, and national security. All
of these ads appealed to mothers with promises of children's healthy and
strong bodies fortifying the domestic sphere as a site of faith and patriotism. Images of children reminded parents of the importance of physical
health, not just for children, but for a strong nation.

CONCLUSION

The close ties between America's ad industry, domestic public information
campaigns, and the federal government's propaganda agencies ensured
that the same professionals, messages, and visual imagery that promoted
patriotic consumerism to domestic audiences also sold idealized images
of the United States to foreign ones. The distinction between domestic
advertising and foreign propaganda during the Cold War was often a fine
one as both routinely used images of children to represent the nation to
Americans and to potential allies around the world. In the hands of government propagandists and corporate advertisers, children simultaneously
functioned as symbols of the happiness and security that could be achieved
through a commitment to democratic capitalism and as symbols illustrat-
ing the nation's vulnerability to the spread of Soviet communism. Youthful
innocence and purity represented American claims of truthfulness and
peace, national innocence, and the good life. But children functioned as
more than just symbols during the Cold War. Indeed, children were mobilized to wage the Cold War as workers, citizens, and consumers; in essay
contests and patriotic pageants; as fundraisers for RFE and as signers of
Freedom Scrolls; and, as we'll see in the following chapter, in their schools.

NOTES

1. Peacock, *Innocent Weapons*, 19.
2. Harry S. Truman, Speech delivered to a Joint Session of Congress (March 12, 1947);
    Life 25.8 (August 23, 1948): 42–43.

3. "Airlift's Camel," *Life* (November 8, 1948): 53. Since 9/11 there has been renewed interest in this quintessential story of American goodwill. See Michael Tunnel, *Candy Bomber: The Story of the Berlin Airlift's "Chocolate Pilot"* (Watertown MA: Charlesbridge, 2010); Andrei Cherny, *The Candy Bombers: The Untold Story of the Berlin Airlift and America's Finest Hour* (New York: Putnam: 2008); Margot Theis Raven, *Mercedes and the Chocolate Pilot: A True Story of the Berlin Airlift and the Candy that Dropped from the Sky* (Ann Arbor, MI: Sleeping Bear Press, 2002). For classroom materials focusing on US foreign aid, see "Audio-Visual Aids," *The Modern Language Journal* 36.8 (December 1952): 407–408.

4. "World Youth Festival," *Columbia Daily Spectator*, LXIX.100 (May 13, 1947): 2.

5. "Red Issue Splits Youth Delegates: Minority Charges Communists Dominated Prague Festival," *New York Times* (October 7, 1947): 5; Joel Kotëk, "Youth Organizations as a Battlefield in the Cold War," *Intelligence & National Security* 18.2 (Summer 2003): 168–191; Margaret Peacock, "The Perils of Building Cold War Consensus at the 1957 Moscow World Festival of Youth and Students," *Cold War History* 12.3 (August 2012): 515–535.

6. Barbara Ward, "The Crucial Battle for the World's Youth: The West Must Surpass the Totalitarian Drive to Capture the Minds of the New Generation," *The New York Times* (November 18, 1951): SM7; "Youth from 102 Lands Swarms Over Moscow," *Life* (August 12, 1957): 22–27.

7. Launched on February 1, 1942, with a broadcast to Germany, the Voice of America's (VOA) first broadcast began with The Battle Hymn of the Republic, followed by the announcement, "Today, and every day from now on, we will be with you from America to talk about the war. . . . The news may be good or bad for us—We will always tell you the truth." The VOA began broadcasting to the Soviet Union in 1947, in an attempt to counter Soviet propaganda. See *The Voice of America and the Domestic Propaganda Battles*.

8. Becky Little, "Digging Up Ads from World War II—When They Pushed Products No One Could Buy," *National Geographic* (December 6, 2014). Available at http://news.nationalgeographic.com/news/2014/12/141207-world-war-advertising-consumption-anniversary-people-photography-culture/. Accessed May 5, 2017.

9. Osgood, *Total Cold War*, 28–32.

10. The increasing reliance on advertising techniques and professional admen created conflict in the OWI during World War II. See Sydney Weinberg, "What to Tell America: The Writer's Quarrel in the Office of War Information," *The Journal of American History* 55.1 (June 1968): 81–86.

11. Peacock, *Innocent Weapons*, 22.

12. Lizabeth Cohen, *A Consumer's Republic: The Politics of Mass Consumption in Postwar America* (Vintage: 2003): 124–129.

13. Inger L. Stole, *Advertising at War* (Baltimore: University of Illinois Press, 2012): 156.

14. Robert Griffith, "The Selling of America: The Advertising Council and American Politics, 1942–1960," *The Business History Review* 57.3 (Autumn 1983): 391, 389.

15. Hixson, *Parting the Curtain*, 14–16.

16. Glassford, "Voluntold."

17. Charles Mortimer speech to ANA conference (October 27, 1948): 2. Ad Council Collection, Hartman Center for Sales, Advertising, and Marketing History, Rubenstein Library, Duke University (hereafter Hartman Center).

18. Quoted in Griffith, "The Selling of America," 395.

19. "Ad Council Reports Improvement in Attitude on Economic Education," *New York Times* (February 10, 1952): 127. Charles Wilson was the President of General Electric from 1940 to 1942 and from 1945 to 1950, where he led an anti-union campaign. He had served on the War Production Board during World War II and became President of the People-to-People Foundation in 1956.

20. Ad Council Chairman Charles G. Mortimer speech to ANA conference (October 27, 1948): 7, Box 16: Campaigns; Folder: American Economic System 1948–51; Advertising Council Collection, Hartman Center.

21. Charles Mortimer, speech to ANA conference (October 27, 1948): 5, Hartman Center.

22. Stole, *Advertising at War*, 168.

23. The American Economic System: A Campaign of The Advertising Council, September 1952, Box 16, Folder: Campaigns: American Economic System 1952–53, Hartman Center.

24. This ad was planned for release in November 1948. Ad Council, *A Campaign to Explain the American Economic System*, Press Kit (September 1948): 10. Box 16, Folder: Campaigns: American Economic System 1952–53, Hartman Center.

25. This ad was planned for release in February 1949. Ad Council, *A Campaign to Explain the American Economic System*, Press Kit (September 1948): 13. Ad Council Collection, Box 16: Campaigns, Folder: American Economic System 1948–51. Hartman Center.

26. This ad was planned for release in May 1949. Ad Council, *A Campaign to Explain the American Economic System*, Press Kit (September 1948): 16. Ad Council Collection, Box 16: Campaigns, Folder: American Economic System 1948–51. Hartman Center.

27. Stole, *Advertising at War*, 170.

28. Griffith, "The Selling of America," 388.

29. Not to be confused with the conservative think-tank founded in 1973, the American Heritage Foundation was founded on May 22, 1947, as a "non-partisan citizen's campaign" to inaugurate the Freedom Train.

30. The American Heritage Foundation, *Good Citizen* (1947), Box 16, Folder: American Heritage, 1947–52, Ad Council Collection, Hartman Center.

31. According to the 1952 award announcement, the Freedoms Foundation was founded in 1949 as a "non-profit, non-sectarian, and non-political" organization to "create and build an understanding of the spirit and philosophy of the Constitution and Bill of Rights" and to "inspire love of freedom and to support the spiritual unity born of the belief that man is a dignified human being, created in the image of his Maker."

32. Robert Stiehl, "What America Means to Me," RG 306.5.3 Records of the Press and Publications Service, Feature Packets with Recurring Subjects, 1953–59; Container 1, Folder 6: USIS Special Youth Packet (September 1953): 1–3; NARA.

33. Note to PAO, USIA Youth Packet (March 1954); RG 306.5.3 Records of the Press and Publications Service, Feature Packets with Recurring Subjects, 1953–59; Container 2, Folder 12, USIA, NARA.

34. Belmonte, *Selling the American Way*, 138, 144.

35. Peacock, *Innocent Weapons*, 43–47, 52–57.

36. President Dwight D. Eisenhower, "The Crusade for Freedom: Truth Our Most Formidable Weapon," *Vital Speeches of the Day* 16.24 (October 1, 1950): 746; Richard H. Cummings, *Radio Free Europe's "Crusade for Freedom": Rallying Americans Behind Cold War Broadcasting, 1950–1960* (Jefferson NC: McFarland & Co. Inc., 2010): 217–218.

37. Belmonte, *Selling the American Way*, 42. The Office of Strategic Services was a World War II intelligence service and forerunner of the CIA charged with conducting espionage and propaganda activities abroad.

38. A. Ross Johnson, *Radio Free Europe and Radio Liberty: The CIA Years and Beyond* (Washington, DC: Woodrow Wilson Center Press, 2010): 11–15, 228–240. Johnson does a particularly good job of teasing out the complex public–private nature of Cold War radio.

39. Hixson, *Parting the Curtain*, 61.

40. Quoted in Friederike Kind-Kovács, "Voices, Letters, and Literature Through the Iron Curtain: Exiles and the (Trans)mission of Radio in the Cold War," *Cold War History* 13.2 (May 2013): 210.

41. "Crusade for Freedom," *New York Times* (January 24, 1955): 22.

42. Cummings, https://coldwarradios.blogspot.com/2010/11/rallying-rfe-1959-truth-broadcast.html

43. "Freedom Crusade Finds Utahns Strong in Backing," *Kane County Standard* (September 15, 1950): 1; "Jaycee Women to Spur S. L. Freedom Crusade," *Salt Lake Telegram* (September 15, 1950): 19; "Schools Sign Up for Freedom," *Salt Lake Telegram* (September 29, 1950): 20; "Over 50,000 Utahns Sign Names to Freedom List," *Salt Lake Telegram* (October 11, 1950): 22; "Freedom Rings: Berliners Cheer the Big Truth as West Gives Them a Big Bell," *LIFE* (November 6, 1950): 47–48, 50.

44. "Jaycee Women to Spur S. L. Freedom Crusade," *Salt Lake Telegram* (September 15, 1950): 19.

45. "Schools Sign Up for Freedom," *Salt Lake Telegram* (September 29, 1950): 20; "Over 50,000 Utahns Sign Names to Freedom List," *Salt Lake Telegram* (October 11, 1950): 22.

46. "Freedom Rings: Berliners Cheer the Big Truth as West Gives Them a Big Bell," *Life* (November 6, 1950): 47–48, 50.

47. "Fundraising Takes to Air," *Life* (February 22, 1954): 37.

48. "Scouts Aiding in 1951 Crusade for Freedom Campaign," *New York Times* (August 27, 1951): 4.

49. Cummings, *Radio Free Europe's "Crusade for Freedom,"* 147, 189.

50. Preston King Sheldon, "Catholics to Join in Day of Prayer," *New York Times* (December 29, 1951): 12; Cummings, *Radio Free Europe's "Crusade for Freedom,"* 133, 141–142, 59.

51. Christopher Simpson, *Blowback: The First Full Account of America's Recruitment of Nazis and Its Disastrous Effect on Our Domestic and Foreign Policy* (New York: Macmillan, 1989): 228.

52. Cummings, *Radio Free Europe's "Crusade for Freedom,"* 17, 164, 182. Apparently, Nikita Khrushchev never threatened, "Your children will grow up under communism," but the quote has been repeated since the 1950s as a direct quote. It originated with Eisenhower's Secretary of Agriculture, Ezra Taft Benson, who said that, in a conversation with Khrushchev, the Soviet leader implied that Benson's children would grow up as communists.

53. Belmonte, *Selling the American Way*, 69, 58.

54. Griffith, "The Selling of America," 405; Belmonte, *Selling the American Way*, 131–135.

55. *Historical Statistics of the United States—Colonial Times to 1957*, Bureau of the Census, Washington, DC. This number, one-third of US households, had been mentioned by President Franklin D. Roosevelt in 1932 and by sociologist Michael P. Harrington in *The Other America* (New York: Simon and Schuster, 1962).

56. Andrew Yarrow, "Selling a New Vision of America to the World: Changing Messages in Early U.S. Cold War Print Propaganda," *Journal of Cold War Studies* 11.4 (Fall 2009): 6–7, 11, 13.

57. http://adage.com/article/adage-encyclopedia/history-1950s/98701/

58. Duke University's Hartman Center for Sales, Advertising, and Marketing History digitized thousands of print advertisements from the first half of the twentieth century. See http://library.duke.edu/digitalcollections/adaccess_TV0213/; http://library.duke.edu/digitalcollections/adaccess_TV0677/; http://library.duke.edu/digitalcollections/adaccess_TV0169/

59. Karen Danna Lynch, "Advertising Motherhood: Image, Ideology, and Consumption," *Berkeley Journal of Sociology* 49, Society & Consumption (2005): 32–34.

60. Catherine Gudis, *Buyways: Billboards, Automobiles, and the American Landscape* (New York: Routledge, 2004): 207–210; Joel Spring, *Educating the Consumer-Citizen: A History of the Marriage of Schools, Advertising, and Media* (Mahwah, NJ: Lawrence Erlbaum Associates, Publishers): 126–128.

61. Arno Johnson, "Americans Must Learn to Live a Third Better," Address before the Newspaper Advertising Executives Association (January 22, 1951), J. Walter Thompson Company Archives, Writings and Speeches, 1918–2000, Box 16, Folder: Johnson, Arno, 1950–51, Talks and articles, #1–7, Hartman Center.

62. Alison Alexander et al., "'We'll Be Back in a Moment': A Content Analysis of Advertisements in Children's Television in the 1950s," *Journal of Advertising* 27.3 (Autumn 1998): 1–3.

63. Arno Johnson, "An Analysis of Post-War Advertising and Marketing," Address before the Advertising Club of Washington, DC (October 17, 1944): 14.

64. Peacock, *Innocent Weapons*, 28–34.

65. Pan American advertisement, Box 19, Folder: Pan American, 1953–57, Elton papers, Hartman Center.

66. *People-to-People News* (June 1957): 1, Cochran Lambie papers, DDE Library.

67. TWA pamphlet, Bortman papers, Box 3, File: Dept. of State Course on Ideological Conflict (1), DDE Library.

68. Cohen, *A Consumer's Republic*, 124–129; May, *Homeward Bound*, 153–156, 172.

69. *Ford at Fifty, 1903–1953* (New York: Simon and Schuster, 1953): 92–93.

70. Arno Johnson, "Memo to Americans: New Age of Promise Ahead," *Family Weekly Magazine* (August 29, 1954).

71. Stephen Kline, *Out of the Garden: Toys, TV, and Children's Culture in the Age of Marketing* (Brooklyn, New York: Verso, 1993): 54.

72. "History: 1950s," AdAge (September 15, 2003). Available at http://adage.com/article/adage-encyclopedia/history-1950s/98701/. Accessed July 17, 2017.

73. "Stranded in Suburbia," Insert, *JWT Co. News* (April 16, 1956), Elton papers, Box 11956, Hartman Center.

5

The Cold War in the Schools

Educating a Generation for World Understanding

Let's follow 14-year-old Nancy Denton through a typical day in the Philadelphia suburb where she lives in 1955. As she dressed for school and ate breakfast, she might hear President Eisenhower on the radio, appealing to Americans to participate in the nation's "vigorous information program [to] keep the peoples of the world truthfully advised of our actions and purposes."[1] On her walk to school, perhaps a public bus drove by with a "Crusade for Freedom" ad banner, urging her to donate three pennies to buy a brick for a new Radio Free Europe studio in West Germany. When she arrived at school, Nancy's teacher may have asked the class to bring used books to school the following day to donate to the needy students at their Chinese "sister school." In history class, she likely studied the democratic ideals of the Founding Fathers and their commitment to democracy and freedom. During gym class, Nancy ran a mile to satisfy the new President's Council on Physical Fitness requirements, to strengthen her body in the name of national security. Art class brought the opportunity to paint a picture of a typical Saturday that would be exchanged with a girl in France. Halfway through math class, the air raid drill sounded, and Nancy and her classmates ducked under their desks and covered their heads until their teacher gave them the all-clear signal. Nancy and her peers studied atomic energy and its potential uses for peace in science class. An afternoon assembly brought the exciting announcement that the Lone Ranger was coming to visit her school to tell the students about his Peace Patrol and ask them to purchase Savings Stamps. Finally, at her Girl Scout troop meeting that evening, Nancy wrote a letter to her Australian pen pal describing her troop's summer camp plans. Perhaps this fictionalized account is far-fetched, compressing into one day activities that American students may have experienced over months or even years. But it is true that each of these activities took place in America's public schools, and, in all of these ways, public schools mobilized American children to fight the Cold War.

THE PROBLEM WITH "DUCK AND COVER"

Whether conceptualized as little Cold Warriors or potential victims of nuclear war, future atomic scientists or United Nations ambassadors, children like Nancy were at the center of the Cold War. Children were called to help contain communism, defend the home front, and befriend children in unaligned nations. Citizenship training was not unique to the Cold War, but it certainly intensified in the two decades after World War II as the threat of communism led parents and politicians alike to question how effectively America's public schools instilled patriotism and a firm appreciation for the nation's political and economic systems. Since the 1830s, educational reformers like Horace Mann and John Dewey had advocated for a system of free public schools that would teach not only basic literacy and arithmetic, but would instill a common political and social philosophy of sound democratic principles. Some advocates suggested that democratic schools would prevent political instability by teaching English and Americanizing the children of immigrants. While learning the three R's, children would become productive democratic citizens. Given the ideological challenge of communism, public schools were charged with teaching "mental hygiene," social skills, civil defense, and more rigorous science and math training to compete with the Soviet Union, all while the school population boomed. At the same time, the public schools became targets for conservative activists who launched attacks against the progressive educational theories that had held sway since the 1930s.[2] Liberal educational theories were "soft" and failed to provide the discipline and moral toughness American children would need to preserve American democracy.

The Cold War experiences of schoolchildren are often summed up by quick references to "duck and cover" and Bert the Turtle. But from the late 1940s through the 1960s, parents and politicians looked upon schools as crucial training grounds for preparing children to live in an uncertain and complicated world. Reading, writing, and arithmetic were no longer adequate preparation. Amidst fears of global Soviet competition, teachers were expected to go well beyond the three Rs and to instruct children in particular interpretations of American history and heritage, democracy, government, economics, and "world understanding." Whether through academic or extracurricular activities, schools provided the most direct way to instill in American youth the fundamentals of patriotic citizenship. Beyond classroom instruction, schools became recruiting grounds for both government and private organizations that looked to the public schools as convenient locations to reach their target audience—children—for a variety of programs. American schools "adopted" foreign schools, sending books, photos, and scrapbooks to "explain" American life. Students collected used books to donate to foreign schools or raised money to buy an American Bookshelf through CARE. They raised funds for Radio Free Europe and signed Freedom Scrolls. They corresponded with pen pals arranged through the International Friendship League, Youth of All Nations, or one of the dozens of pen pal organizations that formed in the postwar years. The US Treasury, the US Air Force, and the Ad Council reached into the schools to mobilize American youth for federal and military programs. The US Information Agency (USIA) highlighted the accomplishments of American schoolchildren in monthly bulletins for distribution to foreign posts and newspapers. As the main point of contact with young people, schools organized American youth into cultural ambassadors, international representatives, miniature diplomats, fundraisers, pen pals, and charity workers.

Simplifying Cold War children's history to "duck and cover" is problematic because it reduces the experiences of millions of children to victims while positioning them as needing government protection. As the most vulnerable of civilians in a new kind of warfare that prioritized the home front, children were the nation's most valuable resource, as well as the reason for fighting. Both women and children were called into service in new ways, as domestic skills suddenly became crucial to national security needs. However, an analysis of civil defense literature makes it clear that the state was unable to fulfill its promises of protection from nuclear annihilation. As national borders became meaningless and domestic life was increasingly militarized, the national government shifted that responsibility to its citizens, young and old, male and female, rural and urban. Citizens were called upon to protect themselves with gas masks, fallout shelters, well-stocked pantries, and "duck-and-cover" drills. The government's continued atomic testing and inability to safeguard its citizens provoked a variety of organizations, particularly women's peace groups such as the National Committee for a Sane Nuclear Policy (SANE), Women's International League for Peace and Freedom (WILPF), and later, Women Strike for Peace (WSP), to create counternarratives. Rather than normalizing domestic warfare and a national culture of fear, opponents of the federal government's civil preparedness movement resisted defense drills and promoted nuclear disarmament and global cooperation instead.

CIVIL DEFENSE IN THE SCHOOLS

The *sine qua non* of Cold War childhood, school-based civil defense programs, have long served as convenient shorthand to describe the general experiences of American youth in the 1950s. Duck-and-cover drills loom large in personal memories—and for good reason. Nuclear attack scenarios typically depicted young people at school, and schools, therefore, had to be prepared. By the early 1950s, most parents, teachers, and administrators accepted civil defense as a necessary component of public education; state and local school districts, and the federal government, responded with an avalanche of information for students and teachers.[3] The best-known example of such efforts is *Duck and Cover*, distributed as a record album, radio program, pamphlet, and, most famously, as an animated film starring Bert the Turtle. Produced for the Federal Civil Defense Administration (FCDA) in 1951, *Duck and Cover* taught the nation's youth how to respond in the event of a nuclear attack by the Soviet Union, which successfully detonated its first atomic bomb in 1949. Officially released as a film in 1952, *Duck and Cover* traveled the nation for nine months as part of an FCDA-sponsored traveling show called "Alert America" (organized and run by many of the organizers of the 1947–49 Freedom Train). Beginning in March, with the endorsement of the National Education Association (NEA), schools across the United States screened the 10-minute film in which the animated main character, Bert the Turtle, cheerfully instructed students in the most up-to-date survival strategies for a nuclear attack. At the first warning of attack, "Like Bert, you duck to avoid the things flying through the air . . . and cover to keep from getting cut or even badly burned."[4]

In the late 1940s and early 1950s, the federal government operated under the assumption that the nation's largest cities would be the primary targets of a Soviet attack. In response, schools in New York, Los Angeles, Chicago, Detroit, Milwaukee, Fort Worth, San Francisco, and Philadelphia instituted regular air raid drills during the 1950–51 academic year. By the end of 1952, 88% of all American primary and secondary schools had implemented civil defense programs.[5] Hoping to alert the public enough to take the drills seriously, but not enough to incite panic, the FCDA distributed short films, radio programs, news articles, posters, and pamphlets to promote readiness in the face of atomic war. Teachers and administrators struggled to walk this fine line between fear and confidence in civil defense programs, following the FCDA's dictum to "alert, not alarm." Records from meetings of Milwaukee's Superintendent of Archdiocesan Schools reveal that, in some cases, excessive emphasis on the horrors of the atomic and hydrogen bombs terrified children, leaving them "with morbid fears" and unable to sleep.[6] Increasingly, teachers relied on information produced and distributed by the federal government, such as *Self-Preservation in an Atomic Attack* (1950), *Survival Under Atomic Attack* (1951), and *About Fallout* (1955), which relied on footage from the wreckage of Hiroshima and Nagasaki and on knowledge learned from survivors of those attacks to provide advice to Americans. Private companies such as Encyclopedia Britannica Films, the largest producer and distributor of educational films of the era, produced *Atomic Alert* (1951) for school use, as well as an educational series explaining the productive uses of the atom. The Civil Defense Education Project, the educational branch of the FCDA, directly propagandized children through lesson plans and films, hoping to indirectly influence their parents.[7] Through all of these means, civil defense programs institutionalized close links between the public schools and the national security state during the Cold War, but they also shifted responsibility for national defense from the federal government to the states, local public school districts, and individuals.

Duck-and-cover drills may have been among the most universal experiences of Cold War students, but they were not the only ones. Prioritizing "duck and cover" reifies children as victims and wards of the state and downplays the far more proactive activities of children in civil defense. A 1955 handbook distributed by the Michigan Department of Public Instruction noted, "With the use of nuclear weapons, long distance aircraft, and guided missiles for delivering highly destructive weapons of war, the civilian population now finds itself in the front line of defense. Civilians are no longer non-combatants."[8] If the domestic front was the new battlefront, all Americans, young and old, were expected to defend it. Teachers conducted lessons on atomic power and provided information about possible nuclear attacks, plans for evacuation and safety, and practice drills. Older students took on leadership roles in school civil defense efforts. In early 1951, Milwaukee's Bay View High School student newspaper, the *Oracle*, warned students that the federal government listed Milwaukee as among the "first six probable targets for enemy air attacks." In response, students prepared and posted signs designating shelter areas and displayed floor plans of the school in each classroom, "showing just where the students in that particular room should go in case of a raid." Students regularly practiced proper safety and evacuation procedures in case of an actual attack. Five years later, another article in the school paper encouraged students to continue to practice air raid drills, educate themselves in the school library, and join the first aid and civil defense crews; boys had the additional opportunity of serving as air raid wardens.[9] A student in another Milwaukee school newspaper asked, "Danger—Are We Prepared?" The writer warned, "Today, the threat of a sudden, devastating world war is constantly hanging over our heads, and we must prepare now for a surprise attack by air."[10] As these examples show, students actively participated in civil defense drills and preparations and urged their peers to do the same. Some were clearly aware of the national security situation and took steps to ensure their own safety and that of others.

As in many other Cold War activities, the Boy Scouts were in the forefront of civil defense. In November 1950, more than 18,000 Boy Scouts in Milwaukee County put themselves at the disposal of Mayor Frank Zeidler. The Scouts offered to serve as emergency messengers, assist rescue units and ambulance services, operate camps for evacuees, assist the Red Cross, and serve in any other necessary capacity. In early 1951, all Milwaukee packs, troops, and posts received instruction in disaster first aid.[11] These were not isolated events. Boy Scouts across the nation participated in civil defense training programs throughout the 1950s and worked with the federal government to distribute information to the public, including the 1958 booklet, *Handbook for Emergencies*.[12] But if the Boy Scouts embraced new Cold War responsibilities, they also saw the possibilities for world friendship. In a foreword to a story in the March 1957 issue of *Boys' Life*, Arthur Schuck wrote, "We must meet this threat [of communism] by increasing the bonds of world friendship among Scouts everywhere. Understanding and the unhampered exchange of ideas strengthens the free world and combats ignorance that breeds communism."[13]

Of course, not all Americans embraced civil defense. Progressives who rallied around Henry Wallace in 1948 made peace and nuclear disarmament cornerstones of their campaign. Pacifists, Quakers, and peace activists garnered headlines by picketing during the federal government's "Operation Alert," a mandatory, nationwide civil defense exercise held annually between 1955 and 1961. Among them was Dorothy Day, the publisher of *The Catholic Worker*, who was arrested every year from 1955 to 1958. Arguing that "peace is the only defense against nuclear war," protesters refused to take cover during the 10-minute drill and were arrested.[14] Many progressive women used the language of maternalism to justify their political engagement, arguing that the best way to protect children from the threat of nuclear annihilation was for nations to work cooperatively toward world peace and through public, not military, control of atomic energy.[15] The peace networks established after World War I, such as WILPF and SANE, laid the groundwork for the emergence of Women Strike for Peace in 1961, an organization that relied on the language of traditional motherhood to wage radical political protests against war and nuclear testing.[16] Young people, too, dissented. As the memoirs of "red diaper" babies attest, many of these children of communist activists did not feel safe or secure in their public schools, particularly during the Rosenberg Trial in the spring of 1951.[17] Many feared their parents would be "found out" or arrested. In 1958, a Palo Alto High School senior named Joan Baez declared herself a "conscientious objector" and refused to evacuate her school during a civil defense drill. As the rest of her classmates took advantage of a half-day, Ms. Baez staged a one-woman sit-in, stating, "I don't see any sense in having an air raid drill. I don't think it's a method of defense. Our only defense is peace."[18]

Despite the actions of individual students and teachers, by and large, public schools reinforced the federal government's containment policy and promoted anticommunism. Some cities and school districts went beyond duck and cover to prepare for the worst. In May 1951, the Logan, Utah Rotarians, with the support of local doctors, instituted a blood-type tattoo program in the name of security and civil defense. The local paper announced, "This area's first civil defense measure, sponsored by the Cache Valley Medical

Association, will insure [*sic*] exact blood-type and Rh factor of all persons living in Cache and Rich counties. . . . Cost of the program will be $1 per person. This includes blood type, Rh factor, and a permanent imprint of blood type and factor in the skin under the left arm."[19] Lake County, Indiana carried out a similar program between spring 1951 and May 1952. Marcia Gaughan clearly remembered the terrifying experience. She and her classmates had their fingers pricked to determine blood type and were seated in "twenty little chairs in a line along the wall leading to an area behind a curtain." One by one, the children disappeared behind the curtain. Gaughan recalled waiting "about an hour, and during that time, as we inched closer and closer to the curtain, we had to witness each of our classmates enter the curtained area and come out crying. . . . Once behind the curtain I had to take off my clothes above the waist. One [person] held me still and the other stuck what looked like a power drill into my left side, turned it on and held it there for a minute or two. Naturally I was screaming and struggling just like the other kids before me."[20] By April 1952, New York City provided identification "dog tags" for all public school students up to the fourth grade; San Francisco and Seattle would eventually do the same.[21] By the spring of 1956, Milwaukee's Catholic and public schools instituted an identification bracelet program. For 50 cents, students received a bracelet identifying their name, address, next of kin, birth date, and religious preference.[22]

Civil defense in the public schools went far beyond "duck-and-cover" drills. Some scholars have argued that the United States of the 1950s could be described as a "garrison state" or a "militarised society" in which national security concerns penetrated all aspects of society, including schools and youth groups."[23] But world friendship and international understanding coexisted with containment as another prominent theme in American classrooms.

THE COLD WAR IN THE CLASSROOM

Because the state actively intervened in the lives of adolescents through the public schools, the crisis of the Cold War was also a crisis in education.[24]

Just as the US entry into World War II politicized daily school routines, "alter[ing] the rhymes [young people] repeated, the cartoons and movies they watched, and the songs they heard," classroom learning changed as a result of the global competition between the United States and the Soviet Union.[25] The Cold War brought long-simmering political debates about school curricula, textbooks, faculty instruction, and federal funding to a head in the 1950s.

In the immediate aftermath of the war, many in the educational establishment advocated curricula focused on promoting peace and cultivating "international understanding." In 1947, the NEA's Educational Policies Commission (EPC) published a report titled *Education for International Understanding*, a collaborative curriculum module created jointly by the nation's leading educators and diplomatic experts. A testament to the high level of support for the United Nations, particularly UNESCO, in the immediate aftermath of the war, educators aimed to teach students to become "world-minded Americans."[26]

Citizenship education came to the fore of history, government, and civics classes; many educators considered global awareness and functional geography crucial to world peace. A 1952 science curriculum developed for New York secondary schools, *Living with the Atom*, provided teaching units on atomic energy and suggestions for integrating its study into a variety of classes, such as Citizenship Education (create a Who's Who booklet of leading nuclear physicists), Math (calculate the number of neutrons released in the first 25 chain reactions of an atomic explosion), and English (conduct a debate on the topic, "Should Atomic Energy Production Be Controlled by an International Body?"). Private organizations created similar lesson plans. For the 1954–55 school year, the *Minneapolis Star* published "A Guide to World Affairs" for junior and senior high schools, as well as community and church discussion groups. Intended to "develop citizens who understand the principles of wholesome democratic government and who are active participants in public affairs," the program offered 26 articles published weekly for classroom discussion, 26 tests based on the articles, additional pamphlets, and a subscription to *The World Affairs*

Teacher, a periodical for social studies teachers that focused on teaching methods.[27]

As Andrew Hartman and other historians have argued, the USSR's launch of Sputnik in 1957 was not the beginning, but rather the culmination of a long struggle over public school curriculum. The Soviet Union's successful detonation of an atomic bomb in 1949; communist expansion in Czechoslovakia, Berlin, and China; and the Alger Hiss and Klaus Fuchs espionage cases prompted conservatives and anticommunists to attack progressive educational ideas and practices that had dominated American education for decades. Since the 1930s, conservatives had targeted the schools and school textbooks for teaching "collectivism."[28] The ideological struggle with the USSR intensified these accusations and opened the door to grassroots reform efforts. From the late 1940s to the mid-1960s, conservatives demanded, with varying degrees of success, a return to morals-based learning, pro-American textbooks that resisted calls for "co-existence," and more rigorous math and science training to compete with the USSR. Anticommunist activists argued that American youth were unprepared to fight their heavily indoctrinated Soviet peers in the life-or-death ideological struggle of the Cold War. Social studies, they insisted, should promote citizenship and civic participation, strengthen democracy and uphold free-market capitalism, and reject dangerous ideas like co-existence and "world friendship."[29] In response to this rising tide of criticism, in 1958, Congress passed the National Defense Education Act, providing millions of dollars for math, science, and foreign language instruction.

By the early 1960s, educators and academics working to revise the social studies curricula promoted a new, inquiry-based approach that has become known as the "new social studies." Their approach advocated a shift from worksheets and memorization to a more active learning style based on problem-finding and problem-solving and the development of higher level skills. Students considered contemporary issues, debated competing value systems, and used games and/or simulations to apply learning to real-world situations.[30] One controversial aspect of this new inquiry-based learning required that schools teach *about* international communism, on the theory that an objective approach to communism would best prepare young people to recognize the obvious benefits of democratic capitalism and resist communism. The Foreign Policy Association provided current events curricula titled "Choices" and "Great Discussions" that were used in 475 high schools by 1957. These guides invited students to debate questions such as "Are the Communists becoming liberal?" and "Are we competing successfully with Russia?"[31] Such efforts were rare, however, as conservative organizations like the John Birch Society pressed for the removal of such curricula on the grounds that they promoted compromise and co-existence with communism. More common was "a single-period lecture given by the American Legion" that had the effect of keeping communism *out* of the classroom.[32]

Social studies and civics teachers engaged with the new inquiry-based pedagogy by practicing student-centered activities such as role-playing, debate, and creative writing. Many encouraged their students to reflect on the meaning of democracy in their own lives and experience. In 1959, six Milwaukee high school students offered the following thoughts. Ann Schwalbach wrote, "democracy gives us a right to choose our friends and to associate with whom we wish. This seems simple enough, but actually it is a basis for our whole society." Howard Bodanske, a student at the Boys' Technical High School, wrote, "In Russia, the people have no choice. They are forced to do the type of work the government wants them to do. Because we have the liberty to choose our life's vocation, most of us will work hard to prepare for it. The enthusiasm will be much greater than if we had to prepare for a job we disliked." Judith Voland echoed these sentiments, arguing that education in other nations was limited to intellectual and economic elites. Under such systems, "These young people do not have a chance to advance themselves beyond the class of their parents. In our democracy there is a chance for advancement. . . . The one who chooses his career will be much happier and he will feel as though he were really performing a worthwhile duty for his country at the same time." Jean Johnson wrote, "To make intelligent choices takes the knowledge which can only be found when there is freedom to seek information. If ideas are wrong, they will be proved wrong when compared intelligently

and . . . with ideas that are better." Ms. Johnson also offered some words
of warning:

> We all should pay close attention to affairs of the United Nations
> because it is in the UN that the United States is leading the free world
> to even higher standards. Unless we begin to realize our responsi-
> bilities, we will live to admit we would rather be governed under the
> communist state. To [do] this, we must become free, critical thinking
> individualists and step out of the general role of conformity. In this
> way we will be controlling not only our own, but also the world's
> destiny.[33]

In English and civics classes, as part of patriotic pageants and Scouting
programs, students regularly contemplated the meaning of democracy in
the United States. Some contrasted democracy to life under communism
as they understood it and prescribed it as the remedy to international
problems. Conservative fears to the contrary, most children seemed to be
absorbing American propaganda; they offered very little in the way of criticism. But some students recognized a more complex reality. One senior
in Rocky Mount, North Carolina who was interested in labor problems
thought that "Russia's methods are wrong, but they're just as entitled to
spread communism as we are to spread democracy." He favored a federal
plan for socialized medicine and was adamant that "Negroes should have
the same economic and educational opportunities as white people."[34] By
1962, some teenagers were demanding a less "black-and-white" approach
to communism, and traditional Americanism versus Communism (AVC)
courses suffered from "an old-fogey image . . . and declining enrollments."
Student expectations for more even-handed instruction in current events,
their interest in controversial subjects, and self-consciousness about their
education spurred more politically engaged learning—in discussion
circles, new textbooks such as the *Communism in American Life Series*
(1957–1966), and engaged instructors, such as Massachusetts teacher Paul
Mitchell, who completely revised his AVC class "so that students could
make up their own minds."[35] Historians Ronald Evans and Campbell

Scribner argue that, by the mid-1960s, student-run conferences and current affairs clubs demonstrated an increasingly activist mindset among high school students and a growing recognition of their ability to influence school curriculum decisions. The inquiry-based methods of the new social studies encouraged some students to question the one-sidedness of AVC classes and to demand a more rigorous and honest approach to studying their own nation's politics, as well as those of the Soviet Union.

The tensions in postwar education between anticommunism and world friendship become clear when anti-Soviet classroom approaches are compared with books such as Lorraine Adele Nieri's *Dear American Friends: Letters from School Children Around the World.* Dedicated "to the boys and girls of the United States," the book included letters from 33 nations that demonstrated the many similarities between American youth and their global peers. Esther Millett, the former executive chairman of the Independent Schools Education Board wrote in the Introduction, "Here then in this book, ready to extend a hand of friendship across the miles, are many students from other lands who have much in common with you." Youth in other countries enjoyed many of the same games, including "skating and volleyball and tennis and even baseball." They collected coins and stamps, joined scouting troops, and listened to music. "The students who wrote these letters did so because they want to work with American students for mutual understanding and to make the world a better place in which to live. They believe that if individuals in every country have a chance to know one another and to exchange ideas there will be less and less chance of future wars. Turn the page and begin your acquaintance with a world of friends."[36]

The postwar "problem" of educating American children should be understood as the domestic side of the global competition with the Soviet Union *and* as an arena for building world understanding and global friendship. In civil defense, physical education, and curricular decisions, public schools functioned as part of America's "weapons system" to prepare scientists, mathematicians, and citizens who would "come to the right conclusions in support of western capitalism and democracy." In short, the schools served the nation's security objectives throughout the Cold War.[37] But America's public schoolchildren also participated in art and pen pal exchanges, fundraisers for UNICEF, and, by the 1960s, in more open-ended curricula. It is clear that at least some American youth were beginning to come to their own conclusions about Cold War policies, communism, and the content of school curricula.

THE COLD WAR OUTSIDE THE CLASSROOM

In addition to preparing Cold Warriors through classroom curricula, the schools also functioned as central locations where voluntary organizations, government-sponsored programs, and a variety of patriotic campaigns could reach American youth. Perhaps no program so candidly aimed to create a people's diplomacy as Eisenhower's aptly named People-to-People Program. American children and youth participated in two crucial ways in this national project—at home, as domestic representatives of the national commitment to international friendship, and as foreign ambassadors of American friendship to children in other nations. As one USIA report noted, "The dictatorships—Communist, Nazi and Fascist—which held their large populations in a vise over the last generation, built their most solid popular support from the cradle. In the Soviet Union, for example, every person 30 years or younger, has known nothing but Marxist indoctrination from birth. Without resort to authoritarian methods, the US too—through private as well as governmental agencies—must make every effort to reach the minds and hearts of the world's youth."[38]

Eisenhower launched the People-to-People program in September 1956, proclaiming, "there will never be enough diplomats and information officers" to make American "objectives and principles better understood throughout the world." If "American ideology" was to win the "great struggle" for global supremacy, thousands of "independent private groups and millions of individual Americans . . . men, women, *and children*" had to establish "person-to-person communication in foreign lands."[39] As International Educational Exchange Service (IES) Director Russell I. Riley explained to a Virginia Women's Club in early 1954, US leadership in world affairs carried "very heavy responsibilities" for the average citizens. Urging the club women to fulfill their civic duties by "getting to know" other peoples of the world, Riley upheld international exchanges as a means of facilitating "better understanding" between peoples and nations and disproving any "false ideas" that foreigners harbored about the United States. These ideas informed American public diplomacy efforts through the 1960s (and beyond), as seen in Secretary of State Dean Rusk's speech explaining the Kennedy administration's approach to diplomacy: "Foreign policy is the total involvement of the American people with peoples and governments abroad." Sharing "accurate information" and American knowledge and skills with other nations, establishing "lasting contacts" between Americans and "free world" peoples, and "increasing our under-standing of other countries" became foreign policy goals for ordinary Americans, including children, throughout the Cold War years.[40]

Historians of Cold War propaganda such as Kenneth Osgood have explored the cultural and intellectual aspects of the People-to-People program among adults, but little attention has been paid to the Youth Committee and others that mobilized young people, such as the Education, Music, Pen Pals, and Sports committees.[41] One of 40 People-to-People committees, the Youth Committee lacked an official budget and relied on "ordinary Americans" and existing organizations such as the Boy and Girl Scouts, 4-H, the National Association of Student Councils, and Camp Fire Girls to carry out diplomatic work. The extent to which children and youth participated in People-to-People would have depended to some extent on their age, the group(s) to which they belonged, and the level of adult commitment to the ideals represented by the People-to-People program. In the 1950s, these organizations were already committed to the ideals of world friendship, and several historians have focused on their activities in this realm.[42] However, it is less clear what meanings young people attached to their participation and what they thought they were accomplishing. It isn't clear if participation in the People-to-People pro-gram influenced young peoples' ideas about foreign policy or commu-nism, or if they understood their actions as cultural diplomacy. Finally, it is unclear whether children imbibed the nationalism espoused by the US

government during the Cold War, or views espoused by liberal or conservative interest groups.

Arthur Schuck, the Director of the Boy Scouts of America, served as
the head of the People-to-People Youth Committee from its inception.
Under Schuck's leadership, the Youth Committee pursued four main
activities: extending youth activities overseas, communicating with youth
groups abroad, organizing youth pilgrimages and "junior ambassador"
programs, and sponsoring exchange visits. Schuck contacted established youth groups to suggest possible activities under these broad topics. For example, he encouraged the National 4-H to increase rural youth
exchanges and undertake letter-writing projects.[43] Between 1948 and
1957, almost 1,000 International Farm Youth Exchange delegates representing 45 states trained abroad in 58 foreign nations, while more than
1,000 visitors from foreign nations trained in the United States. More than
8,000 farm families hosted foreign visitors. In practice, it seems that more
people, goods, and information traveled *from* the United States *to* other
nations. In other words, US policy encouraged Americans to tell others
about themselves and the nation, rather than learn from other peoples in
an equal exchange.[44]

People-to-People committees regularly reported on their successes in
the monthly *People-to-People* newsletters, which were then reprinted in
USIA newsletters (and Youth Packets), as well as in foreign newspapers as
examples of American efforts to establish world friendship and international understanding. The November 1957 newsletter reported the Youth
Committee's accomplishments during its first year, which included a
Youth Activities Workshop at the Pratt Institute that drew 100 leaders from
33 national youth organizations. The Camp Fire Girls sponsored a photo
album project based on the theme, "This is Our Home. This is How We
Live. These are My People." More than 480,000 girls in 3,000 communities participated, sending scrapbooks to Ghana, Greece, Turkey, Lebanon,
South Africa, Israel, Malaya, the Sudan, Egypt, Pakistan, Nigeria, Ceylon,
India, and Mexico.[45] American Boy Scout troops, leaders, and parents had
initiated a fundraising campaign to extend scouting globally through the
World Friendship Fund. The People-to-People Cartoon Committee's new

cartoon became a regular feature in the monthly Boy Scouts of American magazine *Boy's Life*, drawing the attention of scouts to opportunities for cultivating world friendship. The Boys' Club awarded the Boy of the Year and the Family of the Year overseas trips to Cuba, while the Boy Scouts began its first exchange program with Laos and sent a goodwill ambassador to Japan. The Experiment for International Living, a student exchange organization founded in 1932, hosted a conference for 200 foreign youth leaders from 16 nations. Finally, Arthur Schuck addressed an international conference of 600 Scout leaders in Cambridge, England.[46]

Committee reports also provide a window into some of the difficulties the People-to-People program experienced. In 1957, for example, Youth Committee leaders convened in New York City for three days to discuss strategies to advance their work. The committee suggested that the federal government provide financial assistance and modify immigration restrictions to facilitate youth exchange programs. They also noted a recurring problem: a lack of understanding among participating youth of the cultural norms of the countries they visited and the need to work *with* foreign groups with shared similar challenges, such as race or labor problems. A representative of the National Jewish Welfare Board (NJWB) insisted that teaching respect for cultural differences should be an integral part of exchange programs, as "other nations do not want the American way imposed on them."[47] Their discussion highlights persistent tensions in Cold War cultural diplomacy. Numerous scholars have noted the divisions between those who advocated an "informational" approach that highlighted American successes and those who encouraged a "mirror" approach that included a "warts and all" depiction of the United States. The latter argued that foreigners would be more inclined to accept American propaganda if they felt they were getting a true representation of the nation. The former felt that the Soviet Union overplayed American problems and put the United States on the defensive, when in reality American society was much freer than Soviet-style communism. The comment by the NJWB representative also highlights the fact that "world understanding" meant educating the rest of the world about America and not the other way around.

In addition to youth-focused activities, the Youth Committee leaders worked to integrate their activities with non–youth focused People-to-People committees. For example, the Books Committee encouraged young people to organize book drives in their schools and communities and collected children's books for distribution to overseas libraries. The Music Committee planned international performances by youth orchestras. The Fine Arts Committee arranged exhibitions of children's paintings as well as exhibitions *about* children, such as the 1959 show "America as it Looks to Children" at the International Conference of Social Work in Tokyo. Although the Letter Writing Committee sometimes found that adults had little to say to one another beyond a brief introduction, many children created enduring pen pal relationships. In early 1959, the Hobby Committee sponsored a photo contest for foreign students living in the United States, *My Impressions of the USA*. Winner Shin Koyama captioned his photo "America is not only what is tangible and material, but the giving of peace, joy, and security." Just as the USIA reprinted American students' patriotic essays, it also sponsored 200 traveling exhibits of the winning photographs, and Transworld Airlines (TWA) distributed to all its overseas offices counter displays featuring the winning photographs. Throughout the 1950s, the US government attempted to shape the experiences of young foreign visitors, assuming that the positive impressions they brought back to their home countries would pay future dividends as these young people moved into positions of authority in their communities, governments, and businesses. By early 1957, 4-H youth clubs in California had established bilingual correspondence with their peers in Peru; Boy Scouts were helping their Colombian counterparts create handbook materials; and Girl Scouts offered English classes to Hungarian refugees, made layettes, and invited the girls to troop meetings.[48] At the close of Eisenhower's second term, the organization was incorporated by a board of private citizens, with headquarters in Kansas City. The first Student Ambassador Program began in 1962 and continued until 2002, when People-to-People contracted with a private organization to conduct student travel programs.[49]

The USIA also concentrated on particular projects involving children, including expanding the Junior Achievement Program, creating

"sister city" projects, developing affiliations between American and foreign schools, collecting books, encouraging youth groups to raise funds for
the American Bookshelf program through CARE, and cultivating school
newspaper "salutes" and exchanges. One of the best-known partnerships
between USIA and CARE, "American Bookshelf" was a preselected package of 99 books that aimed to reflect "American" ideals, disprove Russian
claims of American materialism and lack of culture, and "build a world of
freedom and peace."[50] For $30, individuals, groups, or organizations could
send the books to a recipient of their choice. The program became a popular service project among schoolchildren and Scout troops. Presented
as "an opportunity to counteract anti-American propaganda. . . . In the
crucial war for the hearts and minds of men," the American Bookshelf
program allowed ordinary Americans, including children, to fight the
Cold War from the domestic front. As Christine Jenkins pointed out, the
American Bookshelf was CARE's strategy for avoiding "objectionable"
books such as *Judy's Journey* by Lois Lenski and objectionable authors,
such as Langston Hughes, who was under FBI investigation in 1953. The
American Bookshelf highlighted American ideals, not necessarily its
realities.[51]

Town affiliation and "village-to-village" projects affiliated with the
People-to-People program were particularly popular among young
Americans. Dozens of examples in the People-to-People and USIA historical records demonstrate how American schoolchildren participated in
these partnerships between American and foreign towns with the goal of
simply establishing relationships and, through them, world understanding. In 1950, the Weston High School student council prepared a report,
"Your Peace," suggesting ways that Weston, Massachusetts, and Pont
L'Eveque, France, could become "sister cities." It is difficult to determine if
the students acted independently, if a teacher or adult encouraged them,
or if they acted on an idea that was "in the air." The students chose Pont
L'Eveque based on that city's similar demographics, as well as on information provided by Operation Democracy, Inc., a State Department–approved
organization that specialized in fostering town-to-town affiliations. Weston's
students proposed sending photography exhibits, book and magazine

collections, films of town meetings and school athletic events, radio productions in French, news bulletins, and letters to present a "clear, convincing picture of American life." They delivered their report "to every door in the community" and urged town leaders to convene a meeting to discuss the proposition. Eventually, Weston formed a "town-to-town" partnership with Rombas, France. The students' report suggested that international peace was the greatest problem facing their generation and that creating an international connection was one practical way for average people to "play an effective part in the crusade for peace." In the first decade of the partnership, Rombas sent six students to study in Weston, "dozens" of friendships were formed, and "the latest pictures and correspondence are on the public library desk." By 1962, seven students from each town had spent a year abroad, and one of the founding students of the sister city program had graduated from Princeton and was planning to join the Peace Corps.[52] As of 2008, the two cities were still exchanging students. Although some of the language and the ideas articulated in the student report were clearly drawn from State Department publications and existing projects, the students initiated the project in their own town. They believed that individual efforts by ordinary citizens, including young people, were essential to an effective "crusade for peace."

In January 1959, the People-to-People News proudly reported on the developing relationships between students in Seattle and Kobe, Japan. At Christmas, the Junior Red Cross made and sent 100 dolls to Kobe; four Japanese high school students visited Seattle for a leadership conference and stayed with Seattle families; Boy Scouts exchanged photo albums, equipment, and uniforms; Seattle schools used movies, slides, tapes, and photos sent from Kobe to teach about life in Japan.[53] Another successful village-to-village project arose between North Conway, New Hampshire, and Arlberg, Austria, in 1965. Rather than exchanging Christmas gifts with other local children, North Conway children decided to send gifts to their sister city instead. The children collected wrapped gifts, included their addresses in the hope of initiating pen pal relationships, and loaded them into a 64-square-foot box. Dedicated by the New Hampshire governor and the Austrian ambassador, the box was transported to Boston's

Logan airport free of charge by Avis and flown to Munich by Lufthansa airlines. Two years later, the two communities built on their shared ski culture to create a Junior Ambassador program drawn from local ski teams. In December 1967, a boy and a girl from New Hampshire enjoyed an all-expenses-paid week in Arlberg to cement the friendship between the two towns.

As these examples demonstrate, children and youth were deeply involved in a wide array of public diplomacy efforts. The People-to-People archives provide hundreds more stories of American children "helping" foreign children throughout the 1950s and 1960s as Cold War policy evolved from staunch anticommunism to world understanding and from international friendship to economic development assistance in the 1960s. For example, in 1964, the students of Rosendale School in Schenectady, New York, helped to build a school in Casa Blanco, Colombia. Rosendale children "donated their own nickels and dimes rather than buy candy" and sold tickets to Saturday movies at the school; Cub Scout paper drives generated profits as well. CARE administered the $1,000 raised in Rosendale, while Peace Corps volunteers and local men provided the labor. In the meantime, the children corresponded, studied each other's countries, exchanged instructions for their favorite games, and mailed handicrafts and art work. School assemblies in Rosendale featured Latin American music and dances, high school students translated pen pal letters for younger children, and children built and displayed a model of the Casa Blanca school. In Colombia, locals dug the foundation, dedicated the site, and raised $250 worth of materials. This project proved so successful that, in April 1964, Sargent Shriver declared the "school to school" project an official Peace Corps program. By February 1965, 14 schools were under construction with full financing, 30 American schools had launched fundraising efforts, and 60 more were in the initial stages of exploring the school-to-school project for their communities.[54] That the program could so easily shift rhetoric from world friendship to economic development reveals the benevolent relationship that had animated most American efforts at world understanding.

International student exchanges and living exchanges were another means of youth participation in cultural diplomacy efforts, although only for wealthier Americans. People-to-People partnered with the Experiment in International Living, established in 1932 and still active today, to take advantage of their established relationships with educational organizations, group travel savings, resources in host countries, and contacts abroad. In addition to sending young Americans abroad, the Experiment in International Living created the Incoming Experiment Ambassador program, which offered cost-sharing assistance to communities that wanted to sponsor a foreign visitor for two months "to create mutual respect and understanding among the different peoples of the world . . . through a direct and personal approach." Young people came to the United States not for formal study, but to live with three or four American families over the course of eight or nine weeks. The family stay was considered crucial because it was in the domestic setting that foreigners learned the most about the United States: "we teach best what we are and what we believe in simply by being ourselves."[55] Like the State Department's Leadership Program, however, only the most elite and well-off foreign children would have been able to afford such a trip.

Despite these many efforts to involve children and youth in a people's diplomacy, at least some young people remained skeptical of their impact. In 1958, a panel of five high school exchange students interviewed Charles E. Wilson, the Director of People-to-People, on the *New York Times'* Youth Forum on the subject, "Who will maintain peace—governments or peoples?" A French exchange student doubted the Russian people had much influence over national policy. Another noted, "The Hungarian people tried [to force government concessions], and we know what happened." A Japanese exchange student suggested that ordinary people might be more effective in directing their efforts against nuclear testing, to which another student responded that only when the United States and the Soviet Union trusted one another could testing come to an end.[56] Created and hosted by Dorothy Lerner Gordon, the Youth Forum was an unrehearsed discussion among New York City area youth on topics ranging from politics and world affairs to science and juvenile delinquency. The program, one of several popular television shows featuring young people exploring current events, was broadcast in various media—live, radio, and television—between 1943 and 1970. The students' comments do not seem to indicate an overwhelming faith in the viability of people's diplomacy to overcome the world's problems.

A similar program, the *New York Herald Tribune*'s World Youth Forum, brought together more than 900 young people from around the world between 1947 and 1972. Founded by journalist Helen Hiett Waller, the World Youth Forum invited 30 teenagers from a wide range of countries for three-month stays in the New York City area. They attended local high schools, lived with American families, and, each week, recorded a television program for CBS called "The World We Want," in which they debated various issues. They visited Washington, met important political figures, and traveled to Virginia, where some of them confronted segregation for the first time. According to historian Catherine Bishop, the Forum delegates were treated as honored celebrities.[57] Both the *New York Times* television show and the *Tribune*'s youth "family stay" program demonstrate the idealism and imperialism involved in mobilizing youth as ambassadors and future leaders during the Cold War. Young people were encouraged to learn about other nations and peoples, think critically about political issues, develop relationships with their foreign peers, and become leaders in world affairs. They also highlight the fact that staunch anticommunism was not the only approach to world affairs available to young Americans throughout the Cold War.

As the Youth Committee of the People-to-People program attests, the US government fully grasped the importance of mobilizing children and young people, both at home and abroad, as cultural ambassadors during the Cold War. At home, grooming American youth for a long ideological struggle began with engaging elementary schoolchildren in art exchange and pen pal programs. Boy Scout, Girl Scout, and Camp Fire Girl troops collected books, organized trips abroad to meet their peers, and sent scrapbooks and newspapers abroad. Many historians have studied American exhibitions at global trade fairs, but few have noted that children's bodies functioned as important propaganda displays at these events as well. At the 1955 Paris fair, kindergarten children played with the American toys on display, "oblivious to the thousands of spectators," in order to humanize the displays of American consumer goods, associating them with real people and friendly faces. What better propaganda than happy children, playing and learning with American-made products?[58] Or young Japanese students, returning home with stories, not only of American democracy and wealth, but of the love, joy, and security they experienced as guests in American homes? Or Chilean schoolchildren learning about the United States through boxes of new books and much-needed school supplies sent from American schoolchildren? Each example demonstrates not only the US government's commitment to Cold War people's diplomacy, but also to the utter pervasiveness of such efforts and the eagerness of many American youth to participate in them. These examples also demonstrate how efforts to promote "world understanding" might have undermined the staunch anticommunist policies of the federal government and led to criticism from young people by the 1960s.

FEDERAL PROGRAMS IN THE SCHOOLS

Both the Soviet and American governments recognized that they were engaged in a battle for the world's youth—the leaders of tomorrow. The Soviet government's Young Pioneers organization had been socializing young people since 1922, but, during the Cold War, Moscow expanded its efforts to reach young people through World Youth Festivals, held every two years beginning in Prague in 1947. Their stated purpose was to bring together youth from around the world in a spirit of friendship and cooperation and to strengthen world peace. The festivals included cultural events such as films, live theater, sports, and excursions, as well as more serious lectures and discussions. About 25,000 young people representing 70 nations attended the first four-week festival in Prague; 10,000 attended the two-week festival in Budapest in 1949.[59] American commentators immediately criticized the festivals for their staged and tightly controlled events, and American youth who participated in 1947 returned to the United States complaining that communist youth dominated the conversations and proceedings. The US government responded to the 1950 World Youth

Festival, held in East Berlin, with a variety of competing public and private initiatives in West Berlin. The State Department orchestrated counterpropaganda campaigns that included an auto show, a display of the UNESCO "Rights of Man" exhibit, additional CARE packages, Theater Week, and Motion Picture Week. The Economic Cooperation Administration (ECA) sponsored its own European Youth Organization. The 1957 fair, held in Moscow, prompted the Secretary of Komsomol, the Soviet youth organization, to warn Soviet youth to "fight against the penetration into our midst of alien ideologies, morals, and customs."[60] The battle for young minds persisted throughout the Cold War.

Throughout the 1950s and 1960s, the USIA waged a simultaneous battle for the hearts and minds of young people around the globe, "particularly those of uncommitted countries and those where Communist influence is strong." As part of its ongoing effort to "tell America's story" to the world, in the early 1950s, the USIA Policy Planning Staff agreed that the USIA should "consider youth as one of its principal, if not its primary target." Devoting a "much more substantial proportion" of its resources and developing programs to foster close associations with youth groups were first steps toward this goal. USIA propaganda detailed living standards, health care, education, and "ordinary Americans" going about their daily routines in suburban and rural communities, working, attending school or community events, volunteering in social organizations, engaging in leisure activities and cultural events, and attending church.[61] Each USIS country plan was required to create specific programs targeting youth, and, under Edward Murrow's leadership, the USIS assigned "youth officers" to posts around the world.

Between April 1953 and June 1957, the USIA compiled Youth Packets for distribution to its posts. Using a combination of news clips, human interest features, documentaries, and radio programs, the stories focused on the daily lives of American youth in the United States, as well as some of their extraordinary accomplishments. A typical Youth Packet might include excerpts from the winning entry in a nationwide radio contest on the meaning of democracy, feature articles on sports stars like Rocky Marciano and musicians like Louis Armstrong, the conservation efforts of the 3 million American Boy Scouts, and the accomplishments of young scientists discovered through a national talent search. Such tidbits of information about American young people might seem mundane, even silly, in the context of foreign policy and a global battle against communism. But the USIA assumed these stories would interest foreign young people in the United States, humanize the American people, and demonstrate the superiority and desirability of "the American way of life."

The public schools provided the most direct access to American youth. As early as 1947, American schoolchildren collected more than half a million Christmas and Hanukkah gifts for children in 16 nations in response to an appeal to "create the one element most urgently needed for peace: world friendship." Under the guidance of The World Festivals for Friendship, Inc., this youthful "Marshall Plan" included a letter with each gift bearing the name and address of a potential pen pal. The 10 schools that donated the most gifts were given awards.[62] We've already seen how the Advertising Council's Crusade for Freedom launched fundraising campaigns and sponsored patriotic pageants in schools and encouraged children to sign Freedom Scrolls. The American Economic Campaign distributed free booklets to schools to teach young Americans about the connections between freedom and capitalism. Art and pen pal exchanges, book sales, and sister cities were all arranged through America's public schools. Civil defense programs like "duck and cover" tied children's daily school activities directly to Cold War preparedness. But other federal agencies, including the Treasury Department, the Air Force, and the USIA relied on the public schools to mobilize children.

In an effort to expand the Treasury Department's stamp savings program, in 1958, the Lone Ranger personally invited American youth to join his Peace Patrol, "a nationwide organization of boys and girls who buy United States School Savings Stamps and Savings Bonds to help build the economic and military strength required to preserve our freedom and insure [sic] the peace."[63] While children read Lone Ranger comic books or watched his adventures on television at home, their school teachers encouraged them to participate in the US Treasury's Savings Stamps program, with a little help from the Masked Man. Americans, mostly children, bought $20 million worth of stamps in 1957, but, as one official noted, 4 million babies were born every year, and "no American has a greater stake in peace than the *young* American."[64] International organizations encouraged American schoolchildren to look beyond their own borders and to accept new global responsibilities as well. The United Nations, particularly UNESCO and UNICEF, worked through American schools to promote a variety of programs. Among the most memorable was UNICEF's popular "Trick or Treat for UNICEF" program. Begun in 1952, the program spread to all 48 states in three years and raised $273,000 in 1955 alone.[65]

The US military used the schools to organize children into "civilian armies." Junior and senior high school students played important roles as "aircraft spotters" in the Ground Observer Corps (GOC), part of the Operation Skywatch Program founded in July 1952. Volunteers became members of the GOC, a World War II initiative revived in 1950 by Air Force Commander General Ennis C. Whitehead. With the belief that the Korean War might provoke a possible Soviet attack, recruiting volunteers was not a challenge. In 1951, 210,000 GOC volunteers manning 8,000 observation posts and 26 filter centers were tested for the first time in nationwide drills. Unfortunately, Whitehead was not impressed by their performance; it took too long for the volunteer sighting reports to reach the Ground Control Interception centers. As a result, the corps recruited additional volunteers to man more observation posts on a continuing basis. Whitehead proposed the formation of a 160,000-member civilian volunteer GOC to operate 8,000 observation posts scattered between proposed radar network sites. Skywatch was the latest iteration of a recruitment campaign that, by 1952, would have been familiar to many Americans. By the middle of 1953, a year into Skywatch, the number of participants had risen to 305,000. Some accounts place peak enrollment at 400,000, while other estimates are much higher. Volunteers manned between 16,000 and 17,000 observation posts, along with at least 73 filter centers. "Operation Skywatch," supported by both Presidents Truman and Eisenhower, functioned from July 14, 1952 through 1958. Eventually more than 800,000 volunteers participated in Operation Skywatch.[66] Truman described Skywatch as "a commonsense precaution," part of a civil defense campaign in "the American tradition, dating back to the frontier days," when all members of a family "had a task to do in defending their homes and their stockades from marauding savages." Eisenhower praised Skywatch as "the greatest civilian volunteer peacetime defense organization this nation has ever known."[67]

Like diplomacy, defense was everyone's job. Historian Matthew Farish noted the emphasis on women and youth in GOC publicity campaigns and argued that by championing the roles these nontraditional groups could play in national defense and by highlighting schools and homes as places for voluntarism, GOC campaigns promoted the idea that defense, like diplomacy, was everyone's job. For example, in September 1954, two young girls from Klamath Falls, Oregon, won "the grand prize in the annual 'Kiddie Parade.'" Aged seven and four, they wore GOC uniforms and carried a banner reading, "We are safe because they watch." This language echoed a prominent GOC recruitment image of a toddler clutching a teddy bear, his mother's eyes gazing skyward, and the slogan, "Safe, because some American looked to the SKY!" With its routine, simple obligations, the corps was an effective vehicle for the education of Cold War children who could counter their fears of nuclear war with positive and patriotic action, rather than simply taking cover. Civil defense began in the schools, where the federal and state governments provided teachers with civil defense manuals describing sky watching as a "most interesting project." Asked about the GOC decades later, alumni of an Arkansas school could still remember the use of "a phone at the press box at the football field at the fairgrounds" for GOC purposes, airplane call letters, and a field trip to an Air Force base. Recalling an initial meeting in the cafeteria, one volunteer recalled it as an "exciting time for me because I actually felt I was helping in the defense of our country." Another student recruited in her high school's study hall remembered traveling by bus on Sundays to the Cleveland suburb of Euclid, where she watched the skies from an observation post set up on the lawn of another school. In Hawarden, Iowa, the observation post was located in Central School's bell tower. Enthusiastic teenage boys held extended vigils at places such as the grandstand at Long Island's Belmont Park racetrack. Unsurprisingly, the BSA magazine *Boy's Life* advertised the GOC through articles that emphasized the suitability of scouts for such patriotic work and repeatedly noted the need for additional volunteers. Ringed by photos of eager young GOC volunteers, a 1953 piece acknowledged the exciting proliferation of Pentagon "defense gimmicks" but reminded the magazine's readers that "the fellows who operate those scientific and mechanical marvels are counting heavily on your two big brown eyes to let them know when and if enemy planes come zooming across America's skies."[68]

CONCLUSION

The Cold War reached deep into America's public schools, far beyond the typical "duck-and-cover" drills encouraged by Bert the Turtle. Although civil defense became part of the daily school experiences of Cold War kids, so, too, did fitness tests, atomic science, and art exchange programs. Global competition with the Soviet Union changed the way children learned across the curriculum, from science and math classes to history and citizenship training. Dozens of new initiatives by the federal government, educational organizations, and private institutions affected the daily routine in schools, from gym class to civil defense drills to visits by the Lone Ranger. In America's public schools, anticommunism and containment co-existed in uneasy tension with "world friendship" outreach efforts and "international understanding" curriculum modules. And, of course, children were not passive recipients in all of these experiences; they actively participated in and shaped them. Older students led civil defense drills, assisted younger children, and launched Sister City programs. Students challenged their one-sided AVC classes or demanded a more nuanced approach to contemporary politics. Some "red diaper" children protested civil defense drills or criticized American foreign policy. In short, American students' experiences in the schools were complex, but understanding that complexity strengthens our ability to decipher the meaning of the Cold War for American youth and their impact on the politics of the 1960s.

NOTES

1. Dwight D. Eisenhower, "State of the Union Address" (January 6, 1955).
2. The extensive literature on public schools and citizenship includes John Dewey, *The School and Society* (Chicago: University of Chicago Press, 1900); Eleanor Roosevelt, "Good Citizenship: The Purpose of Education," *Pictorial Review* 31 (April 1930): 4, 94, 97; David Tyack and Larry Cuban, *Tinkering Toward Utopia: A Century of Public School Reform* (Cambridge, MA: Harvard University Press, 1995); Sarah Mondale, ed. *School: The Story of American Public Education* (Boston: Beacon Press, 2002); Diana Selig, *Americans All: The Cultural Gifts Movement* (Cambridge, MA: Harvard University Press, 2008).
3. JoAnne Brown, "'A is for Atom, B is for Bomb': Civil Defense in American Public Education, 1948–1963," *The Journal of American History* 75 (June 1988): 69.
4. Available on numerous websites: https://archive.org/details/gov.ntis.ava11109vnb1
5. Andrew Hartman, *Education and the Cold War: The Battle for the American School* (New York: Palgrave Macmillan, 2008): 71–72.
6. Excerpts from miscellaneous minutes and memos, Box 4, Folder 6, AS 121, Office Records, Superintendent of Schools Office, Archdiocesan Archives, Archdiocese of Milwaukee.
7. Hartman, *Education and the Cold War*, 71–72.
8. Civil Defense in the Classroom: A Handbook for Teachers, Michigan Dept. of Public Instruction (Lansing: Michigan Dept. of Public Instruction, 1955).
9. "Cooperation and Safety Hand in Hand for Defense," *The Oracle*, Bay View High School, February 2, 1951; "Civil Defense is Vital; Observe it Now," *The Oracle*, Bay View High School (March 23, 1956): 2.
10. "Danger—Are We Prepared?" *The Craftsman*, Milwaukee Boys' Technical High School newspaper (April 27, 1951).
11. "Scout Organization Joining Civil Defense," *Milwaukee Sentinel* (November 12, 1950).
12. "City's Volunteers Rehearse Defense; Boy Scouts Take Their Place in Civil Defense," *New York Times* (December 19, 1950): 19; "3 Million Scouts to Visit Homes Today to Distribute Booklets on Civil Defense," *New York Times* (October 11, 1958): 12.
13. Arthur A. Schuck, "Foreword," *Boys' Life* (March 1957): 11.
14. "9 Pacifists Seized in Defying Alert," *New York Times* (May 7, 1958): 30.
15. Jacqueline L. Castledine, *Cold War Progressives: Women's Interracial Organizing for Peace and Freedom* (Urbana: University of Illinois Press, 2012): 69–70.
16. Amy Swerdlow, *Women Strike for Peace: Traditional Motherhood and Radical Politics in the 1960s* (Chicago: University of Chicago Press, 1993): 233–240. Swerdlow's Conclusion is a thoughtful discussion of the political power of maternalism, while her Introduction offers a personal account of how 1950s domesticity informed WSP politics.

17. Kaplan and Shapiro, *Red Diapers*, 9, 23, 37–38, 70–71, 88, 91–92, 168–171.

18. "'Conscientious Objector' Stays at School During Test," *Palo Alto Times* (February 7, 1958).

19. "Walking Blood Bank Slates Typing Day," *The Herald-Journal* (May 22, 1951): 1. See also Elizabeth K. Wolf and Anne E. Laumann, "The Use of Blood-Type Tattoos During the Cold War," *Journal of the American Academy of Dermatology* (March 2008): 474–475.

20. Interview posted on http://www.conelrad.com/atomicsecrets/secrets.php?secrets=11

21. Brown, "A is for Atom, B is for Bomb," 81–82.

22. *Milwaukee Sentinel* (February 26, 1956).

23. Andrew D. Grossman, *Neither Dead nor Red: Civilian Defense and American Political Development during the Early Cold War* (Routledge: New York, 2001); Laura McEnaney, *Civil Defense Begins at Home: Militarization Meets Everyday Life in the Fifties* (Princeton: Princeton University Press, 2000).

24. Hartman, *Education and the Cold War*, 58.

25. Mintz, *Huck's Raft: The History of American Childhood*, 255–263.

26. Hartman, *Education and the Cold War*, 138–139.

27. "Guide to the Study of World Affairs," 6; RG 306, Records of the USIA, Subject Files, 1953–67, Box 2, Folder: Collection of Books and Magazines V, 1954, NARA.

28. Hartman, *Education and the Cold War*, 91–113; Jonathan Zimmerman, *Whose America? Culture Wars in the Public Schools* (Cambridge: Harvard University Press, 2002): 81–95. For more on the attacks on progressive education as a result of the perceived failure of the United States in the "space race," see Barbara Barksdale Clowse, *Brainpower for the Cold War: The Sputnik Crisis and the National Defense Education Act of 1958* (Westport CT: Greenwood Press, 1981) and Herbert Kliebard, *The Struggle for the American Curriculum 1893–1958* (Routledge, 2004).

29. Ronald W. Evans, *The Hope for American School Reform: The Cold War Pursuit of Inquiry Learning in Social Studies* (New York: Palgrave Macmillan, 2011): 12–14.

30. Jeffrey Byford and William Russell, "The New Social Studies: A Historical Examination of Curricular Reform," *Social Studies Research and Practice* 2.1 (Spring 2007): 41–45.

31. The Foreign Policy Association was founded in 1918 as the League of Free Nations Association to support President Woodrow Wilson's efforts to achieve a just peace. The Association was reconstituted in 1923 as the Foreign Policy Association with a commitment to the careful study of all sides of international questions affecting the United States. Accessed from http://fpa.org/about/.

32. Campbell F. Scribner, "Make Your Voice Heard: Communism in the High School Curriculum, 1958–1968," *History of Education Quarterly* 52 (August 2012): 351–369.

33. These essays were printed in the *Milwaukee Sentinel* on May 2, 1959 and are available at http://www.mu.edu/cgi-bin/cuap/db.cgi?db=default&uid=default&view=1 &db=default&uid=default&Content=cold+war&ww=on&bool=and&sb=&CatA bbrev=---&Neighborhood=---&Decade=---&nh=25&mh=1

34. "A Mind of Her Own," in Maureen Daly, ed. *Profile of Youth* (New York: J. B. Lippincott Company, 1951): 222.

35. Scribner, "Make Your Voices Heard," 363–367.

36. Lorraine Adele Nieri, *Dear American Friends: Letters from School Children Around the World* (New York: The Vanguard Press, 1960).

37. Evans, *The Hope for American School Reform*, 214.

38. "Project No. A1—Organization Endorsement of President's Program," Box 30, File: People to People Partnership 1956 (1), James M. Lambie papers, DDE Library.

39. Press release regarding June 12 White House Conference on People-to-People Partnership, DDE's Records as President, Official File, Box 764, 325 (2). Emphasis added.

40. Loayza, "A Curative and Creative Force," 954; Secretary of State Dean Rusk, "The Essentials of Our Foreign Policy," *The Sunday Star* (March 12, 1963): B3.

41. Kenneth Osgood, *Total Cold War*, 234–244.

42. Marcia Chatelain, "International Sisterhood: Cold War Girl Scouts Encounter the World," *Diplomatic History* 38.2 (April 2014): 61–70; Jennifer Helgren, *Inventing American Girlhood: Gender and Citizenship in the Twentieth-Century Camp Fire Girls*, unpublished dissertation (Claremont Graduate University, 2006); Helgren, "'Homemaker Can Include the World:' Female Citizenship and Internationalism in the Postwar Camp Fire Girls," in Jennifer Helgren and Colleeen Vasconcellos, eds. *Girlhood: A Global History* (New Brunswick: Rutgers University Press, 2010): 304–22;

43. "A Program for People-to-People Partnerships," Bortman Papers, Box 3, File: Dept. of State Course on Ideological Conflict (3), DDE Library.

44. People-to-People Program Annual Report (October 21, 1959): 7.

45. People-to-People Program Annual Report (October 21, 1959): 13; Jacqueline Cochran Papers, 1932–75, General Files Series, Box 106, File: People-to-People Program 1959, DDE Library.

46. "Review of Activities (November 1957), Jacqueline Cochran Papers, Box 89, File: People-to-People Program 1957, DDE Library.

47. "US Asked to Aid Youth Exchanges: People-to-People Unit Also Calls for New Travel Rules to Spur Projects," *New York Times* (June 15, 1957): 8.

48. People-to-People News 1.7 (March 1957): 1–2; File: File: Dept. of State Course on Ideological Conflict (1), Box 3, Bortman Papers, DDE Library.

49. In 2002, the nonprofit People-to-People International began a contractual relationship with Ambassador Programs, Inc. to administer People-to-People travel programs for adults and middle and high school students. The Student Ambassador Program closed in 2015.

50. "The American Bookshelf" pamphlet, CARE, Box 66, Folder 9, FBPA, Mudd Manuscript Library, Princeton University.

51. Jenkins, "ALA Youth Services Librarians and the CARE-UNESCO Children's Book Fund," 215–219.

52. "'Your Peace,' A Report of a Special Committee of the Weston High School Student Council on Town to Town Affiliation"; Theodore Jones, "Opinion," (March 20, 1960), typescript of editorial; Report by Mrs. Henry M. Merrill (January 10, 1962); Mark Bortman papers, Box 24, File: Rombas, France—Weston, Mass.; DDE Library.

53. *People to People News* (January 1959): 3, Cochran Lambie papers, DDE Library.

54. Bortman Papers, Box 3, File: Information Agency 1963–1965–1967[1], DDE Library.

55. Bortman Papers, Box 3, File: Experiment in International Living (2), DDE Library.

56. The *New York Times* Youth Forum was a long-running public affairs program for young people founded by Dorothy Lerner Gordon. Originating as a radio program in 1943, in 1952, the show moved to television and ran until Gordon's death in 1970. The format typically consisted of a group of young people discussing a current political issue and interviewing an adult on the topic. "A 'People's Peace' Doubted By Panel: 5 Students on Youth Forum Question Individual's Role in Influencing Policy," *New York Times* (May 12, 1958): 50.

57. Historian Catherine Bishop is working on an oral history project with World Youth Forum participants. See her website at http://catherinebishop.wixsite.com/history/world-youth-forum

58. Osgood, *Total Cold War*, 222.

59. JCC, "The Berlin Youth Festival: Its Role in the Peace Campaign," *The World Today* 7.7 (July 1951): 306–308.

60. Scott Lucas, *Freedom's War: The American Crusade Against the Soviet Union* (New York: New York University Press, 1999): 97; Max Frankel, "Moscow Warns on Alien Ideas Brought in During Youth Festival," *New York Times* (August 19, 1957): 42.

61. Osgood, *Total Cold War*, 262–264.

62. "US Children Use Own 'Marshall Plan' In Sending Gifts to Youngsters Abroad," *New York Times* (November 8, 1947): 9.

63. Program, Advertising Club Luncheon (June 17, 1958), RG 56, General Records of the US Treasury Dept., Records of the Savings Bond Division, Series: Historical Files of the Office of the National Director, 1941–1969, Container 1, File: Lone Ranger Promotion (6/16–17/58) Folder: Lone Ranger Agenda—June 16–17, 1958 (Includes speech material for events), NARA.

64. "Mr. Stiles' Talk, Washington Advertising Club Luncheon" (June 17, 1958). Emphasis in the original.

65. "Trick or Treat for UNICEF," *Social Service Review* 29.3 (September 1955): 296.

66. http://www.radomes.org/museum/documents/GOC/GOC.html

67. Matthew Farish, "The Ordinary Cold War: The Ground Observer Corps and Midcentury Militarization in the United States," *Journal of American History* 103.3 (December 2016): 629–630. See also David Mills, *Cold War in a Cold Land: Fighting Communism on the Northern Plains* (Norman: University of Oklahoma Press, 2015).

68. Farish, "The Ordinary Cold War," 647–649.

Conclusion

In 1961, 50,000 women marched in 60 American cities to protest their government's production, stockpiling, and testing of nuclear weapons. Many of them middle-class, middle-aged mothers, the women organized around the image of vulnerable children and childhood innocence to challenge the US government's Cold War policies. Women Strike for Peace (WSP) activists used the language of maternalism in service of political activism, as women had for centuries, to frame a radical political movement against atomic testing and the resulting fallout that was "killing our children and our children's children." President John Kennedy acknowledged that WSP activism was a factor in the passage of the 1963 Limited Test Ban Treaty between the United States and the Soviet Union, which prohibited above-ground nuclear testing. Historian Eric Bentley credited WSP for striking a critical blow to the House Un-American Activities Committee.[1] It was, after all, difficult to paint middle-class white mothers as "fellow travelers" or part of a global communist threat.

For 15 years, Cold Warriors had used the image of the threatened child to justify deadlier bombs, increased American military intervention around the globe, and bigger military budgets. In 1947, President Truman described ailing Greek children to arouse public sympathy before asking Congress for $400 million dollars to fight communism in Greece and Turkey. In August 1961, Congress approved a $46.66 billion defense budget, which included funds for a major fallout shelter program. In December, the Kennedy administration "proposed a $700,000,000 civil defense program designed to provide community fallout shelters for 20,000,000 people. Most of the money (for the fiscal year starting July 1, 1962) would be earmarked for matching grants to help schools, universities, and other nonprofit institutions build public shelters."[2] The protection of children and youth, both foreign and domestic, justified larger budgets for national security and increased involvement by the federal government.

Children remained potent symbols of the US battle against global communism. Children represented political innocence and vulnerability. They were the nation's future; they were, in the end, the reason for fighting. Activists, educators, advertisers, and government propagandists seized on these symbolic representations of children for a variety of political purposes, from waging peace to waging war. Across the political spectrum, from communist summer camps to nationalist Boy Scout rallies, children represented the future of the nation. But, more importantly, children were powerful political actors. Juvenile entertainment suggested appropriate roles for young American citizens. Throughout the late 1940s and 1950s, American children worked on behalf of the United States as cultural ambassadors, diplomats, and representatives of their nation. They learned to embrace both anticommunism and world friendship in their schools. By the mid-1960s, however, many Americans, young people included, began to question the nation's ideological positions and global interventions in the name of containment. Educated to believe in world friendship and understanding, many citizens argued that children were no longer the reason to *fight* the Cold War; children were the reason to *end* the Cold War.[3]

By the early 1960s, young people joined the ranks of political activists on both the left and the right. In May 1963, thousands of African-American children marched in the streets of Birmingham and went to jail for demanding their civil rights, laying bare the depths of Southern racism. Young people like Joan Baez, who staged sit-ins to protest civil defense drills in the 1950s, were by the following decade occupying the offices of university administrators, filling the National Mall, and protesting in the streets against the Vietnam War. From the conservative Young Americans for Freedom (YAF) to the liberal Students for a Democratic Society (SDS), politically engaged young people took center stage in the 1960s.[4] Historians have offered many reasons to explain the emergence of 1960s social movements. This book suggests that youthful political activism didn't disappear between 1945 and 1960; youth politics were simply redirected toward a largely shared concern: the "vital center" of American politics, united in the goal of defeating communism. When this vital center began to rupture, young people challenged the status quo from both the left and the right, and youth movements became more visible. And children, important political actors from World War II through the Cold War years, were prepared to seize leadership roles.

When Ronald Reagan won the 1980 election, based in part on his revival of tensions with the Soviet Union, the Cold War heated up again. In 1981, six young people from Vermont established The Children's Campaign for Nuclear Disarmament (CCND) and launched a national letter-writing campaign to President Reagan. Ranging in age from 12 to 22, these young people had a clear sense of themselves as global citizens and agents of change. Twelve-year-old Nessa Rabin feared for her own future, she wrote, and that of her "children and grandchildren [who] may be in danger of a nuclear war." In one of the group's first public statements, they pointed out that the United States and USSR possessed "enough nuclear weapons to kill everyone in both countries many times over" and demanded a say in decisions that affected them "more than anyone else." The CCND planned to collect all the letters written to President Reagan and take them to Washington, DC on October 17, 1981, where they would be read out loud at a rally in Lafayette Park across from the White House.[5] Inspired by the civil rights movement, by the end of the twentieth century, youthful political activism, led and directed by children themselves, had become mainstream.

The importance of children, both literally and symbolically, to American efforts to win the Cold War, cannot be overstated. Bolstered by the Baby Boom, images of children permeated American visual culture from the late 1940s through the 1960s. The sheer number of young people born during the Baby Boom ensured their cultural importance, but the Cold War created new representational and political vocabularies. Popular culture offered children lessons in a benevolent form of national supremacy and encouraged them to imagine their place as leaders in the postwar world. Public and private organizations, from the federal government to the Boy Scouts to cultural exchange programs, propagandized both foreign and American children and attempted to cultivate favorable international relations through "world friendship" efforts between children. Advertisers and propagandists used images of children to emphasize national innocence and vulnerability and to provide evidence of the superiority of the American Way of Life to potential allies as well as to the American people. The global struggle between the United States and the Soviet Union made it necessary to win over unaligned nations through unprecedented efforts at covert and overt diplomacy at all levels—from the United Nations to the nation's classrooms, churches, and Scout meetings.

The Cold War politicized children's activities in new ways as well. Whereas children "helped" the war effort from the home front during World War II, the Cold War put women and children on the battlefield itself. Art and pen pal exchanges made young children unofficial ambassadors for the United States, charged with fostering international friendship through the supposedly universal languages of art and childhood. Civil defense responsibilities landed on the shoulders of students, as did the purchase of savings stamps, the collection of books and pennies, and the establishment of sister cities. Diplomacy and defense became the responsibility of *every* American, including, and perhaps even especially, children.

With the collapse of the Soviet Union in 1991 and the lack of a clear enemy, support for public diplomacy dwindled, and the US Information Agency was abolished in 1999. At that time, USIA broadcasting functions, including the Voice of America, Radio Free Europe, and Radio Free Asia were consolidated under the independent Broadcasting Board of Governors (BBG). The USIA's information and exchange functions became part of the newly created office of the Under Secretary of State for Public Affairs and Public Diplomacy in the State Department. Since the terrorist attacks of 9/11, however, there have been renewed calls for efforts at public diplomacy to improve the global image of the United States abroad, especially in countries with significant Muslim populations. Following the attacks, the Department of State expanded its public diplomacy efforts in Muslim-majority countries considered to be of strategic importance in the "war on terrorism," significantly increased program funding and the number of Foreign Service officers in South Asia and the Near East, and launched new initiatives targeting broader, younger audiences—particularly in predominantly Muslim countries. For example, the Shared Values initiative features a series of mini-documentaries on Muslim life in America to demonstrate that the United States is an open society and that Americans and Muslims share certain values and beliefs. The State Department estimated that the programs reached approximately 288 million viewers in the Middle East, South Asia, and East Asia between 9/11 and September 2003. Future plans included new exchange programs for high school students, expanded programs to teach English, and a continuation of the Shared Values initiative.[6]

The Trump administration has not prioritized a strong State Department, pursuing instead a desire to dismantle the "administrative state" by leaving administrative positions unfilled. Members of Congress from both sides of the aisle have expressed concern over the many vacancies in the diplomatic corps, internal problems with morale, and increasing crises abroad.[7] It remains to be seen how, and if, the United States will use cultural diplomacy to strengthen America's diplomatic relationships and if youth are considered crucial, as they have been in the past, to the nation's future well-being.

NOTES

1. Rebecca Solnit, "Three Who Made a Revolution," *The Nation* (March 16, 2006). Accessed at https://www.thenation.com/article/three-who-made-revolution/. Eric Bentley, ed. *Thirty Years of Treason: Excerpts from Hearings Before the House Committee on Un-American Activities, 1938–1968* (Nation Books, 2002): 950–951. Accessed July 12, 2017.
2. See https://www.jfklibrary.org/Research/Research-Aids/Ready-Reference/New-York-Times-Chronology/Defense-and-Military-in-progress.aspx. Accessed July 13, 2017.
3. "Women for Peace" flyer, Folder: 1971, SF and EB. WFP/WILPF leaflets and petitions, Women Strike for Peace Records, 1961–1996, DG 115, Swarthmore College Peace Collection; Swerdlow, *Women Strike for Peace*, 16, 233–236, 239. The Conclusion to Swerdlow's book offers a thoughtful discussion of the strengths and weaknesses of traditional gender- or maternalist-based political activism.
4. Young Americans for Freedom was founded in September 1960 by William F. Buckley, Jr. Students for a Democratic Society evolved from an early twentieth-century labor-socialist organization and held its first meeting under the SDS name in 1960 at the University of Michigan.
5. Children's Campaign for Nuclear Disarmament letter, July 3, 1981, Folder: Subject File: Children's Campaign for Nuclear Disarmament (1981), Swarthmore Peace Collection; Neil Davis, "'Peace, Not Nuclear Weapons,' Children Say to Ronald Reagan," *The Burlington Free Press* (June 21, 1981); Ailene Lachs, "Children Ask Reagan for Nuke-Free Life," *The Vermont Vanguard Press* (June 26–July 3, 1981).
6. United States General Accounting Office, "US Public Diplomacy: State Department Expands Efforts but Faces Significant Challenges" (September 2003): 2–3.
7. Julia Ioffe, "The State of Trump's State Department," *The Atlantic* (March 1, 2017). Available at https://www.theatlantic.com/international/archive/2017/03/state-department-trump/517965/. Accessed July 13, 2017; Morgan Chalfant, "Worries Mount About Vacancies in Trump's State Department," *The Hill* (May 21, 2017). Available at http://thehill.com/policy/international/334327-worries-mount-about-vacancies-in-trumps-state-department. Accessed July 13, 2017. The Deputy Secretary of State was not appointed until June 9, 2017.

CPSIA information can be obtained
at www.ICGtesting.com
Printed in the USA
BVHW032342291220
596582BV00002B/97

9 780197 532904